SOLD OUT

When You Sacrifice Your Life

MANU PHILIP

Now no one can say Bible stories are boring.
This is an eyewitness news.

ISBN 979-8-89130-796-4 (paperback)
ISBN 979-8-89130-797-1 (digital)

Christian Faith Publishing
832 Park Avenue
Meadville, PA 16335
www.christianfaithpublishing.com

Printed in the United States of America

CONTENTS

Other Books by Manu Philip

1. *Onnu nilkku yesuviney sraddichunookku*
2. *Thottarivo atho kettarivo?*
3. *Nizhalum Porulum oru samaggra veekshanam*
4. *Samudhrathil thurakapetta vizaala veethikal*
5. *Sold Out: When You Sacrifice Your Life*
6. *Mysterious Ocean Walkers*
7. *Route 66: Sky Highway Heaven*

PREFACE

THE SPIRIT OF God has inspired me to write this book in a very special and unique way. Today, we are in an age where media newscasters and interviewers subjugate human minds like self-made deities and see them as such without the knowledge of the general public. Throughout this book, I want to disguise myself as a journalist and take you beyond a few centuries. Although I can fly indefinitely on the wings of imagination, I am quite aware that writing here is not a fiction. Therefore, I can't violate the boundaries of the Bible. It's a lot of interesting news of the overleaf of chronicles, but I'm not going to go into it. A journey through the dark history that no one has ever told to the source of the human race!

The histories of travels are forever since the human being was created. The land, the sea, and the sky were prepared highways for him. The ups and downs, the success and failures at the end of each journey are recorded in the account book of human history. The later marked times on the path of progress gave his journeys the impetus of conquest. As science has grown, man's journeys in search of new lands and exploratory possibilities have continued unabated, and it is not over yet. This means that there is no final exit for travel as long as man exists. A voyage taking advantage of the favorable travel conditions El Niño and La Niña are climate patterns that can affect weather worldwide on ships and paddocks in olden times. The book of Exodus to Joshua records the travels of the nation of Israel, which began in Egypt as a travelogue of a people. Exaggerated and biased tendencies can often be found in travel literature. But we can see that what is most truthful is written in the pages of the Bible. It will benefit you if you have the research and intelligence of a research student, the hands of a magician who tries to capture the soul of the past, and the zeal to grasp divine truths.

I hope that by imagining the biblical characters that have been read many times and combining the burning experiences that burn in the depths of their minds, I will have the opportunity to experience the eventful sequences and official moments that the sparkling have seen. I believe that the mind-boggling eyes of a historian traveler can be found on every page of this work, as the travels to the other side of written history in an attempt to solidify biblical truths. It takes you to the imagination as a visual representation of an event that took place centuries ago. Readers need to understand that my imagination has its limits, limitations, and confines. Readers may not like the limits set by the author. What the author puts on his chest can sometimes make the reader feel nauseous and throw it in the trash bin. One thing I can say for sure is that I am not manipulated or to twist the Word, and certainly I believe all the scriptures are inerrant and God-breathed. It contains sharp life experiences that illuminate the principles of truth, holiness, and righteousness with full of justice and obedience to the Word. The various emotional experiences that occur during the journey have touched the mind intensely and will remain indelible over time. The description of the place, the description of the route, and the description of the view, which includes the features of the area, have been made as imaginative and poetical in language as possible. A feature interview is what suits our work the most.

Although the author appears in the guise of a newscaster, I would like to underline once again that the Scriptures are inspired by God, so that anyone who mistakenly thinks irrationally will write biblical events in chronological order. I was willing to travel as much as I could in search of news outlets. Some likes that way; it will cling to us. Even if we try to pull it off, it will not leave us. The passion for travel was burning like an unquenchable fire in my heart. Even those instilled memories of previous trips still haunt me today. I also fell in love and yearning to travel, and it was a great experience to see unfamiliar forests and people across many lands gently kissing the sun's cheeks hidden in the mist. Rising cliffs, blood-soaked red-historic lands, ruined castles, statues, shattered shrines, stone pillars—all create turbulent waves in the mind.

I know that it is very important to have a perfect hand when mixing the element of imagination and fiction in the spiritual book. Otherwise you will slip away from the target. It will also lead to far-reaching futures. The language used in this book is not immaculate writing mode but mostly spoken. Yet it tried to effectively incorporate the emotional levels of experience. The history and nature of the ancient human life and the region at that time are examined in such a way as to provide a more comprehensive understanding of the social conditions of the ancient peoples, human form, animals, picture configuration, dance, hunting, and so on. I do not dare to study these paintings and sculptures in detail as it takes months to conceive and embody the experiences behind them. The clock of the time cycle is reversed back and forth as the many faces of the Bible are brought into a circle and traversed by epochs, centuries, years, months, and so on. The days of the year were not as systematic as they are today. It was mostly transmitted orally from one person to another and from one country to another. There are hundreds of faces and sights that can be captured by the camera eye. When I pass the microphone to selected characters in the Bible, it is a pleasure to hear them choose God and share with them some of the most important events in their lives, as if on a canvas.

Some people may not like the fact that it provides an opportunity in a different manner for a person who does not normally like to read the Bible to understand the truth of God's Word in a particular way. I have nothing against them. It is not a matter of how many years a person has personally studied the Bible, formally or informally, but how much he has grasped the spiritual truths contained in the Bible. Let us write this journey in golden letters in the memoir anthology. It was a melodramatic occasion to visit our late ancestors. My aim is not to show the power of the interviewer's rhetoric, to create a wave of sympathy, or to amaze the audience with the exciting breaking news presentation style. As if to capture the vastness of that memory, to capture the endless eternity of that memory, to touch the heart of the important people marked in the Scriptures and the lands they were in, to notionally touch our footsteps to the same soul-stirring journeys and the tumbledown cultures they traveled through, and to shine through the light-filled eras and direct cultures of the past. Every law in the world has one exception. Books written in ancient times are rare, and there are scattered objects that reveal certain information like rocks, mountains, oceans, temples, rivers, deserts, ruins of ancient animals, and trees. If you want to study the history of nature, you have to learn the alphabet of the natural language. Everything from the amoeba to the largest animal the blue whale (weighing as much as two hundred tons with a heartbeat that can be heard up to two miles away) is letters that taught us some kind of new knowledge. It's like every punch and comma has a lot of meaning.

Let us begin our travel-interview journey. This journey with me will be an eye-opener for many. In it, I will do my best to describe the expressions of positive and negative emotions, anger, sadness, frustration, fear, anxiety, disbelief, disobedience, ups and downs, and gifts and talents of the characters I am going to tell. Characters with different temperaments, backgrounds, and why they reacted that way in that context, and have tried to emphasize the dramatic moments in the story. After telling a story about a person, I tried to tell the lesson that we should learn from that story. In each story, God weaves mystical secrets, spiritual truths, observations, practical uses, and the place and circumstances in which they lived. These characters are real human beings who, like us at one time, overcame obstacles and lived on the top of this soil. They still exist today as a frightening historical fact in the sandstorm that burns into the depths of the soul. No matter what is lost in the course of time, no matter what the evolution, no matter what progressive ideas are embraced, the scrolls of hidden secrets will be unrolled. Inscriptions, carvings, and paintings are examples of the tribal cultural glory that existed in ancient times. It should not be overlooked in the reading that the marks of noise and sighing, which are very close to the noises and lay still within or between each line. From the first five books of the Bible, the Pentateuch is said to be the law, but it also contains history. When we read these books, we can understand it as a formal statement after a detailed analysis of the scene or as an eyewitness account of what we saw, heard, and experienced after realizing the true nature of the news.

I would like to list before you some Bible characters that have walked with God, who have appeared to God, and who have spoken directly to God. Adam, the first man not born of a parent; Cain, the first murderer in world history; Enoch, who was a follower of the Spirit; and Noah, the comforter. Abraham, the father of many nations and his test of faith; Isaac, the best example of obedience; and Jacob, who overcame temptations by wrestling with God and receiving blessings from God. Joseph, the overcomer of temptation; the story of Moses, the leader who led Israel across the Red Sea; and Joshua, the leader who led Israel across the Jordan, which is described as the Jordan of Death, is shocking. David paints a picture of a long-suffering and merciful God, proving that even God's decisions can be changed by weeping before God; and Hezekiah, who portrayed the image of a long-suffering and merciful God. Examining the chronology of our daily footsteps of life reveals whom we are traveling with.

When I started to write a book of this manner, I referred many books for the subjects dealt in this, especially periodicals such as Assisi, Idayan, and Jeevanum Velichavum; I am thankful and grateful to them. It is worth mentioning here that I have read the book that was authored by the honorable priest Fr. Bobby Jose Kattikadu more than once. I have very much impressed to quote some of his illustrations in this book. When I thought about whom I shall approach for getting a foreword to the book, one name has come to my mind—that was Rev. Fr. Canon Tim Mayberry. I was fortunate to have my request for a foreword to be accepted by him. He read through my book in a few days and wrote an elaborate foreword. I remember Rev. Fr. Canon Tim Mayberry with gratefulness, for reading this and making necessary corrections on my language and idea, and for giving valuable suggestions, and also for writing a masterly foreword, which is like a fine mark on the forehead of the book. I express my sincere gratitude to Christian Faith Publishing and the staff for printing the book beautifully in a timely manner. My thanks to those who encouraged and supported me in my humble effort. I am striving to lend a full shoulder to the growth of the church and the spread of the gospel in the places where the Lord has placed me. The year 2019 has been a big milestone in my personal life because I decided to retire. But COVID-19 has shattered my dream, and I have to wait two years to start as a clergy at the hospital where I used to work. I am thankful to my wife, Joyamma; daughter, Christina; son-in-law, Clinton; son, Steven; daughter-in-law, Asisha Philip; granddaughters, Priya and Aliya; and grandson, Lucas. I hope and pray that the book should be a reason for the salvation of many. I take the freedom to thank the Almighty and Eternal God by offering praises to him.

Yours's humble servant of Jesus Christ,

Pastor Manu Philip Florida
Pazhangeril, Niranam

FOREWORD

WE LIVE IN a busy world. We are rushing like superfast vehicles, engrossed in the routines of worldly life. It is a well-known truth that some values are buried in the confusion of this goal. People are very busy, and there is no time for men to stand. Too busy to even breathe properly. In the race for money and status, we tend to forget many things that should not be forgotten. Roots are being uprooted by the rapid tide of consumer culture. Man becomes a superficial object— without deep roots—who considers only the present to be relevant. Society is becoming nothing more than a group of people with no obligations or memories. When we walk in such haste, we don't have time to see and hear the blooming flowers of the field; the chirping of rickets; the stretching, shrinking of, and soft clicks of worms; and the beauty and the diversity of life. Instead of violent speed, love is the culture of slowness. Life is not worth rushing or hurrying. Don't forget that even when you think you have everything under control in the midst of life's struggle, there are times when failure is waiting on the doorstep.

The Bible is the basic tool for building a way of life wherein communication with God is a day-to-day reality. The pressures and conflicts in the closing years of the twentieth century have made the message of the Bible more necessary than ever before. It must meet the needs of men spiritually, intellectually, and physically by offering answers to the problems posed by a changing civilization and by the increasing need for the stamina to maintain the exhausting pace of modern living. This book offers an amazing collection of fascinating characters ranging from the holiest of the holy to some of the most depraved scoundrels imaginable.

As the author wrote in this book, "The histories of travels are forever since the human being was created. The land, the sea, and the sky were prepared highways for him. The ups and downs, the success and failures at the end of each journey are recorded in the account book of human history." The sights seen were warming to the eyes and heart even after the passing of time. He believes that "the mind-boggling eyes of a historian traveler can be found on every page of this work, as the travels to the other side of written history in an attempt to solidify biblical truths. It takes you to the imagination as a visual representation of an event that took place centuries ago." The various emotional experiences that occur during the journey have touched the mind intensely and will remain indelible over time. "The description of the place, route, and the description of the view, which includes the features of the area, has been tried to make it as imaginative and poetical languages as possible." The author is holding the reader's hand who wishes and yearns to travel. The explicit geography extends from Spain in the west to India in the east, with sporadic references to parts of North Africa, west of Egypt, Ethiopia, Arabia, and Greece and Asia Minor, as well as Italy. The saga of the Israelite's exodus from Egypt is the greatest story of liberation from enslavement ever told. It is a metaphor for all people and all times. This book gives you a great experience to see unfamiliar forests and people across many lands gently kissing the sun's cheeks hidden in the mist. Rising cliffs; blood-soaked, red-historic lands; ruined castles; statues; shattered shrines; stone pillars—all create turbulent waves in the mind.

His comprehensive work is meticulously researched, accurately presented, and fascinatingly written. I have no surprise these stories of the ancients continue to intrigue and inspire us as we search for meaning in our own lives. Just as they fear, hope, aspire, love, and lose, so do we. It is a book that should delight everybody who delights and travels through the biblical lands.

—Rev. Fr. Canon Tim Mayberry
Chaplain, Memorial Hospital Miramar

BOOK REVIEWS

BY TELLING THE history of millennia, the soil of the Bible land and the ancient fathers are made accessible to the readers through this book. The antiquities and broad cultural traditions are attractively drawn in the pages of this book, *Sold Out: When You Sacrifice Your Life*, like in a picture gallery or with the skill of an eyewitness reporter. The writer here takes on the mantle of a world traveler and journalist. Anyone who reads this book will feel like they are walking through these places. Travel provides us with knowledge, experience, exploration, discovery, relaxation, adventures, and creativity. I have no doubt that this book, written in a beautiful language full of flow and rhyme with poetic style, will give readers a heartwarming reading experience as well as spiritual inspiration. I hope miles take the reader into the very heart of the Bible and a new way of reading the Bible for Christians and public alike. The author reminds us that there is so much more there in the Bible to explore. This book is a treasure house of knowledge. No summary of mine can do justice to the richness of this book.

—Dr. Omana Russel, retired professor, Sree Sankaracharya
University of Sanskrit, and senior research fellow,
Indian Council of Historical Research, Delhi

What an amazing concept to look at key biblical characters through the eyes of an interviewing news reporter. "I believe that the mind-boggling eyes of a historian traveler can be found on every page of this work, as the travels to the other side of written history in an attempt to solidify biblical truth." The author's main source of information is clearly the Holy Scriptures. Background information about the setting comes from an informed imagination. In places, he uses extrabiblical literature to provide interesting character and setting descriptions. (All are well documented). Anyone who has enjoyed the late Rush Limbaugh's history books will recognize the similarity of approach to the subject matter. They will enjoy this book. As a retired pastor, I could see using passages from this book as an introduction to sermons, especially one designed around the characters interviewed. I was intrigued about speech and silence, good thought-provoking thoughts. The thought came to my mind that what gives silence strength is presence! Without presence, silence can be ignored, and its message is pushed out of mind. Presence makes silence unignorable. The content of this book is a deep piece of thought that combines logic, thought, humor, influence, and presentation skills. There is not a single line in this book where letters are strung together to make meaningless statements. Everyone who reads this book will understand that Pastor Manu Philip is a prolific writer and author.

—Pastor Leon Hiebert,
daily devotion writer for thirty years (SOAP)

Sold Out: When You Sacrifice Your Life is a very informative and insightful book. It is another amazing volume from Pastor Manu Philip, making the Bible stories interesting. This book is a storehouse of information, and every reader of this book gets insight about the triumph of the Bible characters who lived for God and the tragedies of the unfaithful ones. It is a must-read book written in a very journalistic format—not fiction but facts, historical facts, that I have never heard of. It is a rich resource for every Christian who seeks the forgotten side of history. This book is articulated as educational, equipping, and energizing the reader. It is a multipurpose paperback arming every Christian to stand upright and serve God diligently. Its ten chapters are filled with hidden treasures. This is geared toward the ministry worker, whether lay or professional. Pastors, in particular, should find it relevant and helpful. Above all, it is doctrinal, historical, and very scholastic. This book can alter the way you read the

Bible and change the way you live. I greatly appreciate Pastor Manu for utilizing his time and talents to bring glory to the Lord through his books.

—Rev. Dr. Babu Thomas, senior pastor, Hebron IPC, New York; director, Rakshamargam Ministry; and secretary, IPC Eastern Region, USA

CHAPTER 1

Life Sacrificed for God in the Old Testament

GOOD AFTERNOON TO you all. This is Sky News 66 from Eden. Today is 6000 BC, October 8th. Today's broadcasting has just begun. Time is half past three. It is my honor and privilege to report that these interviews will last for several months. It is time to get ready to let go of the thin heat rays of the afternoon sun. The camera is handled by a reporter who plays the presenter with a white umbrella. The umbrella is designed to control the light when taking pictures. Behold, look! Two people are having a conversation, and perhaps even an altercation, under that giant, overgrown tree. They are the main characters in this story. Come on; let's observe what's happening there. Now Adam walks among the poplar bushes on a green hillside.

Eden has many historic legends. We are now on our way to Eden to see Adam and Eve, the first people ever created. They live in a *perfect sanctuary made by God for His creation.* Eyes and mind enjoy amazing views. Among them, gem trees of all colors are dazzling to see. There were trees that grew rubies, trees with lapis lazuli flowers, trees that dangled gigantic coral clusters like dates. Everywhere, sparkling on all the branches, were enormous jewels: emeralds, sapphires, hematite, diamonds, carnelians, pearls. Gilgamesh looked up and marveled at it all like in heaven. Beetles and bees come to suck the nectar of the fragrant flowers, flocks of sheep scurrying under the trunks, the wind, the waterfalls, the wildlife, the sounds of the beautiful bulls, the peacocks and the hornbills, and the beauty of the river and the forest. The unforgettable drive with *hairpin curves* and steep

1

ascents twists and turns leads to the crest of Hot Springs Mountain. A *rock formation* is an isolated, scenic, or spectacular surface rock outcrop. Bubbling yet soothing sound of the overflowing wild rivers. Calm atmosphere, beautiful flowers symbolize pure love and beauty. Early in the morning, butterflies and bees set out to collect honey. The bud is in full bloom, spreading its beautiful petals and smiling at the sun. A breathtaking journey through the lush greenery where the wind and the cold come together, enjoying the beauty of the rainforest chatting with the winds, and to listen the wild streams amid murmurs of the wind. The tree twigs and snow particles are embracing dawns that are thrilling experience. The butterflies are fluttering their wings over the canopy of sky with golden spots. The views of a completely different and unbelievable era are being captured and transformed into words. This journey is going to lead us to a very proud legacy and autograph of history that can be said to have happened. History also teaches us the truth that nothing lasts forever. If the reader has experienced an extraordinary feeling, he can hold it dear to his chest. I think this travel experience will not go unnoticed and will inspire inviolate obeisance by the readers. In the early centuries of human origins, there was nobody using recordings to document the history that is called prehistoric times. But imagine if there were! Let us open the window to enter the unfolding historical truths that the eyes can believe and the thoughts cannot reach.

We were greeted by crimson red flowers. Flowing rivers, streams, flowering plants, trees, birds, fields, colorful and beautiful woodpeckers, grasshoppers, the moon, the stars, the sun, the moon are open to the eyes and mind. Spring tulip fields, cherry trees, peaches, plum trees—the view never ends. There are no words to describe the scenes that have been captured by the eyes and mind. No matter how much you describe Eden, it's just a small peak at the tip of an enormous iceberg.

Adam (0–938 BCE)

The morning wakes up slowly like a shy bride, and the sun's rays are slowly coming to touch the earth. It is a drizzling snowy morning.

The aurora borealis shines through the ice particles. We greet the morning with excitement and surprise. Adam and Eve are waiting for us near the lake where the stars of the night sky are full. The story begins with the camera zooming in on Adam's face. Adam was the first man created by God. Adam was made of clay. He was given the authority to rule over all things (Genesis 3:8). From creation to the fall of Adam is known as the age of innocence. While God commanded all other things to be created by His words, He created Adam from the dust of the earth with His hands and breathed into his nostrils the breath of life, and man became a living soul. By that, Adam was created in full growth without a parent. Not only that, but God also clothed him with the garments of glory that are not for other living beings.

According to Midrash, Eve's creation occurred while Adam was sleeping, and he neither knew nor even sensed anything when God created her from his rib. With this in mind, a noblewoman asked R. Yose, "But why stealthily?" That is, why did God take Adam's rib without his knowledge, after causing slumber to fall upon him?

He replied, "If a person entrusted you with a single uncia, a small weight of silver clandestinely, and returned to you a Libra = 12 unciae of silver in public, is this theft?"

She asked further, "And why in secrecy?" Why did He create her while Adam was sleeping, and not while he was awake, so that he could see her at the moment of her creation?" In the Midrashim account, Eve was created whole with all her limbs fully developed, as was Adam; according to one view, they were created as twenty-year-old young adults (Rabbah 14:7). She asked another question: "Why is a woman's voice clearer and higher than a man's?"

He told them, "If you fill a bowl with meat and strike it, the sound will be low and dull, but if you place a bone in it, the sound will be vibrating clear tone and high," thus man's body, which is filled with earth, while the woman was created from a bone, and therefore her voice is clear. The rabbis maintain that Eve was the most beautiful woman ever. Adam was the most beautiful creature in the entire world, since he was created in God's image. Eve, also, was God's handiwork, and therefore, no woman was as beautiful as she, even though she was lesser than Adam, for she was a secondary creation from Adam's body (*Bava Batra* 58a).

The songs of sparrows began to be heard from the forest as seen from the banks of the Euphrates. At first, the only sound I heard was from the forest. Over time, small noises that no one normally pays attention to are beginning to be heard with great pleasure in the ears. Scholars believe that geography is the stage for drama that becomes human history. We need to ask Adam some questions and understand who wears the garment of glory and walk with God every evening. Let us open our eyes and minds and wait for the amazing sights.

Reporter: Can you explain me the alluring Garden of Eden?

Adam: It will take a few months to talk about Eden. Geographically, Eden is a natural land. Eden paints a beautiful picture of friendship between nature and man. The Garden of Eden was designed by Jehovah God in such a way that it conveys the full beauty of nature. Nature is covered with lush green hills, narrow valleys, weedy springs, grasslands, mountains, and lakes that stretch as far as the eye can see. When you see the snow on the top of the mountain, it's like putting icing on a chocolate cake. Frozen dew and clouds fly over the mountain. The full bloom flowering shrubs, abounding fruits hanging on the trees are beautiful. The journey through that comfort of coolness is a fulfilling and astounding experience.

It is home to a wide variety of flora and fauna that are full of fruits and flowers that can be grown in all seasons. In the fragrant south wind, the birds were playing music and dancing on the trees. Maple trees, deciduous maple trees, pine groves, and colorful fir trees. Adam described the names of many unnamed, unseen, and unheard of giant trees competing with the vampires to kiss the blue of the sky. Let me write some of the special trees I have seen here. Methuselah tree (oldest known tree), dragon blood tree (upright umbrella shaped tree), Dead Vlei (skeleton-like tree), sequoia tree (largest known living single stem tree on earth), baobabs pine (stores nearly 32,000 gallons of water), angel oak tree (shade that stretches nearly 17,200 square feet), bristlecone pine, flamboyant tree, wisteria tree.

Adam first took us to a roadside view of Eden, near a waterfall where four waterfalls in a still desolate landscape were violently scattered into deep cliffs. Four rivers blessed with the Immaculate Garden of Eden perpetual springs even in summer. It was a cool feeling as the water droplets splashing from the waterfall flew in the wind and hugged my cheeks. There are small and large waterfalls here that attract the eyes and are not limited to the view from the hills. The four rivers in association with the Garden of Eden: Pishon, Gihon, Hiddekel, and the Euphrates. Sheep covered with fur, with pearly mane and red eyes, moving briskly through the woods and hills. That beautiful forest is home to a variety of birds, some with blue eyes, animals, butterflies, and streams. The bees pollinating beautiful umber flowering plants and flowers. The sun rays erupting from the solar system when it hits the water droplets in the flower petals sparkle like a rainbow.

The place is a haven for so many medicinal plants. A miniature version of the universe where sheep graze and enjoy the beauty of nature. The laughter and weeping of nature and the thousands of stars that sparkle like rattlesnakes on the rack where the song falls are not to be missed. The twilight that spreads in the magical golden sky to the island of greenery. When the glorious sun wakes up in Eden, the cold particles form the veil of snow. The winged expressions of love of the robin birds and the red-eyed eyes of the gray partridge birds, which call out to its mate and make a noise, are such a sight to behold. The rivers of Eden gleamed like diamonds in the light of the setting sun on the horizon. A beautiful world where quills sing sweetly, peacocks dance with the rain, and deer leap. A variety of animals roam freely. The atmosphere is filled with the chirping of a variety of birds. Flamingos, hornbills, and waterfowl chirp, and the beautiful lakes shimmer in the sunlight as clear as pearls. Herds of cattle grazing on the lawn, dewy meadows, sweet waters, and golden deciduous trees. Sand grains glowing golden. There the falling leaves do not dry out, and some days they lie in the soil and slowly dissolve into gold dust. The fragrance of the fallen flowers is never lost here. It gives the impression of a spring festival every day.

The curiosity in the eyes created a commotion of nostalgia in the mind. The crickets on the banks of the river, white pigeons in the paddy fields, and the light scent of the flowers of the garden. Flowers, blossoms, meadows, butterflies, spring-bought flowering trees, squirrels jumping on flower twigs, warbling birds. It is a tranquil and picturesque place, full of streams, hills, and lush greenery. We stared without taking our eyes from the topography of the garden. The multicolored parrots were moving their lips and singing something in the blossoming lattices. Wild buffaloes graze on sunny sidewalks. Fearless herds of foxes graze on the shores of the lake, where elephants roam, mighty tigers, leopards, and lions with their heads held high with royal pride.

It's nice to see the thin dark clouds spread over the ocean. Above the great ocean as the majestic magic of the small fog settles in like an illusion of an umbrella spread out. The fragrant south wind and the impingement sound of the branches of trees in the forest, the honey rain of music on the ears. It rejuvenated the mind and body. Even this gentle breeze blown to the grass nips buds, which makes a music that warms the ears. An eternal love poem between wild trees and fog is written here. This forest, which loves the fog that embraces the huge trees, seems to have been denied access to sunlight. Suddenly, a drizzle fell from somewhere. When it rained, the remnants of the rain were amethyst on the leaves which creates irresistible eye appeal just like a lapis lazuli. The trees are immersed in that coolness. In the middle of the forest, which is covered with lush greenery, is a beautiful large body of fresh water. Out of nowhere, two swans fluttered their wings, made a croaking noise, and they conversed in their language with merriment as they took a long swim in that lovely pool. These most beautiful lakes are clear and cold water. We moved on, immersed in the breathtaking views of the Garden of Eden. Everybody will fall in love with the serene Eden, which is a rural modesty. We continued our journey praising God's handiwork, marveling at the natural beauty that lined both sides. I wondered what a great artist God is, who has created so many amazing images in the universe.

Anyone who touches the soil of Eden will feel the spiritual energy and instantly realize that something supernatural is filling them. Eden is an unforgettable experience for anyone who loves nature and wildlife. Only someone who was truly blind could fail to see or understand the sublime beauty hidden here. If you look at nature with taciturn, all the burdens of the mind will disintegrate. We could plainly see there was an amazing world of sky and nature. The cool breeze on the lake caressed us. A valley guarded on both sides by carved horizontal rocks. The Garden of Eden is a beautiful land nestled in the lap of snow-capped mountains. It always gives us an indescribable experience no matter how much we see or experience. Even stones offer ways to tell a story. The sight of the Garden of Eden adorned in the golden light of the twilight in the sky is thrilling to compose a poem, no matter how poetic it may be. No matter how busy if you see such sights, you will not want to ever leave this beautiful land.

Reporter: Why you and Eve banished from the Garden of Eden?

Adam: We fell prey to Satan's scheme by deciding to rebel against God (4004 BCE). Eve ate some of the forbidden fruit, and then she encouraged me to do the same. That brought sin into the world, damaging every part of it. Now tainted by sin, we could no longer be in the presence of a perfectly holy God. God cursed Satan for what he had done and announced the consequences for humanity. Eve's disillusionment was truly pathetic, downcast by the sense of guilt of rebellion, the whole predicament and while heartbroken and dejected. Look at them, standing there so tall and majestic, with outstretched wings and flaming swords! Glorious creatures! But I dare not approach any closer; their assignment is to keep Eve and me out of the garden. It is sobering to think that Eve and I once lived in innocence inside that beautiful paradise.

Reporter: What was the verdict from the Holy of Holies Jehovah pronounced against you and Eve, and why?

Reporter explanations: The righteous God as a Judge of Heavenly Supreme Court is trying the first crime on earth as case no. 1 The Abel murder case is case no. 2, and Achan's was case no. 3. "The Heavenly court has some significant differences from the worldly court procedures. The case is not being investigated by the local police, and all cases will be investigated by the heavenly agency (Universal Law Enforcement Agency, ULEA). There are no subordinate, districts, high court, or supreme courts to decide the case. A litigant who loses in a federal court can appeal to a higher court. For heavenly cases, all cases are final decided by the Supreme Court.

Reporter: What deceptive tactics offered to you and Eve by Satan to disobey God?

Adam: In the Garden of Eden, we had everything we needed or could possibly want. There was only one restriction given by God, and that's exactly what the devil focused. Satan directly contradicted the Lord, saying, "You surely will not die." Satan uses the same approach always trying to get us to focus on what we don't have but would like to possess. He wants us to doubt what God has said in His Word and desire an experience that will stimulate and satisfy our senses. Satan masks his deceptions in beautiful packaging that appeals to our natural senses and desires. Satan promises that there will be no repercussions for disobeying God. Satan came to me and promised that we would become as God, knowing good from evil, if we ate the fruit from the forbidden tree. Satan cast doubt on God's Word and character. Satan is always evil: a liar, deceiver, accuser, false prophet, and more. His one strategy is to kill and steal and destroy. He's the master of deception. Satan may try to deceive you through the influence of people family, friends, neighbors, coworkers, those in authority, etc. Satan disguises himself as an angel light. Because of our disobedience toward God brought about several significant changes that affect us but also the entire creation. We lost our fellowship at the Eden, fell from grace, and separated from God, cursed the ground, and physical death came to the world.

Reporter: What you know about the first family who violates God's commandment case trailed by Heaven Supreme Court (HSC) Case No. 1? (The trials were conducted from the beginning to end by

God the Almighty, who serves as the investigator, the prosecutor, and the judge. The place of crime is the Garden of Eden. The first crime is original sin. The defendant or the accused are Adam and Eve. The second Accused is Satan, the coadjutor, snake is the plotter. For time being, the reporter is the defendant's attorney.)

Plaintiff Jehovah: A legal case was conducted in the Garden of Eden, to bring out the facts of that case and the issues involved, to establish them as a matter of public record, and also to pass sentence on the offenders. Jehovah called Adam and Eve before him for questioning. Though he knew all, he held a hearing, made the charges clear, brought out the facts by questioning, and gave them an opportunity to make expression in their own defense. He obtained a confession from the offenders. Jehovah then made his decision in the matter. Jehovah, God the Supreme Judge, here set the pattern for all further judicial proceedings among his people. Legal cases conducted according to God's judicial regulations were for the finding and discussion of facts for the purpose of rendering justice where possible, justice tempered with mercy.

Plaintiff: The first transgression of humankind leads to the first interrogation of an accused person. Have you eaten from the tree of which I commanded you not to eat?

Defendant Adam: The woman whom thou gave to be with me, she gave me of the tree, and I did eat.

Eve: The serpent beguiled me, and I did eat. We did not deny the facts. My only defense was Eve had given me the fruit, and that God was the one who had given Eve.

Eve, in turn, blamed the serpent. The record shows that these were invalid excuses.

Jehovah: When I created you, I gave you Garden of Eden to live in. I also told that you could freely eat the fruit from any tree except from one called the Tree of the Knowledge of Good and Evil and warned clearly that if you eat from that tree, the penalty would be death. You ate the forbidden fruit, so I have to pronounce the sentence of death. Note that I had not sought your downfall. On the contrary, I had made obedience both easy and pleasant. I had created you without a sinful nature, placed in an ideal environment, provided for all your temporal needs, endowed with strong mental powers, and warned the consequences of disobedience, and entered into personal fellowship with me. So you both can't claim ignorance of the law, which is no excuse anyway. Finally, I have to cast you out of the Garden of Eden. The motive for your disobedience was not appetite, but prides the ambition to be like God. The defendants acknowledged their guilt, all sin is essentially rebellion against God's authority and His revealed will. The measure of God's wrath against sin is the measure of my holiness. Therefore, the case is dismissed.

Reporter: Could you ever thought about going appeal against Jehovah's verdict? Do you think the Lord Jehovah act like a dictator?

Adam: The answer for both questions, my plain answer is no. There is no court of higher authority to which we could have appealed against this sentence. Our Almighty God is omnipotent, omniscient, and omnipresent, and also the Most High God. He is also *the only true God*. There is no higher authority than God.

Reporter: Since you are the first man and woman, and most popular couple in the world, what you learn from your life?

Adam and Eve: Satan can tempt us in the most unexpected ways. Each of us must bear the responsibility for our own sin, and each of us must endure the consequence of that sin. The child of God should resist the devil and withstand him. Know that your actions not only influence you but also other people around you. Know that you can't hide anything from God. God doesn't force us to follow Him. God wants His children to follow Him from the heart. He doesn't need robots that would do anything He commands that would be completely against His plan. Sin separates us from God. Sin will cause a rift between God and man. Run toward God, not away from Him.

We should accept the responsibility and simply endure the consequences of our actions, instead of making excuses and blaming others. Covetousness is an insatiable desire for worldly gain. The spirit of covetousness leads to and is the mother of many other sins. That's how dangerous covetousness is. Sin should be stopped right before we think about it. We will reap what we sow, if we sow the sin of rebellion and disobedience. For this reason, we have reaped its many deadly fruits. You can't hide from God. It is impossible to hide from

God, and yet many of us still try the same mistake. Sin brings temporary pleasures but permanent penalties. Satan is deceitful.

Abel (Approx. 3927–3905 BC)

Eve was a beauty parlor with dreamy blue-eyed, apple-red cheekbones. Cain and Abel were the lilies of the valley of Adam and Eve's married life. The word *Abel* means one who disappears like a breath. Ancient tradition states that Adam had thirty-three sons and twenty-one daughters. From the fall of Adam to the flood is known as the age of conscience. During that time also, Adam and his children sacrificed and worshiped God according to the pattern set by God, although Adam and Eve usually led the sacrifices as the children got older. So one day Cain and Abel brought sacrifices to God out of their labors to please God. But Jehovah did not approve of his older brother Cain and his offering. The resulting resentment culminated in fratricide. Abel became the first martyr on earth, a perfect sacrifice, a witness of righteousness. Abel's life was crushed in his brother's hand, as if it had fallen off a bud before it could develop into a flower.

At the beginning of creation, we find in the book of Genesis that Jehovah God created man and gave him the blessing to fill the earth with children and to rule over the earth. A careful reading of the Scriptures will show that in the first few years, a great crowd had formed on earth. It is not wrong to assume that twins, up to three or five babies, were born in the same birth in favor of population growth at that time. We see Cain as the firstborn of the Adam and Eve couple. But a careful reading of the Word reveals that Abel was born again in the same birth. Scholars believe that Abel was born after Cain and that they were twins. Now Adam knew his wife, and she conceived and bore Cain, and again, she bore his brother Abel (RSV). This is evident in the Hebrew language. The firstborn Cain accepted his father's job. This method has been practiced since ancient times. In any case, when he came to sacrifice, Cain brought out of the ground and Abel out of the flock. Abel's gift was offered by faith, but Cain's was not. Cain apparently knew what God desired and was given a second chance to make the right sacrifice.

Reporter: Why did your brother killed you?

Abel: I think he may be outraged that God is not pleased with his sacrifice. Anger is an intense emotion that sprouts from jealousy. Hate is the by-product of anger Cain probably didn't sleep a wink. I failed to understand the coals of hatred burning in my brother's eyes. One morning, when the sun was shining in the sky and lighting exposed in the ground, my brother called me and told me that we will go to the farming place. The mask of smile that my brother was wearing, I couldn't recognize at all. It was a long way to walk, and it's just like any other day, a beautiful evening in the month of Nisan an early spring. The sun is about to descend in the west. The magpies are fluting the corellas' call. And the red wattlebirds on the blossoming trees. Their loud cracklings carrying in the freshening breeze.

No matter how angry you are, if you see such celestial views, will you allow yourself to commit a heinous crime? My brother has a masterplan in the back of his mind, and he had done everything what he planned. After the execution, he returned with the relief that nobody seen nearby. But God asked him, where is your brother Abel? That question really burned, juddered him. God doesn't need polygraphs, brain mapping, and narco-analysis test to prove something. He doesn't need to question or any kind of interrogation to the accused. God's witnesses do not change the story in the trial for material benefits. Nor can they be influenced.

Reporter: Who are the witnesses brought by the angels of your murder trial?

Abel: God doesn't need to convey him the messages by sentries, adherents, patrolling people, soldiers, moonlight, footprints, fingerprints, or any forensic experts. God has his own investigation teams like hell, death, ocean, spirit, water, blood, voice, darkness, the book of remembrance, the book of the Word of God, the book of life. All of these witnesses will be called by God. Although Cain should have been sentenced to death for this rarest crime, the merciful God granted him a waiver.

Reporter: If you are agreeable, I am going to do a mock murder case trial now. Assume that I am the foreman of the jury at your trial.

Hello, news reporting Manu Philip warmly welcomes to all this evening's live broadcast. Today, the FIR is analyzing the news in the case of Cain, the main accused in the Abel murder case. Joining us in this discussion is Gabriel, the eminent leader of the ruling party from the heavenly studio and the cherubs in charge of security from the Eden studio. We look forward to the archangel Michael on the line. On the other side, Mr. Lucifer, the eminent leader of the opposition from the hell studio. The audience can also participate in this live discussion. Let's take a look at what it would be like to present to the audience the victim and the accused in the Abel murder case, which shook the whole world years ago. Plaintiff and defendant are warmly welcome in today's event. The news that Cain, the main accused in the Abel murder case, had fled the scene and gone into hiding was misleading. For the Lord God had sent him to a place not far from Eden, to a place called Nod. He was allowed to flee on temporary bail granted by the Chief Justice of the Supreme Court, Jehovah God.

Cain was arrested and now been handed over to Eden County Police. After three days of angelic interrogation, Cain was taken into special police custody for the investigation of the Abel murder case. Police teams from different places are being brought to the interrogation center in connection with the case. Lucifer came out and justified before God by saying that Cain is innocent and it is a fabricated story. When Cain killed Abel, Jehovah recorded aerial view photographs of the scene to show geographic relationships of locations or objects. Usually an investigation team uses four types of search methodology that can be considered to search a crime scene: strip search, grid search, zone search, and spiral search. But God have one more tool, which is soul search.

Reporter: What do you want others to know about your faith and tolerance?

Abel: I want others to know that God is very living, and He is very real. I want people to know God is very alive, He speaks to me, and I honestly feel guided. All humans are sinners, which is the problem that we all have. God's love for humans made Him give us free will, but it is this freedom of choice that allowed us to commit sins. Everyone commits sins; no matter how righteous we are, because this is human nature. The belief is that no one can meet the perfection that God requires, as it is impossible to be sinless. As a result, all humans deserve to spend eternity in hell. However, since God is forgiving, He made an alternate plan and frees us from the penalty of entering hell. I would also like to add some historical documents and traditions related to the Abel murder case. According to some Bible scholars, Cain hurried to the field with his brother and spilled innocent blood on his head with a plowshare (Jasher 1:25).

There is no clear record of what Cain did at the end of his life, but according to the twelfth-century Lazore Saint of France, an arrow shot to kill a hunting animal, Tubal Cain, the son of Lamech, is said to have caused Cain's accidental death. Asked if Cain had survived Abel's assassination, John Bairen's article at the Ashland Theological Seminary (BAR, May 2014) states that Lamech had lost his sight and that Cain's accidentally fired an arrow. In Scripture, we read that "If Cain is avenged seven times, then Lamech seventy-seven times" (Genesis 4:24). Some believe that Abel was killed in Swat, Yemen. This is said to be due to a fluid-like blood flowing from the wound of a tree here. The tree is also known as the Brothers Blood Tree, in reference to the story of Cain and Abel, in which the first murder on earth took place. In a Yemeni legend, it is said that Cain and Abel were the first to live on the Socotra Island; when Cain killed his brother, Abel, his blood was the reason the Brothers Blood Tree (dragon blood tree) grew. What makes this tree stand out among other trees in the world is that it bleeds when it is truncated; the bloody liquid is a type of red resin that has no smell or taste (dragon blood tree by Manar 08/06/2020).

Reporter: Since you are the first victim of sibling homicide in the history of the world, you have every right to give your spiritual lessons to the mankind.

Abel: I have learned from a very bitter experience in life that there are certain unwritten rules for human existence. When these unwritten rules are violated, human existence itself is lost. It is not right to turn a blind eye to certain laws laid down by God, and such laws should not be amended in a timely manner. Of course, violating the obligation will result in punishment. Let this experience be a beacon for you to make quick decisions without getting angry in the event of an unexpected situation. Please God rather than men. God looks in the heart. We may fool other people, but we can never fool God. He sees and knows all things. God knows every intention and motivation that we have. Righteousness doesn't always lead to a good life. While it is true that God promises us abundant blessings when we obey Him, we must also realize that sometimes we are going to suffer for doing the right thing. Faith comes with action. Faith is not just a deep or warm feeling inside of us. It is not just a belief in God, but it is a living faith demonstrated through actions. We must worship God in His own term. We must have right heart and motivation when worshiping God. Worship God properly and based upon what God demands of him.

Enoch (BCE 622–87)

Reporter introduction: Enoch walked with God. The space between Enoch and Noah is only two generations. Enoch is seven generations from Adam. One thing is for sure: in Enoch's time, the wickedness and immorality was just as bad as Noah's period. Enoch pleased the Lord. Enoch was taken without death. In any case, Enoch was a prophet who revealed God in the face of cruelty in an ungodly world and paved the way for righteousness. He was a preacher of repentant who walked with God and was in constant fellowship with God.

Enoch was in the world but not of the world. The people of Enoch's day were wicked. Those who live according to their lusts, their god are their bellies, and their glory is in their shame. Four generations of murmurers, complainers, those who always find fault with others, and those who blaspheme God who cannot shed light on those around them! Yet he followed God every day, every step of the way. Enoch was the first person on the list of ancestors to be taken without death.

Enoch had no deathbed, no burial, and no funeral. There was no need for a coffin. Three Enoch's are found in the Bible (Genesis 4:16, 17, 5:19). His name means "dedicated." I can say with confidence that the meaning of the title of this book is very appropriate with the meaning of Enoch's name. What is written about Enoch in the New Testament is that he had remarkable faith. Genesis chapter 5 is a depressing chapter in the Bible. It records the deaths of many. Every human being is born into a dark world full of adversity and contradictions. In the middle of this burial chapter, as the horrible form of death's monstrous mockery in the dark, we can see a silver lining of light from Adam, the seventh Enoch. Enoch did not die. He walked with God and was taken to heaven.

Reporter: How can a frail man walk with Holy of Holies and glorious God?

Enoch: The question that is often asked is whether weak men can walk with God, who is majestic in holiness, who dwells in heaven has more radiance than the sunlight and glorious. For those who please God in anything and everything, the answer of my life gives is of course possible. Just as the breath of life is necessary to sustain life, so the devotee experiences every moment of his life longing for the presence of God.

If the devotee didn't feel the experience, the presence of God is like the drowning person is suffocating their life in the depths of the ocean. Man cannot take a step forward by his own strength. It is my life experience that the full spring of God's love will be given in the path of life. God is the great treasure of mercy as big as an ocean. We can walk with God because He helps us in our weaknesses and makes up for the shortcomings in our ways. Is it not possible for two people to walk together without getting along? If two people want to walk together, they must have the same mind, goal, and interest. Do not forget that we are the property of a compassionate owner.

Reporter: What is the meaning of walking with God means?

Enoch: To walk with God means to live an immaculate, sinless, honest, holy life. It means one who lives in fellowship and obligation to God alone without any attachment to anyone else. One who walks with God can also mean one who make up the hedge and stand in the gap before God.

Reporter: Explain to me how you ascend to heaven without dying?

Enoch: Actually, I don't prefer to answer this question. However, I will partially answer to your question. I did not suffer the same fate as Adam and the rest of his descendants. I did not die. I walked with God. Since the creation to my time, I am the only biblical figure that did not see death. It is possible that someday in the future, we will experience physical death. It may be that God desired to save me without experiencing death due to our faithfulness in serving and obeying Him. Whatever the case, God has His purpose, and while we don't always understand God's plans and purposes, we know that "His way is perfect." I preached to the people about the coming judgment of God (Jude 1:14–15). This can easily make people angry and lead them to persecute me. Perhaps God rescued me by taking me and preventing people from killing me.

There are some very relevant things in my life that were taken without death. As a warning to this generation, I had a personal fellowship with God and faith in God. Noah was the grandson of Methuselah, my son. The name I gave my son was not just a name; it was a message of danger to that period. The name literally means "it will happen on the day he dies." I did this because I received a special revelation about the judgment to come from God.

Human life is something that has not been defined since the time of man. Life is a mystery that there is no assurance to happen tomorrow in a shaken and reversals of the world. As a person who has walked with God, I can tell you what to keep in mind and step forward for a spiritual life. One must set an example for others, to walk according to the law, to walk in truth, to walk in the light, to walk in good works. Life is like a voyage. The circumstances of life are like the weather. Sometimes there's smooth sailing; sometimes there's storms. We are caught up sometimes in these storms because we are sailing on the sea of time between two eternities. When the storms of life are raging, pray to God stand by me.

Reporter: What spiritual lessons did you learn in your life?

Enoch: It is not easy to live a life pleasing to God, but you know something is worth doing if it is difficult. Though we may suffer, we know that a great reward awaits us. If someone is walking with God means walking in faith. There are things in this life that really do not make sense if we use our human eyes. However, with the eyes of faith, we are able to see the promises of God and be assured of God will execute judgment. Most people go on with their lives not thinking about the consequences of their actions. God will protect His people. God shows that He is able to protect His people during persecution.

Noah (1056–2006 BCE)

Reporter introduction: Here we come again with a topic that is as relevant as it was discussed in the last episode. Occasionally there are waves rushing hide and seek in and out of the sand dunes. Thoughts roared through the endless sands, but I listened intently to the sound of the sea. Evenings are the gift of God to the sun artist. The golden rays fading across western horizon whispering good night because sunset is the sun's fiery kiss to the night. It was on such a nice evening that we met Noah.

The word *Noah* means comfort. Noah is the tenth generation since Adam. Noah was righteous and upright among the wicked generation. Noah walked with God (Genesis 6:2, 9). The Bible describes the righteous as Noah, Joseph, Jesus, John the Baptist, Simon, Joseph of Arimathea, and Cornelius. Noah's faith was a responsive faith, and Noah believed in the revelation given by God. Noah was the first man to build the ark, to witness the first rain and the flood, to see the rainbow, the sign of the first law, to preach righteousness, and to build the first altar. The rainbow that appeared in the sky still bears witness to the unpredictable flood of Noah's day. The rainbow symbolizes God's protection and God's promise to never destroy the earth again with a worldwide flood. Noah was a man of the covenant. Noah was the conservator of a traveling museum.

Reporter: Why did God say I destroy all the earth and flesh?

Noah: When man's wicked deeds became displeasing to God, God said, "I will destroy man, whom I have created from the face of the earth." That's it. The time when God saw that the wickedness of man was great on earth, and that every inclination of the thoughts of his heart was always evil. God realized that as the number of men increased, so did their wickedness. God repented and grieved over the creation of man. But God counted me righteous and upright among them. Moreover, in that generation, I received the grace of God (Hebrew 11:6–8). Adams's responsibility was to pass on the truth of God to the succeeding generations. He failed at this, and as a result, the world became so wicked that God had to destroy everything which had breath. Now it was responsibility to pass on the truth of God to my family. Unfortunately, after several generations, the truth became clouded in obscurity, asks you to build an ark, man became idolatrous.

Reporter: Why didn't you question God when He asks you to build an ark?

Noah: Now, no shrub had yet appeared on the earth, and no plant had yet sprung up, for the Lord God had not sent rain on the earth (Genesis 2:5). My friends and neighbors questioned me, "How can you make it strong enough to hold together in rough seas?" The skeptics frequently assume that someone living in my time would have been wholly incapable of building something as large and sophisticated as the Ark. As you all know they were capable of building cities, making musical instruments, and working with metal (Genesis 4:16–24). Don't underestimate the people; those who lived before the flood would have been highly intelligent. Even though building such a large ark was going to be an enormous job, I did not doubt. I and my sons set to work building the ark according to God's instructions.

It took a long time to build, and my friends and neighbors laughed at me for building such a huge boat on dry ground. But I was not discouraged by the jeers of the wicked people. I trusted the Lord completely and was only concerned with doing the Lord's will. On the seventeenth day of the Hebrew month of Cheshvan, rain began to fall. In addition, jets of steaming water shot forth from the depths of the earth. The downpour continued for forty days and forty nights, until the face of the earth was entirely submerged, covering the summits of the highest mountains with water fifteen cubits deep. Finally, on the first day of the Hebrew month of Tishrei of the year 1657 (2104 BCE), the water completely subsided. Close to two months later, on the twenty-seventh of Cheshvan, the ground fully dried.

Reporter: Explain to me the intricacies of how you build a gigantic ship without seeing a ship ever.

Noah: The project of the ship building was according to the blueprint that was given to me by Lord Jehovah. The ship's design, drawing of plans, sheer plan, body plan, and half breadth plan was overseen by God. People walked around looking at the noise of the work being done in the workshop. It was built of strong gopher wood over a period of about sixty years; the ark was plastered with fine-grained hinges on the inside and outside. Gopher literally means atonement. I was the first to build a ship according to a certain design to survive the flood. The hull is an important part of the ship. The hull has the strength to survive and resist all adversity at sea. The hull is reinforced with several separating walls, chambers, and girders from the inside of the ship. It is built in the shape of a fish to move very effortlessly through the water and to reduce resistance. Its bottom is well-smoothed. The front of the hull is called the bow, and the back is called the stern. Shipbuilding is still built on this same simple basis.

The ship is as old as human history. Today, the technology of shipbuilding has come a long way. Spacious interior, the modern ship features gold-plated pillars, upholstered carpets, and stalls selling a variety of food and soft drinks, Wi-Fi, and ship crews such as angel-like beautiful girls. The ark that I built by God's command had the same foundations as the modern-day ship. For about 120 years, God warned me that I would survive the coming flood. But no one is listening. I testify that God is the provider of protection for the righteous who obeys God, even if the heavens will disappear with a loud noise, and the heat will melt the whole universe. God is the one who give protection even if it is only for a single righteous person obey God. Those who decide not to conform to the world, but to flow against the flow of the fallen world, then God will be with you. There is no doubt that a minority will see to walk with God even in a time when the majority are living according to their own desires without wanting to follow God.

Reporter: Was there any enough space for all the animals in the ark?

Noah: Naturally, there are many skeptics who question that there is millions of species in the world far more than the number that could fit on the ark. It usually turns out that skeptics simply did not fully understand the situation. (As per the estimates published in 2014, there are fewer than 1.8 million documented species of organisms in the world.) Land-dependent, air-breathing animal ones that could not otherwise survive the flood are boarded on the ship (Genesis 7:21–23). Conversely, for marine animals don't have any threat about this flood. Many skeptics assert that the Bible must be wrong, because they claim that the Ark could not possibly have carried all the different types of animals. This has persuaded some Christians to deny the Genesis flood or believe that it was only a local flood involving comparatively few local animals. But they usually have not actually performed the calculations.

The measurement I have got from God to build the ark was measured 300×50×30 cubits (Genesis 6:15), which is about 140×23×13.5 meters or 459×75×44 feet, so its volume was 43,500 (cubic meters) or 1.54 million cubic feet. To put this in perspective, this is the equivalent carrying capacity of 340 semitrailer trucks, each of which can hold 37 1,200-pound slaughter steers, 90 500-pound feeder calves, 180 250-pound hogs, or 300 125-pound sheep. This would be a line six lanes wide and half a mile long. If the animals were kept in cages with an average size of that is 75,000 cubic centimeters, the 16,000 animals would only occupy 42,000 cubic feet. Even if a million insect species had to be on board, it would not be a problem, because they require little space. If each pair was kept in cages of 10 cm (4 inches) per side, or 1,000 cm, all the insect species would occupy a total volume of only 12 cars. This would leave room for five trains of 99 cars each for food, my family, and range for the animals.

Tabulating the total volume is fair enough, since this shows that there would be plenty of room on the Ark for the animals with plenty left over for food, range, etc. The Ark has carried compressed and dried foodstuffs and a lot of concentrated food. The cattle fed mainly on grain, plus some hay for fiber. Foodstuffs would have been only about 15 percent of the Ark's total volume. Drinking water would only have taken up 9.4 percent of the volume. The upstairs closed room is 101,250 square feet. In the language we understand, it's about the size of 21 basketball courts.

Reporter: Why you never hesitated to build the ark and warn the people for the flooding?

Noah: If you ask me what is the secret of not showing any reluctance to warn of God's flood at a time when I have not seen rain with the shipbuilding that has lasted for hundred twenty years, I have had the good fortune to walk with God and have no doubt in the words of God. I did everything according to God's plan. It had never rained, not even once prior to the flood, yet God told me He was going to flood the earth with rain. After I and my family had entered the ark, God closed the door of the ark. Suddenly, dark clouds rolled across the sky. The wind began to blow. Nature had begun to unleash all its beauty and terror. The clouds quickly spread over the sky like black monsters. Lightning bolts sharpened the silver sword and heavy rain pounding the roof and windows of the ship. Not a speck of light fell on the earth. The clouds obscured the sun and the moon. Rain fell for a period of forty days and nights. The floodwaters had been rising for 150 days. We were inside the ark for a year and seventeen days. When the waters rose on the earth, the ark began to move. The phenomenon of heavy ships floating on water is a blessed physical property of water. The force exerted by seawater against the weight of a ship is called buoyancy. It was a flood that engulfed even the mountains. The water rose to a height of 20 feet, the highest mountain in the world. The waves roaming in the dark desolation filled the brain with whiteness of delusion. All life on earth was wiped off the face of the earth. Only the people who were in the ark were left alive.

Reporter: Describe me the ferocious Great Flooding?

Noah: I do not know where to begin. The mountains erupted. Landslip and eruptions were constantly happening. The storm was blowing with a terrible devilish appearance. The gentleness of nature was abandoned. Inability to see even those standing nearby due to the dust stormed around. The sudden gust of wind seemed to be the angel of death. People could be seen running helplessly to escape the rising water level. The destructive force of the wind blows through the trunks of the trees like the music of death. The wildness of nature was rocking the land with vigor. Thousands of lives were lost in the swamps and tornadoes. The intensity of the flood increased. After two days and two nights, many climbed on the slippery tree branches, hoping to save their lives. They knew that at any moment, death would reach the tops of the trees where they were sitting. There are dark days and dark nights.

Strong currents carry the prey of wild animals such as wild boars, lions, and tigers. The flow of water seemed to be faster than the storm. Everything was in the light of lightning, and we saw it from the first day we were on board. The wind that God sent was not an ordinary wind. The fountains of the deep and the windows of the sky were opened. Only whistles and shouts in the flood. Human dreams and lost paradises were submerged under the water. God caused a wind to blow on the earth for those in the ark. So the water stopped flowing. The foundations of the deep are closed. The rain stopped. As the waters receded, the ark rested on Mount Ararat. The ark rested on the seventeenth day of the seventh month (Nissan) at Mount Ararat. Jehovah placed a bow in the cloud as a sign of the law. At infinity, the spectra began to spread, and the stars began to appear. After months of voyage, we set foot on the new earth that had been cleansed by the flood. The birds and animals that were our companions disappeared during the journey. We started a new life with the newly built altar.

Reporter: Based upon your life experiences, what are some words of advice that you would give to this generations?

Noah: We can walk with God, even in a generation running with the devil. One person's faith can lead to the salvation of many. True faith expresses itself in obedience. Our obedience may make the disobedient feel guilty. Even mature believers can fall into serious sin when they let their guard down. God speaks to human beings a truth that can be seen throughout the biblical narrative. We can never go wrong when we listen to God. In a chaotic culture, we can find favor in God. God keeps his promises and covenants. We can grieve the heart of God with our sin. God always provides a way for us to begin again with Him. We will not always understand God and His ways, but we can trust Him. We can obey God even if the world thinks we are foolish. All things are possible with God. God is able to do far above what we know, expect, and even understand. That was true of Him then, and it's still true of Him today.

Abraham (2050–1875 BCE)

Reporter introduction: After a lengthy slumber, the sun is waking up slowly, crackling with activity, and hurling blistering pulses of energy into space. Today's voyage to the ancient city of Ur in ancient Mesopotamia, on the banks of the Euphrates Tigris River in the Middle East, the birthplace of Abraham. Ur is a town located between the Euphrates and Tigris rivers. Although it is densely populated by farmers and shepherds, there are occasional skirmishes between the two groups. Abraham is called the father of many nations, patriarch, progenitor, ex-father, high father, the father of the Hebrews, the father of the believers. The city is named after a man named Abraham, who is called by many adjectives, such as the Exalted Father, the root of the good olive Israel. Abraham was one of those whom God changed his name.

Abraham is known as God's friend. He is the crowning example of obedience to God. With a name that is revered by all the three major nations of the world alike! Through a covenant, God called Abraham out of the city of Chaldea and promised to give him and his descendants the most beautiful piece of land in the middle of the earth. Abraham's selflessness, courage, unselfish nature, lowly and partial nature, faith, and obedience lived in tents and waited for the city that God had built and had foundations. He was looking forward to the city with foundations, whose architect and builder is God.

The history of the nation of Israel begins with the call of God to Abraham, who leaves the city of Ur. Ur, located in Southern Mesopotamia, was one of the largest cities in the kingdom of Sumer what is today Southern Iraq. Ur was a highly centralized, wealthy, bureaucratic state, and controlled much of the trade into Mesopotamia. Imports to Ur came from many parts of the world: precious metals such as gold and silver, and semiprecious stones, namely lapis lazuli and carnelian. The boundaries on God's map are not the boundaries drawn by man. God is the one who draws maps for His people. Human knowledge of God can't encompass the infinite dimensions of his greatness. He does not have to learn anything, and He has not forgotten anything. We don't have a tape measure long enough to see how big He is. We don't have a calendar old enough to see how long He's been around. There is no limit to His existence, no limit to His power, no limit to His knowledge. God told Abraham to go to a place he had never seen or heard of. God's calling is so unexpected and humane. It would be impossible to understand with the intellect.

Reporter explanations: A famous Midrash shared by Judaism and other traditions depicts Abraham as a little infant abandoned in a cave by his parents. They were afraid that Nimrod would kill their little child since Nimrod's astrologers had told him a baby had been born who was destined to shine to the entire world.

Abraham cried and cried because he was so hungry. God sent the angel Gabriel, who gave him milk to drink until Abraham grew and was three years old. One night he decided to leave the cave. When he went out, the world was dark. He looked up at the skies and saw the twinkling stars. He was amazed by so many millions of little lights. He said, "These must certainly be the most powerful forces in the whole universe. These must be the gods." But then came the dawn and the stars disappeared. "No," said Abraham. "Those little lights can't be gods because they have disappeared. Something else has outshone them. I won't worship them anymore." Then the sun rose and shone in all its glory. Abraham said, "This is the most powerful force. This is God. I will worship this." But towards evening, as the sun set, Abraham understood that the sun is also not God. Out of the darkness, the moon rose and shone its light, and Abraham thought, "Yes, this time I have found God."

At that moment, the angel Gabriel came down and took Abraham to a fountain of pure water. "Immerse and purify yourself," said the angel. Afterward, the angel revealed to him that HaVaYaH, the One God, holds power and dominion over the heavens above and the earth below. God created the entire world. When Abraham heard the words of the angel, he prostrated and prayed to HaVaYaH, creator of heaven and earth. Abraham understood that a subordinate power has no option but to submit to a higher power. What he sought all his life was the highest power of all—in the knowledge that if he could discover the secret of ultimate power, he himself would be able to channel it and wield it for good. (Rabbi Mendel Adelman, Chabad.org)

Reporter: What kind of mixed emotions came to your mind when God spoke to leave your home town to a place never seen?

Abraham: I remember when Sarah and I packed up and left Ur. Our relatives, neighbors, and friends thought we were crazy. It's bad enough to leave the comfort and safety of city life; they were criticizing that we traveling to an unknown land at the command of some invisible God. Faith means obeying God even when we don't understand His revealed will. Taking matters into our own hands can cause problems for us and others.

Many thoughts went through my mind when God commanded me to leave my homeland of Haran, my homeland, my relatives, and my ancestral home. A journey where you are not sure where you are going or where the journey will end. The journey from Ur to Haran was not that difficult, because Haran was the border of our land. At that time, no one was crossing on the other side of the river of Haran. Beyond that, cultures, costumes, and diets are all different. That is why the journey with the family that started from the city was interrupted when it reached Haran. My brother's son and father did not want to go beyond that. The word *Haran* means parched. Haran is located on the banks of the Balik River, a tributary of the Euphrates River in northern Mesopotamia. The city wall of Haran had more than 180 gazebos and 6 massive walls. Today's city has nothing close of that with the famous town of the old Haran. The Babylonian religion was started after the flood by the Nimrodites of the Ham tribe, who were notorious for turning people against God. Ur is the richest and most densely populated area in southern Mesopotamia. It was a sophisticated caste center. These were just behind the Euphrates and Tigris rivers that flowed into the Persian Gulf.

Many ruins that shed light on the ancient culture of Ur are still found there, lying in ruins in Babylon. The huge temple tower, which was a skyscraper, remains indelibly, inscribed in the history books as a symbol of human arrogance. The Bedouins, now known as the heirs of the desert, can be found there in droves. The great city of Babylon was the meeting place of all the abominations, immoralities, and evils of the Western and Eastern nations. The city of Haran tells the story of human history and Babylon, the cradle of human civilization. So we decided to give up our hometown before the voice of God. If we prefer to go the choicest place of Canaan, then we had to leave Haran. The roots and familiarities of our connections of Ur had to be cut off. The natives are idolaters. According to the revelation, I made the decision to leave Ur. My father Terah and his brother's son Lot and family are set out for Canaan from Ur.

Reporter explanations: The world-famous story about Abraham's breaking the idols shows the wit and wisdom with which he exposed man's folly and self-deception when he worships idols and other products of his own activity. Abraham's father, Tera, was an idol manufacturer. Once he had to travel, so he left Abraham to manage the shop. People would come in and ask to buy idols. Abraham would say, "How old are you?" The person would say fifty or sixty. Abraham would say, "Isn't it pathetic that a man of sixty wants to bow down to a one-day-old idol?" He was pointing out that if you are searching for the ultimate power, it's no use looking at ephemeral, man-made objects, no matter how impressive. The man would feel ashamed and leave.

One time, a woman came with a basket of bread. She said to Abraham, "Take this, and offer it to the gods." Abraham got up, took a hammer in his hand, broke all the idols to pieces, and then put the hammer in the hand of the biggest idol among them.

When his father came back and saw the broken idols, he was appalled. "Who did this?" he cried.

"How can I hide anything from you?" replied Abraham calmly. "A woman came with a basket of bread and told me to offer it to them. I brought it in front of them, and each one said, 'I'm going to eat first.' Then the biggest one got up, took the hammer, and broke all the others to pieces."

"What are you trying to pull on me?" asked Tera. "Do they have minds?"

Then Abraham said to his father, "Listen to what your own mouth is saying? They have no power at all! Why worship idols?" (Midrash Bereishit 38:13).

Reporter: Can you explain your journey to a place that you never seen?

Abraham: A journey with a large entourage on foot without any preconceptions or knowledge, leaving the city of Chaldea reflecting the light of antiquity and reform. The journey started as God commanded us to leave our homeland where we were born and raised and the house where we used to crawl, walk, climb, and run and to a new place. Migrating to a different place is so hard in many ways like missing good friends, community, social structure, familiar sites that defined my comfort zone was overwhelming, especially when it is suddenly and permanently. Moving is never easy. It's always hard to say goodbye to a place you have loved. I felt so full, I thought I might burst. The trails alternate between sun-drenched deserts, scorching deserts, meadows, and new cities. The rocks and the ever-hot sand dunes look like an ancient image of Arabia. The greenery of the wild interior is lush with plants and trees. As you walk, tall trees form a leafy canopy above your head, blocking the sun and casting dappled shadows over ground. The trees are as tall as like hitting the sky, so the sun occasionally comes up like a guest. To meet the arrival of winter, the leaves fell on the roadside in dormant condition.

A journey of herding sheep on a dry summer season is very difficult. During the extreme cold, the lawn is to turn brown and appear to be dead. These areas become pitch dark in nights and turn to a mystery after dusk. Nature's daily masterpiece: sunset. The sun was setting in the west, scattering the colors. The sun was waiting to set in the sky, which was painted with saffron and red. The color of the sky slowly changed. The sun went down with enchanting beauty. The blazing sun wishing good night and disappears and never returns till tomorrow morning. The atmosphere was filled with the crickets' chirp. They primarily chirp at nights and is created when the front wings are rubbed together and is amplified by wing surface, and foxes howling. The cuckoo echoed mysteriously in the depths of the vast forest. After dusk, the wild boar and the woodpeckers are disturbed. There have been no instances where unimaginable horror has crept into me. The slow rhythm of the depressing noise is the disturbing noises. The blanket of darkness spread around, and the darkness slowly began to spread. Moon's light began to spread through the blackness of the night makes the journey difficult.

Reporter: Do you have any hard time to believe that you are going to have children in your old age?

Abraham: Walking with the clock of time, Sarah and I regretted not being able to have children despite our age. So it was only later that I realized that my acceptance of Sarah's advice to seek an alternative way which causes and the mental agony was excruciating pain. Although I was not at all skeptical of God's promise, but Sarah didn't believe. Sarah couldn't get pregnant for almost ninety years. Sarah dealt with all the hope, fear, anger, and disbelief that accompany trying and waiting to have children. Sarah, with tears in her eyes, kept complaining. So I went to a famous doctor and ask about his opinion. The doctor said sympathetically to Sarah, who was sitting in front of him with hopeless grin. "See, Mrs. Sarah, we can go for a surgery, but I can't give you an assurance that we will able to correct the deformity. I'm extremely sorry." Sarah left the room with confused eyes, determined to see the black blanket in front of her and the twinkling light of fireflies (Lampyridae) to challenge the passing night. Sarah unilaterally decided to have a child from Hagar, our servant. It is safe to say that she was not in the mood to reconcile her decision with God's counsel.

Reporter: You being the father of faith, can you advice the believers some of your spiritual life lessons?

Abraham: The greater the cost, the greater the sacrifice. Sacrifice doesn't always come with answers. Obedience both relies on God for strength and expects God to deliver. What God requires, He provides. God is always at work, molding and shaping us for His purposes. This sometimes comes by sacrifice by testing and by trusting. Faith means obeying God even when we don't understand his revealed will. Faith is the complete obedience to God, even when the motives hidden in God's heart are not revealed. Belief is a feeling of certainty that something exists has never been seen but actually exists. Until then, following God will cause us to have a great deal of turmoil in the world of friends and family. Don't ignore it. It is a faith that is unshakable, courageous, obedient, steadfast, and adventurous. Unquestioning obedience is often difficult, but the result can be astonishing.

Job (Approx. 2100–1650 BCE)

Reporter introduction: I would like to share with you an eventful life story that is even more intriguing than what was discussed in the last episode. It was a journey to the land of Job in Edom, called Uz, whose name means "tormented big." Uz was a tribal kingdom located between the land of the Philistines and Egypt. The biographies of Job are the experiences of his salty tears and swollen eyes and are discussed here. This is a sobbing story. I want caution everybody to grab some tissues handy to wipe the tears. The city of Uz in Edom, the land of Job, which is afflicted; Uz is a nation located between the land of the Philistines and Egypt. It is located in the southwestern part of the Jordan and is inhabited by the Shemites.

This is a heart-wrenching tale of loss and curiosity, terribly tragic and perfectly heartbreaking. Job lost everything and everyone in his life. The unexpected turns and tragedies are so devastating. It is a long journey about 293 kilometers from Hebron to the southwestern Jordan (Uz—the land of Edom). We were on the way to Uz, the sky darkened with clouds and darkness spread. Strong wind brings rain, thunder, and lightning. After a while, the rain slowly subsided. Then it rained. Raindrops fell from the trees and from one leaves to the other leaves of the plants, and the flowing rain water created a four-part music party in that atmosphere. The sound of rain is one of the most relaxing sounds in existence. This sound alone eases away stress and makes everything outside look more calm and quiet. The fragrant breeze was blowing the leaves. Though it was supposed to be a rainy morning, the rain clouds had cleared. After traveling a short distance inland, the views are breathtaking and stunning. Everywhere, there are only sand dunes around, except the views of the local nomadic tribesmen driving the camels. They live in tents with camels. Above the head as the sun blazed, baked sand at the bottom, and small forts and caves at the top of the hill could be seen in many places along the way. The road is full of dangers. The rays of the morning sun began to brighten the hills.

Streets view with lush greenery full of oil palm and other types of crucifixes. Herds of sheep grazing in the pastures could be seen in large numbers along the way. The silver plate of the moon gave white to the sky. Most conservative scholars believe that the book of Job is at least as old as the time of Abraham. Satan departed, and tragedy began to fall upon Job like a trip hammer in rapid staccato blows. The Sabeans attacked, fire fell, the Chaldeans raided; the house was blown down and killed all his children. Each report came on the heels of the preceding one. In a few minutes time, Job learned of the loss of all he valued: possessions, crops, animals, servants, and children. Yet he did not curse God or shake his fist at Him. The greatness of Job's reverence of God is the fact that heaven, hell, earth, God, Satan, and man all agree on this. He possessed immense wealth for everything from cows, sheep, bulls, elephants to camels. He was a man who was testified by God to be righteous and true. At the same time, the children and the house were destroyed, the beast's wealth was plundered, the crucified lands were set on fire, and the whole body was wounded with worms; those who thought they were loved covered their noses and walked away in pain. Friends blamed, ridiculed, and tore his heart out with words, and thus he became a nugatory life rejected by all. A dark cloud of questions and thoughts lingered in our minds. Why did this happen to the pious Job? A group of people say that it is useless to worry about their life except to sympathize instead of railing or murmuring. Job is not a Hallmark movie; Job is real. Job had been lying in unrelieved misery for months with open sores all over his body. Job cries out to God in the darkness of his despair. A strong person is not the one who doesn't cry. A strong person is the one who cries and sheds tears for a moment then gets up and fights again. Sometimes painful things can teach us lesson that we didn't think we needed to know. The subject matter is the pathetic inversions in the drama of life. Life can be more tragic than death.

Reporter: What was the first encounter between God and Satan and the strange conversation about you?

Job: The living man could not ascend freely and was invisible to the naked eye, but Satan went to God and complained about Job in the heavens, then God said to him that everything he had was in his hands. In a way, I was handed over to Satan. This is not a fictional story; it is an event in my own life. Satan's entire authority is under God. He can do nothing in the lives of a passionate worshipper of God. God determines our suffering; only God gives and takes life. To do anything against to a child of God, Satan requires permission from the Sovereign God. The accusation cut deeper than any sword, and that's the greatest weapon of Satan. God does not need to tempt me to know my heart's position, but the temptation I faced was only a coddling of God in the face of Satan's strategic need. God does not tempt us. This may come as a shock to many people, but God does not trick, tempt, or give us opportunities to sin. This is contrary to His nature. Satan thought that I would deny God and curse him. Satan laid land mines to my health, wealth, prosperity, and family relationships, which was hidden and camouflaged to making them seldom seen and difficult to locate and was waiting for an explosion. He tried to use my wife and friends for that. But the game went awry, and he failed miserably.

Reporter: What was the encounter between you and your friends and the strange conversation?

Job: You know that the reaction of my friends who came to comfort me after learning about the tragedies that befell me was not pleasant. Eliphaz, Bildad, and Zophar came to me to show sympathy and comfort. But it is safe to say that they enjoyed rubbing salt in my wounds. Think about what Eliphaz says, has the innocent ever been ruined? Those who plant injustice will harvest disaster, and their reign of terror will come to an end. They were saying harsh words and ridiculing me. Bildad says that there is no end to your fervid speech? If you are innocent, God will arise and save you. When they kept on jeering toward me, I began to lament to God the day of my birth perish, and the night that a boy is conceived! Why did I not perish at birth and die as I came from the womb? I know the fact that no one on earth can be immortal. I know the fact that all human beings begin life by being born, and all human beings die. I was in deep sadness especially for the loss of all my children. I was not afraid of the stalks that Satan launched earthworm to make my life miserable. You know why I say earthworm. They move away from light and will become paralyzed if exposed to light for too long. Nothing prevails before my God who is brighter than sun. Words should restore and heal the wounds. I did not give up hope even as I plunged into the vortex of fear in the darkened corridor. I will cross the sacrificial shore of this tragedy that I am trapped in because of the mind-numbing sluggishness and heart-wrenching exhaustion. I relied incessantly on God in His mercy. I spent those painful times building great walls of tolerance for the great floods of crises. Those who tried to isolate and ridicule me did not show even the slightest bit of animosity. I learned survival lessons in a tainted world.

Reporter: Why your friends accuse you when you are in great misery?

Job: It's a lesson I learned from my experience that periphrasis can do more harm than good. My friends did not understand the harsh language of silence. Instead of sympathizing and shedding tears for the grieved one, they were giving lectures on philosophy of great truths. Words, among other factors, are vital to the survival of human civilization. It is very difficult to heal the wounds caused by the inappropriate usage of words. The tongue has no bones. But it is strong enough to break a heart. It is so easy to let our brains slip out of gear while engaging our tongues. A tongue, without cerebral guidance, is a vehicle out of control. Someone is most likely to get hurt. To keep one's lips sealed is more dangerous than stopping the flow of a river. The presence of friends alone was enough during my worst grief. Speaking of which, it should have been better than silence. It is not right to think that anyone can say anything because he has a tongue. May our speech be such as to bring joy and comfort to ourselves and others? Likewise, do not forget to examine whether our speech is harmful to others in any way. Silence has its own value. Therefore, when we use words to break someone's silence, it must be healing the wounds. Time has advised me to look for meanings behind any smile, to look for differences in meaning even in familiar words, and to be wary even of those who believe they are saints. The loneliness of the lonely days and nights of the mind, the silent sighs, and the scorching heat of the desolate corridors left deep wounds by the friends. But God had given me the strength to break through the great wall of untruth before truth. I was defending myself against the Great Wall of Silence. I have learned that silence is better than words to heal some wounds in the mind.

Reporter explanations: Silence speaks the language of the heart where words become irrelevant. J. C. Chandor's *All Is Lost*, the film, is an exception to the film's concept. At the beginning of the film, there is no dialogue except for the conversation between the passenger and the rescue (SOS) over the wireless phone. Waiting for a small glimmer of hope, he received no good news. Eventually he drinks the bitter water of loneliness and spends his days as a stranger even to the sea. The film underscores the film's concept of interacting with the audience through the diversity of scenes, not through the abundance of dialogue. The empty vessels make the most noise in this world. Even spirituality is degenerating into a kind of rhetoric lapse that pierces the ears. Those who are devoted to God are treated as fools and fanatics and treated like the rubbish of the world and the filth of everything. God can sometimes seem to maintain a kind of cruel silence, not just silence (aggressive silence).

Reporter: What were your good dreams of your future wife, and in reality, what was your experience?

Job: I understand the meaning of your question. The first question can be answered, and the second question can only be answered in part. Real life experiences have completely toppled down my perception of my wife. As a star of my dark life, I wished she could turn my nights into the moonlight by giving her own eyes. Even when the volcano inside in me is tried to explode, I dreamed of a soothing touch on the journey through the ascents and descents of the disease. Though I thought that the obligation promises of commitment would console for the rest of my life, but she moved away like a stranger who was left alone halfway of my life. Even though I was disappointed by the sarcastic words, I quietly tried to hide my sorrows in a sigh, expecting that there would be something magical about to have a dramatic change. She saw my deformed body, covered her nose repulsively, and asked me to deny God and to die. Her every word was just like fire, which burned my mind. It is impossible to describe in words the altruism that comes with hurting accusations and sharp sarcasm in the midst of life's ups and downs. I still remember once said to me, "I trust you as if my soul were yours. I am willing to sacrifice my life for yours or simply for your well-being." What's the meaning of those words now? Husband-wife relationship is a coldish fire that melts two people joins together. Therefore, the term *spirituality* of a family of two is most ambiguous when combined with the term *family*. Caring is its manner; love is its way. The word *spirituality*, which associates with a loving God, is most purposeful when meld with the word family.

The love of the world is like a rain that widespread changes in weather patterns change in minutes, and sometimes suddenly, and within a few moments, it suddenly fades away in some way. But I do not like to remember the moments when I was shocked by the strange expressions of whether relationships are so fleeting. They purposefully disown me and walk away unexpectedly, but the snivel still linger somewhere in my chest. I did not receive the loving care, unconditional care, sincerity, and loving treatment of my life partner, but she also advised me to deny God and commit suicide. When anybody is going through the distressed mind, the better half should give comfort and to lean on to them. But my case was different. This kind of situation anybody will think and wonder what is the use of a partner if you can't lean on them. Crises are the cornerstone of a person's true identity will reveal.

Crisis does not change the nature but reveals the real character of a person. The little candle flame that was left in my life, the heavy wind was relentless and competes to blow off my test of faith. Friends and relatives signed the pages of my death book, saying that there would be no coming back to life and abandoned me. All I could do was to pour out the sorrows and wounds of life to God.

Reporter: How did you withstand despite of all the troubles and your friends were accused that you are a sinner?

Job: I didn't deny God, even though everyone around branded me as a sinner, because I am convinced that my Redeemer is alive, that my witness is in heaven, and that my guarantor is in the heights. All those whom we consider to be our own leave us at a time when comfort and support are essential, and when we realize the presence of God gives strength, energy, and vitality of comfort is sprinkled on the wounds that are filled with pain, while pouring oil on the coals of sorrow. The comforting words of my friends seemed to be aggressive, uttering painful words that a thousand heartbreaking hedgehogs pounded into the body together. My friends surmised that God as inferior to the common man. It seems to them that they have come to argue for God. They deliberately forgot that my God is comforter and merciful. True friendship is tested in the hour of adversity. When you are in trouble, many professed friends will be shy of you and insult, betray, and cause the deadliest wounds. Don't offer counsel when you don't understand what people are going through. Avoid throwing gasoline on the fire and escalating the painful feelings by saying or doing inappropriate things.

People are seen to rejoice when they are happy, and there is no one around when you are in deep trouble and sad! There are so many comrades in happiness, and when sorrow comes, you will be left alone to stand on your own two feet. Human life is like the life of a mayfly. Mayfly also called one-day fly transforms while they move. Within their short life, they transform at three stages of their life that lasts only for one day, teaching us how to live our lives effectively. The mornings and evenings of suffering were slowly passing by. One night when I finally broke the boundaries of waiting, I asked God a question from the slums of sleep. Do you have eyes of flesh? Do you see as a mortal sees? Whatever I acquired due to the hard work in my lifetime was lost in one day. For a while, I was devastated. It's hard to imagine anyone who has faced a day like me. I faced catastrophe after catastrophe. On that particular occasion, I was engulfed in a sense of humiliation when the guilt of asking vain questions to God.

Everything happens for a reason. Evil is never part of God's plan. God brings good from bad situations.

The hand of God's deliverance will be revealed only in due time. God's time may seem too late for us. God never misses the time. God's never early, never late, but always on time. Our timing isn't God's timing. For us, God's timing often feels like a long, desperate delay. God's perfect timing does two things. It grows our faith as we are forced to wait and trust in God, and it makes certain that He and He alone gets the glory and praise for pulling us through. God then gave me the joy of being like a child who has got back a toy that he once thought was lost. But everything got doubled. There is no place that you can find the unconditional love except God's presence. There is no doubt that only God can remove all sorrows and bring happiness and lead you into the greener valleys.

Life has infinite diversity, there are unbelievable scripts, and there are surprising possibilities and strange endings. It convinces us that God's purpose for us is to dedicate every sight and event in the journey of life to the fine work of the heavenly Master. Accusations like thorns and sword like life experiences and pains relied on the grace of God. My friends and even family members' scoffings, I didn't pay much attention. When rainwater droplets that rebound the leaves of the *Colocasia esculenta* plant, I shook off all the negative charges against me. When the black clouds moved, then only the moon will appear. I can briefly describe what people in the world have to say about how they will react in their time of trouble, but what I have learned from the coal experiences of life is that it is best to rely on God. God has the answer to all diseases and problems, even though sometimes they are not revealed! God's grace bestowed me greatly the only reason that I did not deny God while fighting from the middle of the battlefield of life.

Reporter explanations: The sun is saying goodbye to the day; the pure clouds were shining on the western horizon. It's almost dark, and we are going to wrap up today's journey. Up in the sky, the moon smiles as he lights the candle. A thousand springs blossomed on the moonlit night bathed in the moon. Despite many trials in life, God finally gave Job the opportunity to experience God's love and care in abundance. The book of Job gives us the message that there is a God waiting for us at the end of all suffering. God may have opened the windows for us when the door was slammed shut against us. Even as dreams lay in heaps of ashes, those noble words that my Redeemer is alive were uttered by Job, the Bible's example of endurance. One tragedy after another, the anchor of hope continued unabated. Disasters like waves pounded one after another, and there were huge beasts. The servants were hacked to death by the enemy, and ten of their children were killed in the storm. Lifesavers are those who do not act with vengeance intensity without trying to understand the reality or assess the real situation. Such people try to remove the annoyances of the hearts of others and to remove the turmoil of the mind.

Reporter: Give us some life lessons that will benefit the believers.

Job: God's people are not immune from pain. In fact, it often seems as if theirs is more severe, more frequent, more unexplainable, and more deeply felt than that of the unbeliever. Bad things happen to good people. In the midst of suffering, we must never lose our hope in God. Friends may fail us in the midst of our misery, but God never does. Even in the midst of God's silence, His presence is with us. Wisdom comes from fearing God and turning away from evil. God is with us in the midst of our storms. Our God is the God of the storm. Our God is in complete control. God is the creator of the universe; He is mighty and powerful. Sometimes, in the midst of our suffering, we sin, but God accepts a humble and repentant heart. Sometimes your best friends will fail not only to help and supportive but they gave poor advice and accuse us. When you repent and forgive others, the blessings will follow you.

Jacob (2006–1859 BCE)

Reporter introduction: The beginning of the month of Sivan, the first month of summer after spring. I got a chance to see Jacob when the temperature was thirty to forty degrees Celsius. At first reading of Jacob, we learn that he was the one who usurped the inheritance and then stole the blessing from his father. He was forced to flee from his own parents and circumstances in which he was born so as not to be reduced to ashes by his brother Esau. God had prepared for him many gates of God's grace where he never knew. The man who crossed the Jordan few years ago in fear and anxiety about what will happen to his life. All he had was a stick in his hand, but he came back in two groups. We can learn from the life of Jacob the essential life advice that we only reap what we sow. Whatever is sown, it will be returned in a hundredfold increase. If you sow artifice, you will reap artifice. Sow only the good, think only the good, and desire only the good. The Bible introduces many people whose names have been changed by God and who have multiple names. One of them is our protagonist Jacob.

It does not seem wrong to say that Jacob was a man who tried to help God and save himself by lying. In this connection, an incident on the pitch of football legend Maradona comes to my mind. He hits the ball with his hand at a crucial moment. He was one of the athletes on the field who profess that he is a Christian. The ball was touched with the hand against the rules of the game, but the referee did not pay enough attention and ruled it was a goal. Later, when journalists asked Maradona about this hoax, he said that the hand you saw was not mine but God's. On November 25, 2020, the media reported that the legendary football legend, which rose to prominence on the field at the age of sixty, had disappeared and part of history. Winning the 1986 World Cup has become part of the history of Maradona telling with God's hand and my head. All success is temporary. Its energy does not last forever. God is not the sponsor of anyone's deception. God is not a reed sway back and forth in the wind to protect our own interests. Jacob's life experience shows that God scrupulously keeps all record of each person's accounts and that the rewards will be strictly paid.

Reporter: Traveling one place to another like a wanderer, tell me the Paddan Aram trip.

Jacob: My whole life has been a long journey from one place to another like a nomad. The journey from Beersheba to Paddan

Aram after the usurpation of the patrimony from Esau is unforgettable (1760 BCE). The next day was an unexpected escape, because I
had to leave before Esau returned from the hunt, so I could not sleep
that night. Moments gave way to minutes, minutes to hours. The
confrontation between the pros and cons of the important decision
about the travel was heartbreaking, but in the end, it was decided to
go according to the mother's opinion. In the depths of my mind, I
was working on the finishing touches of the final decision without
my permission. It was a situation where we could not wait for a clear
decision to emerge. I had to leave the love that had been stored in
my mother's heart for me. My mind was not even strong enough to
think that I would have to leave the land where I grew up, played and
dreamed and felt safe and protected. Childhood memories are the
strongest that stick with us for a lifetime. It was early in the morning,
and I was in a hurry to say goodbye to everyone, hiding my sadness
and laziness in my sleepy eyes. It was the curiosity of a journey to an
unknown place. The village is waking up as usual from the slumber
of sleep. The red rays of the sun were beginning to spread the colors
in the village. The light at sunrise is filtered and scattered by dust
particles and moisture in the air, which in turn produces the beautiful color in the sky. Because my mind was upset so much, I could
not enjoy the sounds of the birds in the morning, the beautiful glow
of the rising sun, and the touch of the cold breeze. I had to travel
completely unfamiliar terrain, through the woods alone, without a
compass. All I know was "the sun rises in the east and sets in the
west." None of the servants or slaves in my father's house is with me
now, in a journey that changed the course of my life.

My trip was flagged off by my loving mother. An ocean like
love of my mother's is like a lamp in my path. There is nothing in
this universe that can equal the mother in endurance, strength, and
love. I watched as a thin smirk spread across my mother's lips as she
rescued me as tears fell on my body. Knowing that the roads were
deserted, that thieves were lurking, that there were thorny paths to
cross, that there were reptiles lurking by the side of the road, and that
they would have to deal with the ugly faces, the deceitful vampires,
and the occasional discoloration like a chameleon. I was traveling

through a forest path full of stones and thorns. Contrary to expectations, a thousand enticing hopes and dreams left and set off for an unknown place. Village roads are without much traffic. It was an afternoon when the date palms and *Sabal palmetto* tree branches sway and make loud whistling of the gusty winds. The heat of the sun increased slowly. The tapered gravel hurt the bare feet. Without the mental strength to resist, life was a race held tightly in the hand.

The howls of wolves, like the terrifying siren of hell, awoke the fears of lightning. Certain places I have to climb hills, because of the poor visibility, howling winds and rain makes very difficult. It was known that the heartbeat sometimes reached its climax, when it hit the stones and thorns; I have to limp and walk. By dusk, the sun is shining vibrant red. Twilight begins with the unfolding of the black curtain. The intensity of the sunrays diminished because of the nightfall. The sun is reluctant to go back; the day began to cover the rays of darkness with a forceful push away from the darkness. Some nightingale sings along to sleep. I could not find a cave or a safe place to sleep. As the sun was setting, at Luz, I picked up one of the stones and lay it as a pillow. The presence of God that I had there was a relief to my lugubrious mind. God made it the door of heaven (Bethel). From there, I realized that I was not an orphan; I am guarded by the Almighty God. In short, I finally reached the house of my mother's brother Laban. I traveled some four hundred miles north across the Euphrates River to Haran, the home of my uncle Laban. Sometimes I long to visit Bethel once again, where I first saw God atop the stairway with angels, and where I promised to follow him with a few conditions, of course! Then I'd like to stand again on Penniel's soil where we wrestled together. It was there my name changed.

Reporter: Did God spoke you to go back to your hometown?

Jacob: One night I was in my bed, I had a divine vision from God and ask me to return to my homeland. That vision still lingers, simmers in my mind. When grazing sheep, we sometimes go to distant places in search of food. In such cases, I do not come home for three to four weeks. I lay down to rest for the night, thinking that I have to return in one to two days. I forgot the surroundings and had a deep sleep. Suddenly I heard the same vision and voice again at Bethel, so I submitted myself to the voice of God to go back. Even though I knew that my return to the homeland would not happen soon, there were many occasions I tried. A return to my hometown was inevitable. Preparations for the return trip with the family began in secret. Years ago, I walked alone, now I became a large group. We started our journey by trampling on the baked sand grains till dusk. The darkness of that day was more intense than usual. There were no stars in the sky. There was not a shred of light left to penetrate the pitch dark moonless night. The gusts of the freezing wind rain in the background were no different when the pitter-patter sound of the rain. I can even hear the rhythm of my inhalation and exhalation. The mental anguish of an aeon lingered in me. After twenty long years, I was in a hurry to enjoy the cool shower of love reunion with loved ones. In the meantime, I met my brother Esau on the road of Seir, which I am not describing here. Esau ran to meet me and embraced me; he threw his arms around my neck and kissed me. And we both wept. I felt like tears rained from my eyes. The children were very upset, because they have no clue what is happening, and they never expected such a scene. It was very difficult to hold the mind that was caught in the flood of memories. It's been years since I've stepped foot in my childhood house. It was a time when the views were blurred with tears.

Reporter: What was the result of the meeting between you and Esau?

Jacob: Let me tell you a little bit about the meeting with Esau. Moisture-laden winds are blowing from the west with thunder and deafening roars. When you walk in the beauty of nature prepared by God, all the sorrows of the mind will be removed, and you will get good energy. The return trip was inevitable when my mind was disturbed filled with nostalgic memories of homeland. I remember the twists and turns of guilt and the days when I was blindfolded bygone times. I walk through the middle of the cornfields bordered by palm trees. Even though it was raining and the wind was blowing, I could see the protagonist in a vague single glance from a distance. It was this face brutality that I ran away unwilling to be seen for more than twenty long years, with a sigh and a touch of memories. As soon as I saw that face in the distance, lightning flashed through my head, because anything can happen. Here comes that moment that has frightened even my sleep for twenty years. Yet I realized that the confidence I had gained in last night's prayer was stirring my nerves. Before I could say anything, Esau turned all my thoughts around and hugged my neck and started crying. We both burst into tears. I leave the part saying that the one who came to take revenge cried like a child only because God spoke to him. Finally, after many years, I was able to step on the steps of my house and see everyone.

Reporter: Did you believe that the severe famine happened in Israel because of God's doing?

Jacob: I am very much convinced that the famine in Israel was ordained by God to see Joseph. It was early in the morning, and I was in a hurry to travel with everyone, hiding my depression and laziness in my sleepy eyes. I awoke to the sound of the heavy booze of the soldiers sent by Joseph to take me to Egypt. I put my wrinkled hand over my eyes and looked up at the sky in the distance. The gray hairs are messy and tousled that had fallen on my face due to the wind. I do not hesitate to say that the physical and mental problems that surround me with disability and helplessness have cast a shadow over my final days of life. The onset of caducity attacked neither my every organ not only the feelings of loss of physical strength, but it was reflected in sight, hearing, and movement. I got a new strength when I heard about Joseph is alive and he is in charge of Pharaoh's storehouses. Tears welled up in my eyes, and I got into the chariot that Joseph had sent. Now I had an opportunity to look back on the past. My wrinkled face of old age glowed up when I saw Joseph; all the lake of sorrows disappeared. The meeting, which took place after twenty-two long years, was soul-stirring. I stared at Joseph for a long time, spreading the fragrant flowers of love on the faded black old fatigued eyes.

Reporter: Do you have any remorse that you tricked your brother first then your father for getting the blessings?

Jacob: I have often wondered if I have the good fortune to play my brother first and then my father and receive the blessings. From the house I thought was my own, I left behind the garlands of prosperity. As expected, I went to my mother's brother Laban's house. Eventually the wedding went smoothly. I could not be identified as the bride's face was covered with a blanket because of the custom. The first night was dark and white. At the end of the wait, that morning came. I was so energetic until a while ago that I suddenly felt like a balloon pricked with a needle and the air blown away. It was only when I was deceived that I learned the pain of cheating others. The shock and frustration I felt when I found out that I was married to Rachel's older sister Leah, even though I was engaged to be married to her younger sister, Rachel, is beyond words. About this, when I asked Laban, he mocked me, saying, "It is not the practice in our place to marry off the younger before the firstborn." I realized that there was no one to speak for me or to stand by me. I was the victim of a deliberate deception. Instead of cheating on my father and brother, the history repeated itself in my life.

Those words hit my ears like thunder. Those words burned in my heart like coals falling on cotton, which catches fire. Like a wild horse out of control, I was engrossed in wild thoughts and sorrows. My condition was like a man escaping his house for fear of rats but confronted to fight with a tiger to spare his life. I wept so bitterly that cause's blurry vision. The problem was that memories of what happened kept popping up in my mind. But I decided to forgive that way my grudges toward Laban lessen its grip and help free from the control of the person who harmed me. For me, it was an escape from not knowing what life was stored for me. I remembered my mother's words that you will face in life that you can even trust your own eyes, which make illusion. If you slightly slip, then you will fall down to laugh and the rocks that fall down if you slip one foot. No matter how much coal of truth is covered with ashes, smoke will continue to rise from that coal. All truths will come to light. Whether the fair is rewarded or insulted, no matter how harsh the mantle, it will come out. My parents gave me the name Jacob appears in the scripture only 446 times. But the word *Israel,* the nickname God gave me, appears 2,540 times in the scriptures. The deceiver Jacob disappeared without a trace. What is the significance of the sword you raised against me? Now tell me, which of these am I, Jacob the deceiver or Israel the father of the tribe?

Reporter: What good advice you can give to this generation from your life experiences?

Jacob: It is possible to pursue the right goal in the wrong way. We should never place conditions on our promises to God. We should show proper respect to everyone in our life, even those for whom we don't have strong emotional feelings. We shouldn't be afraid to place all our trust in God, even in difficult times when we are tempted to take matters into our own hands. Intense spiritual struggle often produces great spiritual blessing. What we sow in our actions toward others, we will reap in their actions toward us. God knows who you are, and He knows what you are thinking. He knows what your life is all about. God does not need our help to fulfill His purpose in our life. All He needs is our obedience. God had not forgotten you, and God has not forgotten you. God has a plan for your life, and His plan does not change. He will allow us to go through times of struggle so that we will seek His face. God wants you to be obedient to Him no matter the circumstances. God will definitely bless you for your obedience. My own personal experience, I want you to remember, we will reap what we sow.

Joseph (1915–1805 BCE)

Reporter introduction: Joseph's story in the Bible is enough to inspire and guide anyone. Joseph came to his life stage as a gentle breeze turned to storm through the history like a hurricane. The one who came as a criminal became the steward, the one who was labelled as guilty became the master, one who was convicted proven innocent, and slave became the slave master. Jail man became a prison officer. The lawbreaker became the prosecutor. The one who were ruled became like monarch. The man who was dragged down the street for sale became the master of all the barns in Egypt. Sold for twenty pieces of silver, he reached an invaluable height. The man who was sold into slavery gradually rose to become the prime minister of Egypt. The man who had been in prison till yesterday without getting his hair cut and wearing nice clothes is now proudly seated near the throne doing all the pedicures and manicures under the leadership of the head hairdresser of the royal palace. Overnight, Joseph became prominent and respected in the community. Joseph was a man of unwavering faith, unwavering willpower, and unconditional masterly love. One who has the zeal and determination to stand up for truth and holiness. He not only resisted temptation but also resisted it. Joseph was honored by Pharaoh with a new name, Zaphenath-Paneah (savior of the world, or bread of life). God did not allow him to end up in a dungeon or a prison. The hand of God spread throughout his life.

Reporter: Please share your testimony in brief and your childhood days.

Joseph: I was sold into slavery, brought to a foreign land, accused of rape, and thrown into prison. Yet even then, my spirits were high. God's faithfulness really clicked in. I could have been desperate and bitter. The circumstances of our lives are not as important as the way we respond to them. Sin is always wrong, even in a foreign land where no one knows or cares about us. Those who live godly lives will suffer persecution. In due time, God will exalt and reward the one who honors him. God is able to use human sinfulness for his glory. When I look back to my life from a political prisoner to prime minister, I arrived here in chains as a seventeen-year-old boy, and now I have been unable to express God's faithfulness in a foreign land of Egypt for ninety-three years. In the early days of my youth, now I'm in my advancing years of my life, I had many nostalgic and painful memories. There are many familiar faces behind my transition from my father's beloved son to the son of tears. From the very beginning, the brothers thought that hearing about God-given dreams was like a swing in the mind to the horns of some never-ending childish desires.

When I reached my brothers, they stripped my robe and threw me into an empty well. When the Midianite merchants passed through, the brothers pulled me from the well and sold me for twenty shekels of silver to the Ishmaelites who were taken me to Egypt. My journey was through a wide path in the middle of the sand dunes.

Reporter: What happened when your father sent you to inquire about the whereabouts of your siblings?

Joseph: My father once sent me to Dothan, about fifty miles south of Shechem, to inquire about the welfare of the brothers. I was walking alone through the woods, mountains, and I heard the burbling sound of the river. Small birds fluttering their wings rhythmically, the grass glows green, and the hills are affluent look giving a beautiful natural beauty. Little did I know that the journey would end on the brink of disaster? It was that wet afternoon when my brothers threw me into the dry well after taking all the food parcels from me. Nothing can substitute blood relation. But my beliefs about relationships were faded that day. I was shocked to see the cruelty of the brothers who shared their joys, sorrows, dreams, and hopes and ate together. I begged the brothers for my life, but I saw a kind of horrible cruelty on their faces and eyes. The world will often show you a fake love first and later throw you into the abyss. You may not even see a flake of hay to catch hold of and escape, but if God has given you a dream, you will not end up lying in the enemy's dry well without fulfilling it. When you are caught up in these dramatic scenes of life, you have to rely on God for help.

Reporter: What happened to you at Potiphar's house?

Joseph: At first, I was very happy to be the caretaker of Potiphar's house. Later I realized that the mistress's steps were wrong and crossed the boundaries. She cast her eyes upon me that is, she looked at me with enticing eyes, and she said to me, "Lie with me." In the absence of her husband, she assumes authority, and she commands, "Come to bed with me, now." I realized that my life was going to be ruined in the house of Potiphar's wife, and I hesitate to do any immoral acts for the sake of physical pleasures. I sensed the siren of temptation trap with blots and blemishes and extremely dangerous. She may have been attracted to me because of all the radiance of adolescence, handsome in appearance, pleasant in personality, energy, and well favored by all. Also she saw in me so many other traits not found in others. Potiphar's wife had become the owner of a conscience that had never been awakened due to her misguided life. Potiphar's wife had unquenchable desires, blind ambition, and was relentless in her efforts to seduce me and made several failed attempts to seduce me. I was aware of the potential ramifications of refusing the seduction attempts of Potiphar's wife and of her power over a slave from a foreign country, yet despite all this, I courageously overcame the temptations. A person who believes that the material body is the only component that makes her who she is will find it very difficult to make life choices that require overcoming urges and instincts. If the body is what defines existence, the body's desires become the ultimate ones to be fulfilled at any price. It was an encroachment on my fundamental rights. All her attempts to subdue me were unsuccessful, so she started threatening me with accusations. She must have thought that if I don't understand the consequences, then let me suffer. What an outward appearances of the hypocritical world. It is a world of total chaos. Temperance distinguishes man from animals. Man is different from all other life-forms in a number of ways. Man can think analytically. He is able to reason and philosophize about life. Man is an ethical being. He can distinguish between right and wrong. He can and does make moral judgments. Man alone of all earthly creation can worship his Creator, creativity, invention, imagination, abstract reasoning, will, and conscience. Like Adam, I did not want to sew fig leaves together for clothing to cover my nakedness. I was able to stop the unwholesome thoughts and not to unlock the door of my mind. I was not ready to ignite or cut it out the passage of my moral consciousness, which lead to do sin. It was not for Potiphar's wife to break my morals, which were viciously illuminated by illusions and illusory feelings of prohibition. Is it not possible to ants crawling in a fire pit? I have a strong conviction that I am a child of God. The woman's sanity plummeted in the face of her vile feelings. At first, she looked at passionately then the gesture of persuasion, and I ruthlessly rejected that demand. Later, when she changed her strategy to force me that even didn't work out also. As there was no other way around, she accused me and invent a story, and I have been victimized. Sometimes there may be some unexpected diversions in our trajectories. But I did not succumb to temptation because of my holiness of life, my fear of God, and my sense of righteousness. You may have met people who sold their lives for a pittance for momentary physical pleasure. But I don't want to give up. If we had known that the price God has given us is more than we can determine, we would not have sold ourselves to the enemy for a paltry sum. In everyday life, some may try to seduce us by filling us with magical expressions of hard-wired ecstasy. We live in a world of deception. As the web of deceit grows, it touches more and more aspects of the relationship until the very foundation of the friendship of marriage is entangled in the deceit, and the very foundation of the relationship is threatened.

Reporter: How you released from the Jail?

Joseph: Prison and release from it is a memory I will never forget. When Potiphar's wife grabbed my outer garment, I left it there to escape and ran away. She used my clothes as a proof that she thought this news spread in public. Does anybody need any bigger proof to sink into the depths of misunderstanding? The woman made up a false story with bit and tassels to put it together. So my name was tarnished without me making any mistake. It was a blow to my pride. I have sleepless nights, and I felt like one night is like a century. Dark narrow rooms with no light in the granite forts built only for criminals. It took days to adjust to the conditions in the prison. Days and months of loneliness, the cracks of grief pierced my mind. It was dark in the sky above the pale trees as I stood holding on to the iron railings. The day is always boring. The prison building stands tall with lot of violent criminals and innocent people stories. There was no one to come to the solitude of my prison life. Isolation is more terrifying than orphan hood. I had a journey through the rough path of life. The days and nights were tossed from the calendar without a trace. One day, Pharaoh had a dream. The court magicians and intel-

50

lectuals could not interpret that dream and its meaning. According to the cupbearer, a man with a divine spirit capable of interpreting dreams was imprisoned and ordered to take me to the palace. It was about seven o'clock in the morning, a nice cool morning. Early in the morning, the cold wind greeted me with a hug. The cool breeze was blowing and caressing my hair like waves crashing in the wind. The signatures of the lives lived within the four walls of the prison. It was too late for me to realize that every color that runs through relationships is a combination of lives. Such people will fail if they do not know how to run hard or soft.

The eastern snow-capped mountains form a colorful universe. The sun was shining like the majestic display of the tail feathers of a thousand peacocks together all in its glory up in the sky. In the morning, two of the king's soldiers came to my cell. The locks of the chains on my hands and feet were opened. Although I have seen the iron gates were open and close for the prisoners freed many during my stay in the jail, but today it was my release day at the least expected time. Pharaoh had two dreams. The next day, Pharaoh asked his magicians and wise men to interpret his dreams, but they could not. Then the chief butler remembered me and told Pharaoh about my ability to interpret the dreams. Pharaoh decided to release me from the jail. Thus the king's dream and the meaning are revealed. Eventually I was elevated to the position of prime minister of the country. That news created a wave of mixed emotions in the prison and in the whole country.

As a result, I earned both the respect and confidence of the Pharaoh, who made me his second in command over all Egypt and was given a gold seal of authority, and he had me ride in his second chariot. The king gave me gold chains and gold necklaces to wear and silk scarves in my hands. Pendulums are hanging, pearls are shining, flowers and fruits are hanging throughout the procession routes. Royal banquet clothed with special garments, the decorated carriages were designed to resemble the boats used to transport the important palace officials. The red carpet was rolled out and lit the streets. The procession with beating of various kinds of big drums and small, royal symbols and majesties add to the journey. Silk cloths, pearls, jewels, various ornaments, embroidered umbrellas, dancers, singers, flute players, all accompanied. The king's throne was adorned with large gemstones and coral pearls made of five precious metals. Years later, I saw the sky, and a new world opened up in front of me. Along the way, princes, ministers, generals, civilians, and people were watching in amazement. It was a huge celebration of curiosities and surprises. It seemed strange to me that all the Egyptians knelt before me, a foreigner, one-time slave, and prisoner. My life story begins from a deserted well and ends in the palace for giving me great position, which I can never imagine. I was brought from a prison dungeon overnight and have been elevated to second in the land. No wonder if this sounds like a myth. If God has planned to bless one's vision, it is useless for an entire empire to stand against it. God's plans must have taken place at the right time. If God had not visited me, even as a slave, I would have had to spend time as a slave in a small hut covered with palm fronds. But in my later life, I was able to sleep comfortably on the soft mattress inside the palace, the high-tech arrangement to hold the cold atmosphere. I didn't forget my past life.

Reporter: Please share your spiritual disciplines, practices, and lessons.

Joseph: Without much introduction, let me tell you I was sold into slavery, brought to a foreign land, accused of rape, and thrown into prison. Yet even then, my spirits were high. God's faithfulness really clicked in. I could have been desperate and bitter. The circumstances of our lives are not as important as the way we respond to them. Sin is always wrong, even in a foreign land where no one knows or cares about us. Those who live godly lives will suffer persecution. In due time, God will exalt and reward the one who honors him. God is able to use human sinfulness for his glory. Jealousy can wreck even a close family relationship. My coat had been taken off and stripped, but not my character and integrity. Always do your best to be diligent and productive. Always remain faithful to God and people around you, and then God will protect you in the midst of dangers and adversities. Run away from sin at all cost. Success do not happen overnight promotion; blessings and prosperity come from God.

Moses (1526–1406 BCE)

Reporter introduction: Moses was the greatest statesman the world has ever seen. He was a mighty warrior, a prophet with personal influence, and a brilliant leader. You can see that Moses was given many descriptions in the Bible. The most gentle of all human beings on earth. Moses was faithful in the house of God. The builder of the Ark of the Covenant, the one who bought the law from God and gave it to Israel, the most respected and elite prophet of all three major religions, Judaism, Christianity, and Islam, who spoke face to face with God, who was a friend of God, who divided the Red Sea, and led the people of Israel out of the land. He was raised to the royal palace, the first and last man to be buried by God, known as the faithful in every planet of God, the God-fearing leader, the unquestionable leader of Israel, the Redeemer, the uncrowned King of Israel, and so on.

Reporter: How did you survive as an infant in Egypt? Share your melodramatic childhood days?

Moses: A time when the unbroken tears of separation from the loved ones of those slain in the grip of slavery melted into the roar of the Nile River. The Dark Ages, when the Israelites were deafened by the vulgar years of the rulers who whipped their slaves. A slave is defined as one bound in servitude as the property of a person or household. The work that the Egyptians forced on the Israelites were evil in motive and cruel in nature under very harsh conditions. They were deployed for construction of buildings, pyramid, and go to war. These slaves mourn their unfortunate births and fall under the yoke of the feudal system of the Egyptian society and end up dying and perishing in the land. I was born at such an unpredictable time (1571 BCE). I was kept in hiding for three months because Pharaoh plotted to kill the newborn Hebrew boys during childbirth. As a last ditch effort, they decided to float me in a basket out of reeds and covered it with tar. My parents had to make that decision even though they are in an ocean of grief and sorrow. Papyrus plants growing in the swamps on both sides of the Nile are reminiscent of mangroves. Princess Bithia came to the Nile River, and she noticed that a basket was swaying and roaming in the bushes. This event marked a turning point in the lives of Princess Bithia and the entire Israelites.

Reporter explanations: Jewish tradition and mythology say that the princess believed that the goddess Nile gave birth to her slave child Moses and gave her a gift. The Egyptians worshiped the Nile as one of their god. Perhaps no river on earth has captured the human imagination quite like the Nile River. The Nile is associated with many gods and goddesses, all of whom the Egyptians believed were deeply intertwined with the blessings. Tradition claims that the daughter of Pharaoh suffered from leprosy, and she went down to bathe in the water to be cured of her disease. The whole innocence of this earth shone brightly on the face of that child, and the mind of Princess Bithia was greatly attracted. Usually at all time, the princesses were never allowed to go anywhere without a maid. When Bithia saw the reed, she sent back all the maidservants into the palace, except Amata, her faithful servant. The princess ordered her maid Amata to bring the reed basket. The basket was not within her reach. So when the princesses reached and stretched out her hand for the basket, suddenly a miracle happened. The princess's hand began to stretch. As per the legend, it says that it stretched about sixty cubits (Sekhel Tov, Buber [ed.]). When she touched Moses's ark, she was miraculously cured, leading her to take pity on the child and love him so strongly (e.g., Rabbah 1:23).

Reporter explanations: Here is another story about baby Moses. Moses was very handsome, everyone desired and attracted to see him and don't want to take off their eyes from him. Moses's life was in danger, despite the daughter of Pharaoh's guarding of the infant. One time, Pharaoh held Moses and hugged him. Moses took Pharaoh's crown from the monarch's head and put it on his own. Pharaoh's magicians, who were sitting there, explained, "We fear that this child will take your crown and place it on his own head, lest this be the one who we prophesy will seize the kingdom from you." Some of the magicians said to kill the child, and some said to have him burnt. Jethro was sitting among them (as one of the magicians). He told them, "This child is witless. In order to test him, set before him two bowls, one containing shiniest gemstone, and the other a burning coal. If he stretches his hand to the coal, he is witless and does not deserve to die, but if he stretches his hand to the gemstone, he did this with intelligence, and he is to be put to death." They immediately set before him the gemstone and the burning coal, and Moses put forth his hand to take the gemstone, but Gabriel pushed his hand away. Moses took the coal and put it in his mouth. His tongue was burnt, thus causing him to be "slow of speech and slow of tongue" (e.g., Rabbah 1:26).

Reporter: Why did the burning bush not burn up?

Moses: I was eighty; I was living peacefully as a shepherd in the desert. Once a young and handsome prince, now I became an old forgotten shepherd. One day, as I was tending my flock, I passed a bush that began to burn and continued to burn, without burning up. So I thought this is beyond my comprehension something supernatural. "I will go over and see this strange sight why the bush does not burn up." I heard the voice of God coming from a burning bush. The invisible, self-perpetuating, and self-reliant God spoke to mess out of the fiery bush and identified himself as "*I am who I am*." God had plans for the next forty years of my life. These forty years was a time when God transformed me into a great vessel in his Hands. God ordered me to go and force the Pharaoh to let my Hebrew people go. At first I was afraid; I didn't think I could do this. Then God gave me special powers. Whatever happened, this was a turning point for me. Fire is often used to indicate the presence of the divine. Fire is pure energy. Yet here the fire does not consume the bush, for it was heavenly fire. I have been asked me to remove my sandals to step in the holy place.

The arrogance of the luxuries of the palace is no more. When I see injustice, I close my eyes, ears and hearts and become so angry that I commit even murder to solve the problem. One day, after forty years of wandering in the scorching heat of the desert, I reached Horeb, the mountain of God. There God called me and set a trap by the fire near the bush! The heat of the fire seemed to have more power in the mind than the heat of the flames. The fire spreads in the bush. But what a surprise! Unable to contain this curiosity, I walked toward the bush. That miracle was about to come closer, and suddenly a supernatural sound calling Moses. *Moses*, I could not believe my ears. Since then, my life has become something else. It was the presence of God that strengthened through the blazing fire. In the meantime, the bush is still green. God told me that I had been commissioned to lead Israel into the land of Canaan, where milk and honey flowed. These were words that were pleasing to my ears, but I refused, saying that I could not. I once wanted to resist the Egyptians who were persecuting Israel and to deliver God's people. But my first attempt at it failed. I later realized that it was because I had relied on my own intellect and power without God's commission. God led me back to life when I realized that the decisions I made in the immaturity of age were wrong. The deliverance of the people of Israel was always on my mind. But I had to wait until Horeb. God had prepared for a ministry of miracles and power at Horeb. There God molded me. The staff in my hand has now become God's staff. It is not possible in writing to describe the sights and experiences seen there, but it can be fully understood once experienced. The indistinguishable sounds heard there were astonishing. There was a pleasant smell, even in the cool breeze that blew in and out at Sinai.

Reporter: How the Israelites crossed the Red Sea?

Moses: After God's appearance in the bush, the journey across the Red Sea was very difficult, because of their abstinence and disobedience and forgetfulness of God's promises. When they came to the shore of the Red Sea, rose up against me, I said to them, "Do not be afraid. Stand firm and you will see the deliverance the LORD will bring you today. The Egyptians you see today you will never see again. The LORD will fight for you; you need only to be still." An east wind in God's treasury was enough to make the mud of the depths of the Red Sea rock solid. The water wall on their left and right protected them like an army. God has provided everything for the last forty years' long journey; still they are an ungrateful people! I felt like I had to back off many times, but I couldn't resist the one who called me. The small villages after crossing the Red Sea and the rugged desert that stretches to infinity were a cause for concern. The journey with these murmuring people was very arduous.

Reporter: Briefly explain me how difficult to climb Horeb and the experience.

Moses: Booming thunder and bolts of lightning accompany with the cloud covered Mount Sinai, bearing aloft two heavy tablets inscribed with the Ten Commandments. I descend Sinai not once but eight times, and more and more laws keep coming all the time. God asked me to ascend the mountain once more, this time to receive the monumental evidence of the encounter at Sinai, namely, the two stone tablets written by God. God inscribes two sets of tablets, and I convey laws to the Israelites time and time again. The Israelites have been led from Egypt to Mount Sinai by God himself, who appeared by day as a cloud and by night as a fire. At God's summons, I ascend the mountain, where God instructed to offer a covenant to the Israelite people. After some preparation, a sound and light presentation takes place. From the cloud-covered mountain, amid thunder and lightning, the people overhear the voice of God saying the "Ten Words." The Ten Words are not the laws themselves but rather a sampling of divine pronouncements, offered so that the people may hear the divine voice speak to a prophet. God invites the Israelites to be his treasured people forevermore, as long as they agree to obey his commands. The Israelites immediately accept the offer, though they have not yet heard the terms. Stricken with terror, the people beg me to excuse them from listening any further to God's voice and pledge to obey.

Beyond the dense view of the green meadows and rainforests, the hide and seek of the mist playing the harp to the mountains is a sight to behold. The way is a very difficult and tedious journey. Only when we know firsthand how far things are from expectations and beliefs can we realize. What a pleasure to see the white-clad mammoths with the warm breeze of a snowy morning. Something calling from a distance has made this morning so beautiful. The rocks are protruding into the atmosphere like a cape. Darkness and fog spread over the hilly path that was blocked by rocks. There are dangerous rocky paths in the middle of the greenery. A small path like the forest must have been formed when shepherds and sheep walked by. It took a lot of hard work to jump from one stone to the next. Knee-high bushes lie on their backs, tilted and trampled. Hairpin curls that curl like a snake. Each curve seems to hold your breath, as if eager to sink into the depths.

Going forward through the green hills bathed in mist, nothing could be seen beyond a ten-meter mark due to the snow. I listened to the song of the murmuring cold wind that was born on the top of the snow-capped Sinai Mountain. The contrast of the surface could be seen when climbing to the slightly elevated plateaus, which are atomic ridges beyond the path where the leaves gather. Mount Horeb, with its inaccessible and unsightly head, turns into an everlasting silence, without a trace of materialism. The foot of Horeb is the place where God first appeared to me. I have climbed Mount Sinai seven times, eight thousand feet. But what I see more than that is that the glorious Lord God descended from the heavenly throne to Horeb. It was an easy opportunity to see God and accept the stones. The glorious God shines like the rising of millions of suns. I am able to speak of that splendor, even if I use selected prefixes, even from the vocabulary of the soundtrack.

Reporter: Why did you take the decision refusing to be called the son of Pharaoh's daughter, rather chose to suffer affliction with the people of God?

Moses: The decision to suffer with God's people rather than the temporary indulgence of sin has never seemed to me a foolish one in later life. I felt that the rod of God's authority was more desirable to me than the scepter, borne by Pharaoh's emblem of authority and sovereignty. I saw the title of the Redeemer of Israel greater than the name of the son of Pharaoh's daughter. What I found more precious than the royal anointing that Pharaoh's courtiers might have organized was the appearance and commission of Jehovah appeared in the bush. I thought it was better to be a humble servant of God than a Pharaoh's prime minister. I deserve the contempt of Christ more than all the dazzling pageants of the palace and all the treasures of Egypt. I have not misunderstood the chains of prestige that Satan holds as ornaments. My opinion is to resist sin to the point of sacrifice. If the nature obeys the rod of God-given authority, then all the emperors of the world will come under it. As the son of Pharaoh's daughter, I was confined to a rocky pyramid. But the people know me as long as the world exists, as the redeemer of Israel. I see the greatness of the anointing of the King of kings and Sovereign Lord of the entire universe. The Christian Jewish Muslim people around the world have always accepted me as a greater prophet than a small community in Egypt offers. What a blessing it is to be able to see the invisible God in the realm of the unseen; I got that luck. I know there is no greater achievement in this world than that. After my death, there were no pyramids in my name, no skyscrapers, no gilded towers, just wild flowers. I consider my choice to be superior to everything else that evens the place where my body is buried in the bush.

Reporter: Why didn't you allow entering the Promised Land?

Moses: To answer your question, you have to go back a few years, back to a not-so-comfortable youth. There were many occasions when I felt like I was alone in the days when I wandered in the desert looking after Jethro's sheep, like an elephants, which may be the most protective moms on the planet. God appeared to me in the bush one day and called my name and ask me to lead Israel. From then on, I was no longer the shepherd of Jethro, but the servant of the Lord of the universe, who gave me the appointment order directly. I have no goals of my own in later life, and I have no right to myself. In that case, I have no right to complain that I was not allowed to see the land of Canaan. If I have been humiliated in it, it is God's problem. You should not complain that God did not allow me to see the land of Canaan, which was so close to God. I have prayed three times to change that decision of God. Lord Jehovah standing tall, clothed with splendor and majesty in the courtroom, pronounced his decree of the judgement. The book of Exodus 20 is known as the cemetery chapter of disobedience and disbelief. Many people are skeptical why I didn't get a huge homegoing service for forty days. God has hidden even my burial place from the eyes of men. God does everything rightly and with foresight. God may have hidden my tomb to avoid the people to make this place as a holy place. There is no pyramid on earth in my name, not even a marble tablet. There was only one person to officiate at my funeral service. He is the Creator of the entire universe. How wonderful that God Himself has taken the responsibility of performing the final acts on my inanimate body.

Reporter explanations: This is how Ivan Powell described from his imagination how the Lord took Moses at the peakiest of his glory. There he died in the land of Moab. He buried him. Moses slowly climbed to the top of Pisgah Hill to become the focal point of the most sacred event of his life. Perhaps he was the last to look back on his followers who were most dear to him. At Jehovah's command, he continued his journey to meet God. We do not know what thoughts filled his mind at those last moments. According to a Jewish tradition, when Moses was ready, God took his soul away with a kiss and then carried the body in His everlasting arms of His beloved friend into his grave, which was prepared for him. There the flowers may have bowed their heads and saluted respectfully, and the birds may have sung beautiful songs above his grave. Imagine for a second in your mind about the awesome occasion. When God realizes His love for His devotee, the heart of any one unknowingly bows and praises to God. Death benefits us because it leads us to the pinnacle of holiness, to heaven and to God.

Reporter: What are the lessons you have to share the world about your leadership?

Moses: God's way is the right choice, even though it often means denying ourselves the pleasures of this life. There's no use in trying to excuse ourselves from God's service. We shouldn't try to do everything ourselves. Fellowship with God will bring radiance to our lives that others will notice. Our goal in life should be spiritual, not worldly, success. When you look at the dry path in the watery sea, a fiery sign in the sky, bread falling from heaven—all are amazing experiences. The ultimate event: the giving of God's law and granting me brief glimpse of God. Four decades later, it all seems more fiction than fact, as I stand here on the barren slopes of Nebo, looking westward toward the land of milk and honey. God uses the humble, not the proud. True humility is finding your confidence in God rather than in yourself. God will fight our battles for us; God never loses a battle. Choose the treasures of heaven rather than the treasures of this world; our worth are not found in physical success. Our worth is found in the eyes of God. Develop a strong relationship with God. He expects a total surrender of our lives and follows the perfect will of God in our lives.

David (1040–970 BCE)

Reporter introduction: David is one of the most frequently mentioned names in the Bible. The Bible highlights many of David's characteristics. One who is by the heart of God? God-pleasing man, anointed, image of the Messiah, shepherd, soul mate of Jonathan, King Saul's son-in-law, skillful harpist, warrior, warlord, musician, author of seventy-three psalms. He has many adjectives such as "destroyer of the giant Goliath," "role model King." David was the youngest of Jesse's eight sons and born in Bethlehem. Bethlehem city is ten kilometers south of Jerusalem and was the birthplace of David and Jesus. David was a man who fought valiantly to fulfill his responsibilities.

David was feeding his father's sheep. Once there was a lion, and another time, a bear attacked the sheep. He chased that wild animal, killed it, and took the sheep from its mouth. God honored that kind of courage and dedication. When his father sent him into the wilderness, God sent his prophet and brought him out. God testifies about him that I found my servant David and anointed him with my holy anointing oil. The name of the LORD God was magnified in David, and he magnified his name among the great men of the earth. He ruled the country for forty long years in accordance with virtue, justice, and truth. All who opposed him were defeated before him, because he had the divine promise that my arm would strengthen him and that the enemy would not defeat him. Saul's tactics, Goliath's power, and the organized power of the enemy nations were shattered by the anointing shield of Jehovah.

The sun is beginning to set at the west. At the sound of a beautiful harp, Prince Jonathan, the son of King Saul, aimed his horse toward that place. When he reached the river bank, he found out the source of that sound. A young man sitting on a rock is playing the harp melodically. Gradually, Jonathan became David's best friend. Jonathan introduced David as a harpist, and later at Jonathan's request, Saul appointed him as a harpist in the palace. It was David's practice to play the harp whenever Saul is possessed by an evil spirit. Jonathan used to tell me playfully that when I play the harp, he saw butterflies circling around, sparrows, and pigeons flying near him, and beetles and bees swarming to prepare the background music for it. The flocks of sheep scurrying on the trunk below, the fish in the river leaping to the top, the spotted deer raising their heads in the distance, the peacocks flapping their wings, the quills responding with sweetness, and the sound of the parrots fluttering.

Reporter: In a few words, give us your testimony.

David: From the highest rooftop here in the Jerusalem palace, I can see the Judean hills, where I once tended sheep for my father. But one day, Samuel, the prophet, visited our little town and changed my life forever. I have memories, memories both wonderful and unpleasant. If we are faithful in little things, we will be entrusted with greater responsibilities. Spiritual growth takes time. God has given each of us the necessary equipment to fight our spiritual battles; we should not try to use another person's armor. Dishonesty is always wrong. Sin leads to suffering and shame, no matter how godly the sinner. God is often more concerned about our response when convicted of sin than about the sin itself. I have an intimate relationship with God. God is very real and very living in my life. In every adverse circumstance, I put my trust in God, believing that He has a great plan for my life.

Reporter: How did you face Goliath?

David: I was just a shepherd who went to inquire about the welfare of my brothers. I have nothing to say but that it was God's appointment to reach the mighty Goliath. King Saul summoned me, to defeat a warrior, when many retreated in fear. I had no armor, no training, and no experience of warfare. Even Saul one time, anointed person who had the entire soldiers of the country, experience, the royal throne, the scepter of power, and the royal robe behind, still he couldn't stand before Goliath. It was a time when the spirit of God was departing from Saul, who had lost his anointing. The enemy army and Goliath had a sword, a javelin, an iron-tipped spear, bow, scepter, and a suit of armor, and a large army was behind him. All I had in my possession was a stick, a sling, and five stones. But I will look at Goliath and call out, "I will cut off your head." If one thinks rationally, one cannot slash one's head with a stick, a sling, or a stone. It takes faith to say that.

Reporter: Why did God reject King Saul and chose you as the king of Israel?

David: It seemed unnatural and coincidental to everyone back then that God had chosen me. My entire family was not mindful of me, and even the great prophet Samuel was considered as a candidate. Lord rejected Saul, the first king of Israel. But in the Lord's book, nothing is a coincidence with God's agenda. Samuel filled the horns with anointing oil and came into our house, and all my brethren, except I, were present. My presence did not seem to be an inevitable fact in their calculations. But God told Samuel to call me as soon as possible. Things came to an end against everyone's understanding and perceptions. I was anointed king over Israel. I was a poor country boy who slept in caves and jungles. I was ill-favored even in my own house. I was as disgusted and unsympathetic to everybody around me. I used to pluck the fruits, drink the honey of the forest, and drink the water from the wild stream from the forest. In my life, God was the first thing. I have learned from my life experience that the life cycle does not move in the same rhythm. My life as a mere shepherd was full of uncertainty and emergent, but I never sank into the depths of anxiety. When I faced setbacks and hardships in my life, I moved forward without questioning God's love and justice. I shed many tears of gratitude to the God who placed me in the kingdom of Israel, which I am not worthy.

Reporter: Why did you spare your enemy Saul's life and waited for God's time?

David: Despite having plenty of opportunity to destroy Saul, I ran through the caves, the wilderness, without laying my hands on God's anointed King, and waited for God's time to come. On many occasions, King Saul tried to kill me by throwing his spear. Saul has been searching for me in the wilderness and in the caves, like a dead dog, a single flea. Although I am an anointed king, I spent so many days and nights in the woods and caves. I have been running; forest roads are very difficult to navigate with hills and trench, amaryllis. Eagles, wild hillocks, wild boar, bison, and screech owl were often seen. Sleepless nights are no exception. When spent in caves and caverns, the forest turns into a dark abyss of mystery in the dark, and the roar of foxes, snails, howls, and the chirping of beetles add to the heartbeat raises. Only the grace of God did not fall when the salt and bitterness of tears paralyzed life when there were tragic moments of ridicule death threats and isolation from my wife, father-in-law, son Absalom, and closest friends. God's work is a mysterious way; God's ways are invisible. I have learned that any celestial body in the world that can be built without God will melt away. So I waited patiently for God's time. If there are no waves, then how can you say it is an ocean? If there are no waves like the water in a well, just call it a pond or puddle. He stilled the storm to a whisper; the waves of the sea were hushed. They were glad when it grew calm, and he guided them to their desired haven. Though their waters roar and foam and the mountains quake in the surge that He may lead a tranquil and quiet life in all godliness and gravity.

Reporter: Why didn't God allow you to build the temple? Tell me about how you built so many palaces.

David: God did not want the monument dedicated to him to be associated with violence and bloodshed, which would certainly happen if a man likes me to build it, because God did not want to be remembered and honored as a God of violence who sheds much blood. God wants to be remembered as a God of peace and honored by people who work for peace. I prepared all the materials like iron, bronze, cedar trees, and other necessary items that could later be used when Solomon carried out the actual construction. The palace is divided into two parts, east and west. In the spacious courtyard of the palace, there are endless views of sculptures and works of art, no matter how many times the camera eyes are closed and opened from the visitors all around the world. The marble statues are numerable. I have a head office that is highly sophisticated and the most import-ant room in the center of the administration.

The stone pedestals on which the generals stood with drawn soldiers on either side next to the throne. The roar of thousands of imperial powers, who have risen from their thrones, has pervaded many empires. But my throne was exceptionally different from all. Anyone who came here had the impression of having reached any magical world. All the walls and the palace are decorated with gold. There are oil paintings as historical evidence on the walls. Wonderful and unbelievable sights any one will be humbled by the architecture that evokes the sculptural skill of ancient man. In fact, I do not have the words to describe the interior wall views and decorations of the palace. This is an absolutely indescribable creation. Inside the cor-ridors and ramparts inside these massive palaces, a shred of history abounds. The past sounds like an invisible presence. All these are just a memory. There are gardens in those courtyards full of spring, and the forest and the canopy are covered. The lanterns, which stood out in the splendor of the majesty, the lampposts on the sidewalks are kept for a relic. There are many prison cells at the bottom of the palace. Emperors and kings built prisons in the basements of palaces where they could live comfortably or beyond a call.

Reporter: As an influential king in Jewish history, what did you learn from your life lessons?

David: Never judge anybody by the appearances, position, education, age, or anything else; the Lord sees into the heart. In life, there is always a solution with God. There are times when circumstances present us with opportunities to take revenge against those who may have wronged us. Hold your friends close, but your enemies closer. Doesn't worry about what others may think, even your spouse, for worshiping God? We must recognize when we sin, ask for forgiveness, and accept rebuke. There is a time for prayer, a time for mourning, and a time for resume living. Don't get stuck trying to undo the past. Treasure your friends, and treat them with loyalty and devotion. Any complex situations, there is an answer, not the way our human knowledge. To worship God, the position is not a hindrance. God is very real and very living. Turn your scars into stars. Do not compromise or knuckle and discharge from your deputation. It is not by sword or spear that the Lord saves and not to be afraid or dismayed because of the great multitude, for the battle is God's; that's my experience. Also, I know there is no proportion more than contrition.

Elijah (900–848 BCE)

Reporter introduction: The sun peeked over the horizon; the sky had pink like a sea of cotton candy, with the light of the sun coloring the clouds above with a pinkish hue. Sunrise is the moment when the upper rim of the sun appears on the horizon in the morning. The peace and tranquility that you feel watching the sun rise over the horizon can't beat. We went out to see Elijah early in the morning. You have to go up and down this hill. A small board saw the home of faith, the place where the disciples of the prophet were trained. From there, you can turn around and walk a hundred meters along the small road to reach the front of a small house. Elijah was an old man sitting on an armchair outside the seating area, reading a scroll. Sometimes he is preparing the lessons to be taught to the disciples the next day.

The prophet himself is a textbook who introduces the Bible in one word as Elijah the Tishbe. God has anointed Elijah, the wonderful man who had performed so many great miracles. Anointed by God, even though Elijah was rough in nature, eloquent, teacher. Elijah was a man who walked in obedience, a man who experienced God's provision, and a man who held belief when situations turned dim. Elijah was a prayer warrior. He had fed by ravens sent by the Lord, multiplying a widow's grain and oil. Elijah raised the widow's son from the dead. Elijah hated and confronted evil; he prayed, and fire from heaven fall atop Mount Carmel. Elijah struck a heavy blow against the evil forces of false gods. He was an instrument for miracles against Israel's idolaters. Elijah was a man with a nature like ours, and he prayed fervently that it might not rain, and for three years and six months, it did not rain on the earth. Then he prayed again, and heaven gave rain, and the earth bore its fruits. He got up, ate, and drank then strengthened from the heavenly food; he walked forty days and forty nights to the mountain of God. Elijah prayed, then the fire of the Lord fell and consumed the burnt offering and the wood and the stones and the dust and licked up the water that was in the trench. Elijah parted the Jordan River twice. Elijah is the boldest of the all prophets.

Probably no other prophet has faced so many questions and criticisms in such a short period of time. He was known as a man who evoked the majesty of the people through the extremes of his masculinity and vitriolic. He was very solemn; at the same, he was also able to throw the answer wrapped in pure humor into the minds of his opponents without fail. A face untouched by artificial adornments, a noble temperament, a gentleman, and at the same time a man of demeanor and modesty, and not a hypocrite who does so only serious if it is necessary to do so. If you ask me why the spiritual world stands out first and foremost for the life of Elijah, I would say that it was the ascension of Elijah accompanied by fiery chariots and horses.

Reporter: Why did God dry up the brook of Cherith?

Elijah: The experience of Cherith was a sample shot of God to prove that God can work through any ordeal in life. I don't blame if some people think that if it was God who told Cherith to hide by the stream, then why God allowed the river to dry up a few days later. Cherith exemplifies a separation. I felt that I have run out of my pride. Hunger weighs more than granite when weighed on the scales of (false pride) vanity. Sometimes God sends us to the drying Cherith brook to teach us not to rely too much on God's gift rather than God. God expects obedience and faith from His devotees. God chose to supply my needs through a brook, not a river nor a lake nor a well. It was a brook that would dry up very soon. God's provision was with me, and though hard times came and the provision in that location started to dwindle, God still had other means available for me if I would simply wait and be obedient to the Word of God. God always has a way. And in the same way that God commanded ravens, He would also command a widow to provide for another remarkable way. Now God asked me to go to Zarephath, which has a distance of about seventy-five miles. Zarephath literally means melting. Then God sent me from Cherith to a widow's heart literally melting with anxiety attack. Unexpectedly, the conversation started in protest but ended in hope. It's drilled into our brains that giving up are a bad thing. *Giving up isn't losing.* She thought that she would feed the prophet then she will starve to death. Because she gave to the prophet, the grain in her pot was increased and multiplied. God had a plan behind sending me to a widow who could not live in this time of famine, without sending me to the house of a prince in the land of Israel. It was only later that I realized that God had a plan to feed a family by giving the flour in an empty pot and the abundance of oil in a jar with only a few drops to dry. In the heat of nature, birds fly to distant lands in search of fresh water. The earth dried up and split as a sign of disaster. The animals die en masse without drinking water. In the meanwhile, I saw there a sigh of relief at the thought of how to move forward in the abysmal state of poverty was the plan that the widow and I had in mind.

Reporter explanations: Fire can be destructive, but it can also illuminate. It is a holy pure fire from the Lord. This fire of the Lord cannot be extinguished by water. It is not a natural fire that can be extinguished by natural extinguishers. God sent fire from heaven every time a sacrifice was consumed. However, in the Old Testament, there are at least eight very significant recorded occurrences of fire from Heaven:

1. Sodom and Gomorrah were destroyed by fire from heaven.
2. Fire from heaven destroyed Job's flocks.
3. Fire from heaven devoured Nadab and Abihu.
4. Elijah called down fire from heaven upon King Ahaziah's soldiers.
5. Again he sent unto him another captain of fifty with his fifty, and the fire of God came down from heaven and consumed.
6. Fire from heaven consumed David's sacrifice.
7. The sacrifice at the dedication of the Temple was consumed by fire from heaven.
8. Elijah's sacrifice on Mount Carmel was consumed by fire from heaven.

Reporter: Why do people call you as the prophet of fire?

Elijah: In my life, there are so many occasions God answered me with fire. In a way it's fitting; fire seems to have accompanied throughout my ministry. It was God's fire that fell from heaven to consume the sacrifice on Mount Carmel. Then who could forget witnessing that mighty wind, fearful earthquake, and roaring fire on Mount Horeb? God spoke to me in his still, small voice. Finally, I prayed down great sheets of fire to consume my enemies who were trying to arrest me. Finally, my fiery ride to glory. How ironic to remember the miracle of miracles; I am only the second person in history to leave this life without dying! Not bad at all for a prophet who once sat down under a juniper tree and requested God to take away life and also sat beside a dried-up brook, having to depend on ravens to feed. We must learn that the lowly "drying brook experience is often necessary to prepare us for the lofty" Mount Carmel event. God's provision will never fail for those who give their all to him. God expects us to build the altar, gather the wood, and prepare the sacrifice. Then, and only then, will He send the fire of his blessings. We are never closer to defeat than following our moments of greatest victory. Finally a chariot of fire and horses of fire and parted between me and Elisa.

Reporter: Why did you chose Mount Carmel to prove whose God was the one true God?

Elijah: Carmel is the highest point in Haifa, facing the Mediterranean Sea. The word *Carmel* means the place where the goal can be achieved. These are women who engage in prostitution as part of rituals associated with temples. When superstition and lack of education combined with the masculinity of men, they left their bodies and became timeless. I chose this place, which is the center of impurity, to prove that it is the gods. The need of the hour was to reveal the true living God. One hot summer day, the sun shines overhead. It was hotter than usual. Dry and dry crucifixes, deciduous skeletal trees, blowing hot winds, desperately men and cattle, and people rushing to collect water with clay pots, and dusty roadside plants. Summer heat engulfs Mount Carmel. The prophets of Baal were to stand idly by in the scorching sun.

The 850 prophets of Baal and Azera were ready to prove that the true God is the one who answers the fire at their command. Obeying the command of the great sage, who was famous for his magic, he was ready to do anything, and he meditated with his eyes closed in reverence. They claimed to have bowed their heads before these witches. According to the five elements theory, everything in nature is made up of five elements like earth, water, fire, air, space, and they believe that each element are assigned to a god. The chanting of mantras rang out, and the hours passed away with a roar, screams, and shouts. They did not like what I said jokingly when they did not get any answer even after hours. Their head down and look sad in their eyes, clenched their fists, smashed their hands, and calmed the anger in their minds. Their eyes were as red as fiery coal like the eyes of an alligator in the night time. The main priest was sitting on a sukhasana position (cross-legged) chanting the mantra (slogan) near the half-moon sacrificing altars. I see the chief priest was experiencing excessive sweating of the face and head due to anxiety and the wrinkles in the face and the long unibrows that connect together, which makes him serious and cruel-looking. The blood was dripping from his self-inflicted wounds, and blood ran down in his cheeks.

Carmel was a heavy blow to their self-esteem. Yet they were not ready to give up. The chief priest yelled with some chanting loudly and trying to cover up the commotion. When the people were insulting them, they could not bring fire to their sacrifice even after hours of prayer. So the main priest was cursing them and yelling at them, saying, "You don't know the power of Baal." The Baal prophets said Baal is going to send fire and burn everyone to ashes. The mind-numbing smell of joss stick, some kind of powder, lingered there. However, the main priest slowly began to realize that the scene was not so favorable to them. About noon time, the false prophets had leaped about the altar and performed all of the rituals they believed necessary to call Baal's attention to their contest. They continued all afternoon screaming and crying and cutting themselves until their blood gushed out. Now it is my turn; I repaired the altar of the Lord and cut the wood and the ox in pieces and laid them on the altar and prayed. The fire fell from heaven, consumed the offering, the stones, the dust, and licked up the water out of the trench. When the people saw this, they fell on their faces crying "the Lord he is the God." Immediately the sky grew black with clouds; the western wind began to blow. In order to light a fire on the altar, the altar must be built according to the Word, the wood must be stacked on top of it, and the sacrificing animal must be cut into pieces, and all other necessary preparations must be completed. No power can hold its own in the face of prayer and worship. I prayed a small with an unwavering confession of faith. Suddenly, a sphere of fire leaped from the sky and ignited as if it were a peony barium firework scattering on the altar. The altar and its surroundings were ablaze with fire. It felt like a thunderstorm and an earthquake. The assembled people trembled. There were shouts in the air that Yahweh is God. The people chased away and caught all the magicians, and they were scattered like terrified ants who had thrown away all the sacrificial offerings. All the 850 Baal prophets were led to the river Kishon, with their faces covered and their hands tied behind their backs. There their blood flowed like a river. I saw King Ahab hiding his face and walking near to his chariot. He snorted like a rat was chased by the cat in front of a roaring crowd. He begged me with his eyes for his soul. I said to Ahab, "Go, eat and drink, for there is the sound of a heavy rain." I bowed low to the ground and prayed with my face between my knees for rain.

Seven times I prayed with my head between my knees, until I saw a little cloud about the size of a man's hand rising from the sea. Within seconds, lightning bolts slammed into the earth's crust. The atmosphere was rough, and the sound of rain could be heard in the ears. A mad wind that had stirring everything up. Sweeping wind take of the dead leaves, which provided shade for the soil, rose like walls. When the dust clouds became unbearable, there was no other way but to close the eyebrows. The wind began to blow harder and harder. Dark clouds came, and darkness spread over the air. God sent a torrential downpour that challenged the cyclical cycle of the seasons. It was darker and lonely that night than usual. Three years later, a torrential downpour brought madness to the dry land, thirsting for a drop of water. It was as if every raindrop was calling out and praising the name of the living Lord.

Reporter: Describe your extraordinary spiritual life lessons?

Elijah: God provides in unimaginable ways. God's power moves with us to bless others. God we serve is alive and will show up when you call upon. The trials and tribulations that we encounter in this life are sometimes the result of our own lack of fidelity to God. Anything we place in our lives as being more important to us than God are idols, false Gods. Trials are happening not because of our personal sin but are opportunities to turn to God because his promises to us are real and unchanging.

Elisha (892–800 BCE)

Reporter introduction: On our quest for Elisha, we passed small villages, streams, small hills, dusty farmland, and vast deserts of sand dunes. Pine trees covered with snow at night. Robin birds fly through their branches and sing dawn chorus. The beauty of the dew falling on the leaves in the morning sun is beautiful; it looks like diamonds. The whistling sounds of large wheat field ready for harvest in gentle winds touches the heart as a relaxing music. The long journey, which started in the morning, is covered with raindrops and the shoots sprout forth.

We arrive at Elisha's courtyard one evening when the rains cover the soil. The elongated yellow grain harvest of maize fields of a wealthy peasant family on a sunny summer day is a spectacular look. We are planned to stay here tonight, accepting Elisha's hospitality, as we have no choice to return. We walked through the wide veranda of that house. The veranda ended in front of a curtained room. Although a farming family, Elisha lived in a house that was financially better than usual. Elisha was devoted 90 percent of his time to the soil and his family having vast paddy fields of harvesting and threshing and barn houses. When Elisha had the call of the prophet came, he was to give up the ox and the plow that had been plowing forever. What came to my mind in connection with this incident was that no fisherman can become a disciple of Christ without leaving his own boat and net. Discipleship demands a complete surrender and a radical change by denying them, so Elijah, the son of Shaphat, followed Elijah like a shadow. Elisha had value-based training in the home-based school (gurukul) system. The school where students live along with their mentors and receive education, moral values, and life skills under their guidance. Elisha performed the greatest miracle of all the prophets in the Old Testament. The one who resurrected the son of Shulammite woman.

Reporter explanations: Elisha was a farmer, the son of a man named Shaphat, from the ancient town of Abel-meholah near the Jordan River. Elisha, the wonder worker, a people's prophet, and maker of kings—his miraculous breath woke the child from the slumber of the grave and the last His bones restored life to a dead man.

Reporter: Explain the miracle performed for the widow.

Elisha: The sudden demise of her husband, who left her children behind, was very painful. The death of a parent in childhood is a traumatic experience. Losing a parent in childhood impacts lifelong experience. The untimely demise of her husband cast a shadow over her happiness. The next few days and nights were very sad and sleepless nights for her.

I can understand her situation about coping with the loss of her husband when she was young could bring a host of challenges of shock and confusion and the grief can be intense. She said at times, she felt so empty without him that she didn't want to live anymore. Despite of all the consequences of the poverty for not always having enough food, not being able to dress luxuriously, and not having a comfortable bed, she was able to move on with her life with a smile and no complaints in the midst of such shortcomings and problems. Her family life was as peaceful and calm as a river. All of a sudden, she lost her husband. She lost all her colorful dreams, as sad and tragic as a bird that can't fly anymore. When some relationships are on the sidelines, we never really know the value of it. We realize its severity when we realize that it will never be recaptured. In the days when the anguish of boredom touches the grave, the voice, "Man, you are dust." A family plunged into the profound depths of poverty. She was suffocating in the throes of life. She said her parents were not so happy that her husband step into the prophetic ministry. When she became as a widow and wore the black attire, they never turned to helped her. In this particular situation, she has nobody except her pillow to embrace; she willingly accepted all the tears and sorrows despite receiving the sharp arrows of neglect. She tasted the bitterness of the harsh reality of life's journey. Her children were too small to understand the severity of the atrocities and insecurities created by the news of the eviction process of the financial institution.

The shock of her husband's separation was not completely removed. She has often wondered if she should leave the hometown as an orphan and go somewhere else. There was a terrible mental anguish on her face. The bitter experiences of the hot days of poverty led to half-starvation, extending to a full starvation. Suddenly one day, she decided to come and see me. She signed and submitted a mercy petition to me with tears in her eyes. She stared into my eyes with a look on her face expecting something from me. She realized that the fountain of sympathy was pouring somewhere in me. I could understand the grief of being evicted and losing home. She also said that the debtor was going to take her two children and enslave them. The grievances of the financial burden and the burdens of the heart were lain before me. The widow's words touched me, and I see her tears streaming down in her cheeks. Her mind was more benevolent than the body. It was heartbreaking that the babies were crying non-stop, rubbing their hungry stomachs. The power of those tears was enough to help them to perform any miracle. I realize that to simply pacify along with her is not enough; I have to do something. It's true that those heartbreaking scenes forced me to do some miracle for them. I said to her, "How can I help you? Tell me, what do you have in your house?" "Your servant has nothing there at all," she said, "except a small jar of oil." Then I said to her, "Go. Sell the oil, and pay what you owe. You and your sons can live on what is left."

Reporter: How far did Naaman travel to see you, and why?

Elisha: It was fun to watch the sun rise in the morning. The darkness of night begins to clear. The stars in the sky begin to grow dim. The eastern horizon of the earth glows with orange-colored light. The sun looks like a ring of fire. The birds wake up in their nests and begin to chirp. I was thinking in mind that every sunrise is an invitation for us to arise and brighten someone's day. At that moment, I was fully immersed in that thought. It was about nine o'clock when a battalion of soldiers and neighbors arrived in my courtyard. Someone is seated in a chariot, but everything is covered except the eyes. It was learned that General Naaman, the commander of the Syrian Rapid Action Force, had arrived. The strong leader of the Aram army, but unfortunately he was a leper. They handed over me a letter from the king of Aram, asking him to cure Naaman's leprosy. Naaman knocked many doors for cure, but no result was seen.

It was then Naaman's wife heard from the maid (slave girl) about a prophet that could heal his leprosy. Despite all the comforts in the house, it was a sad atmosphere. The maid saw her mistress spending hours tossing and turning at night. The maid girl saw the grief burning like coals in her mistress's chest. The mistress treated her well, even in the pain of a needle piercing inside her chest. One night, she told her mistress that if her master had gone to one of the prophets in Samaria, he would have cured his leprosy. It was considered a great blessing to have such a maid. At this time of loneliness and emotional exhaustion in life, the maid's comforting words seemed a great blessing. That is how Naaman came to my house.

The slave girl was very decent and noble. Her radiant face, gentle smile, and spirited speech made her a favorite of all. Some lives are thus blessed births that illuminate the inside of all who interact with them. If the paths they have taken are canals of intense sorrow, the journey continues, leaving some signs of hope for others. Doesn't it feel like a joy to see a grasshopper pulverizing out of a rock! A maid who has no great privileges, but this small act had revealed that there is a God in Israel.

Reporter: Explain the story of Naaman, the leper.

Elisha: Naaman was the commander of the army of the king of Aram (Syria). He was highly respected, courageous, a national hero. His name, Naaman, means pleasant or gracious. However, he was a leper. A leper was considered unclean, disfigured, and loathsome. A young girl whom he had captured from his many battles with the Israelites who was enslaved in his household took pity on him. She told her mistress, Naaman's wife, "If only my master go to the prophet who is in Samaria will heal his leprosy." Naaman asked permission from his boss, the king, to travel to Samaria to meet the prophet. Naaman took ten talents of silver, six thousand shekels of gold, and ten changes of clothing. The Syrian king gave him a letter of introduction to the king of Israel, believing that the unnamed prophet was in the employ of the king of Israel. When the king of

Israel opened the letter, he was alarmed, knowing that he definitely did not have the power to heal leprosy. He thought that this was a ruse so that later he would be blamed by the Syrians for not healing their commander. Realizing he was in deep trouble, the Israelite king tore his clothes. When I heard that the king of Israel had ripped his clothes, I said to the king, "Send the leper to me. Then he will know there is a prophet in Israel." And so it was that Naaman raced with his horses and chariot right to my doorstep. I told him to go wash in the River Jordan seven times to be cleansed. Naaman was in a fury, but finally he obeyed and got healed.

Reporter: What can we learn from the Shulamite woman?

Elisha: Once, on the way to Shunem, a rich woman forced me to come for a meal, and I used to go up there for food every time I went that way. Most often I used to go from one mountain to another and from one cave to another. When I came to the city of Shunem, the Shulamite woman received me with all honors she told her husband, "I am sure it is a holy man of God who comes this way regularly." When I wanted to return the favor of her hospitality, I promised that God would bless with her a child. Through her response, "No, my lord, O man of God; do not lie to your servant." The fact that I was unaware of her barrenness revealed that her personal suffering had not stifled her willingness to serve others. I prayed for her for having a child, and she got a child.

When the child became older, he went out to watch the harvesters as a recreation, but tragically, an accident befell him, and he died (as per the Midrash). The Shulamite woman went to Mount Carmel and fell before me, with her face to the ground. She spoke to me, saying, "Did I ask my lord for a son? Didn't I say, 'Don't mislead me'?" When she was childless, she felt like an empty vessel. Now, too, she is in the same situation, but her feeling of lack is more difficult once she has been filled and then emptied. Her loss at the death of her son returns her to her former condition, which is now much worse. She told me that she felt the grief of her son's unexpected separation, like the state of a sailor in the middle of a wave in the dark. I went in the room and closed the door and prayed to God. The lad sneezed seven times and opened his eyes. God heard his prayer and restored the life to the child!

Reporter: Why your servant couldn't see the army of angels leading horses and chariots of fire?

Elisha: My disciple got up and went out early morning; an army with horses and chariots had surrounded the city. "My lord, what shall we do?" the servant asked.

"Don't be afraid," I answered. "Those who are with us are more than those who are with them." And I prayed, "O Lord, open his eyes so he may see." Then the Lord opened the servant's eyes, and he looked and saw the hills full of horses and chariots of fire all around us.

Reporter: What spiritual life lesson you want to share?

Elisha: Do not let personal or family responsibilities get in the way of God's calling. Any crisis that hinders the progress of the divine cause must be overcome by the power of the Spirit. If our personal life is to have the fragrance of God, it must penetrate the lands and make us aware that there is a true prophet in Israel and that any deadly disease can be cured by going to him. In order to perform a great miracle, we do not need any shows that shake our minds; all that is essential is that obedience with our faith is enough. Sometimes things don't turn out the way we expect. Listen to good advice even when you're in a bad mood. Put your pride aside, and obey God. God's miracles aren't for sale, and God's gifts are priceless. God doesn't have just one way of doing things, and no situation is hopeless. Sometimes we have to go the extra mile to see results. The brighter the light of God's glory, the darker the shadow of my sin will be displayed. Cleansing is achieved only through confession. God will pour out judgment, but there is an opportunity for reconciliation and salvation in Him. When we humble ourselves before God and share the desires of our hearts, the Lord will hear us and bless us. When we have a heart after God, His Word, and His will, God will be apt to bless those who have a relationship with Him. God shows us that He is no respecter of persons.

Daniel (620–540 BCE)

Reporter introduction: Daniel was a servant of the Most High God, one of the young men of Judah whom Nebuchadnezzar, king of Babylon, carried away to Babylon. Daniel was a hero of prayer. Daniel literally means God's judgment, or "God is my judge." Daniel is a man of prayer, a man of wisdom, and a righteous man. God said about Daniel "a man greatly beloved" in three times. In another occasion, God said to Daniel, "Do not be afraid, you are highly esteemed." Daniel was a relative of Zedekiah of the tribe of Judah.

He was filled with the spirit of wisdom that was sent into exile in Babylon. Abel, Noah, Joseph, Job, Daniel, John the Baptist, Cornelius, Joseph of Arimathea, Zechariah, Elizabeth, and Simeon were all directly or indirectly called righteous. Adolescence child-hood is an important stage in the formation of a person's life, with a combination of vibrancy, cheerfulness, influence, pride, and glory. In adolescence, most of the attracted fame and worldly pleasures are of colorful life. Daniel has a strict discipline and matured enough to say no to the enjoyment experiments. At such an elated and joyful turn-ing point in life, there are no restrictions on anything. The waitresses are ready to discharge any orders for Daniel. Daniel learned that his success came from God only so he opened the windows toward Jerusalem three times a day down on his knees.

If you can open your eyes and mind and look through one of the corridors of adolescence where the flowers of dream are in bloom, you can surely experience of a spiritual spring in any desert drought. Sometimes the seals of fire stand for the truth, so it does not matter that the enemy will wrote your shortcomings and guilt. When the farmer separates the hull from the good grain, but there is a chance that sometime a few good grains accidently fall into the chaff sack likewise Daniel was a nobleman that can find in a sickening world. Daniel ran his life without making a mistake like a clock witnessing changes with the passing of time seeing and hearing everything. Later chariots rolled through the wide streets that Daniel had cut down as a role model.

Reporter: Can you describe about Babylon and the palace?

Daniel: Here I will tell you something about Babylon and its monarchy. Cumulus clouds look like fluffy, white cotton balls in the sky. They are beautiful in sunsets, and their varying sizes and shapes can make them fun to observe! One thing is sure that today because of these cumulus clouds do not generally rain, you're in for fine weather. The calm cool breeze blows across the meadow. The sun shines across the grass while it dances slow makes whispers of the wind. The Euphrates River is blessed with never-ending springs. In the twilight of the setting sun, the flow of the river would seem like a silver lining. The lunar image is shaken by the occasional wave of calm water. Babylon in those days was a land of palaces, forts, towers, astronomy, architecture, literature, and fine art, all built on the banks of the Euphrates River. The city wall was 56 miles long, 300 feet high and 25 feet thick. The city has 250 towers, 450 feet high, 8 majestic entrances, and 100 brass gates.

The statue of Baal, made of gold and weighing 50,000 pounds, was erected. The heavy iron gate, full of hedges, remains of old trenches, and walls all around. Techniques to reach the hideout by making a path that only one person can climb through the lion's mouth. The colorful windows and doors were etched and stained glass with eye-popping views. The walls and pillars are not known how many years old, but they have century's old stories to tell. A watchman watches with his right eye at the end of a long pipe from the tower to the entrance to the castle wall built around the palace. The dazzling views, the majestic forts, the palaces, the mansions, the traditional weapons, the folk culture bathed in ornaments and colors. Doesn't it feel like history from centuries ago is greeting your arrival with its strong hands?

Babylon in Mesopotamia was the cradle of faith. The faint moonlight on the field seemed to dim the many burning torches. The moon is the smirk of nature; the desolate ground and the dark castle on the other side are reminiscent of a dream world. I am sitting in the dark shadow of the fort. A few feet below is deep trenches long, deep ditches dug as protective defenses are most often associated with war. In this deep trench, human bodies may have been piled up in the past. The blood was flowing like river mixed with in the muddy water. In ancient times, Babylon was at war with one another. Thousands of human beings may have worked to build a large fort and moat to save the country from its enemies. The walls are made of granite. No one knows about the devoted soldiers who fought for country, but their perspiration and pain spattered in those granite slabs. The sound of horses' hooves still seems to linger in this atmosphere. Soldiers marching in shining belts and boots marched on the camp and on the battlefield in the vigor of youth. Their eyes were filled with blood and dead bodies. Those who enjoyed the sound of ties falling like a musical melody, while the soldiers were moving like lightning.

Reporter: Why did you refuse to eat the king's food?

Daniel: In the third year of the reign of Jehoiakim, king of Judah, Nebuchadnezzar, king of Babylon, conquered Jerusalem. The king asked to bring some of the king's descendants and some of the nobles, who were young men in whom there was no blemish, but good-looking, gifted in all wisdom, possessing knowledge and quick to understand. The king wanted to train these young men at his royal court to serve in Babylon. And the king appointed for the young men a daily provision of his delicacies and of the wine that he drank. But we made a determination to keep separation and holiness in the food without contaminating us with the idolatrous royal banquet in the face of any obstacles. We were disturbed by the fact that the food was first brought before the idol and then served. We were not ready for a compromise because those who side with God would give in to small things that would make other victories insignificant. There is no point in using Vicks balm where surgery is needed. When in trouble, we were reluctant to do as the ostrich hid its head in the sand, believing it was safe. Listen to the words I spoke boldly to Ashpenas, the chief of the eunuchs!

We will not eat the king's meal; instead, we eat only vegetables and water. Leopard-covered table in the dining room outside the last reception room. The table was lined with gold-plated tablecloths and chairs. Flowers and leaves were lain out on the table in glass water mixed with different fruit juices. Expensive carpets were spread in the halls and living rooms. The waiters competed to serve delicious food on plates. In silver bowls, mutton and chicken are served alternately with delicious dishes. But we asked the king for a little adjustment in terms of food, and he agreed the terms. I tried to understand that the knowledge of this world, which assumes that the pulse of the world is only through success, is wrong. The world is trying to win the math test with the strength of the first lesson learned by adding one plus one equal to two, but God does not work by the formulas we are familiar with. It is when life's crises come upside down and changing opportunities of our faith are created. Those who walk around wearing a mere outer garment of faith cannot survive crises. Some things may seem trivial to us. But we realize their value only when we know how great it feels for others. It is when others are proud and overjoyed at what we think is trivial. Although it may seem small, we took the matter very seriously. By eating only vegetables and drinking water and refusing the king's wine and other delicacies, which may have included pork and other foods forbidden by the Law of Moses.

Reporter: Why did you get thrown into the lions' den by King Darius?

Daniel: Half of the sun was swallowed by the sea. The sun is just a few moments away from slowly tilting its head toward the sea. The sky looked at the moon and the stars in the comfort of the cool breeze blowing from the river bank. Sitting on the east bank of the river, one could see the palace grounds. On either side of the river were towering towers. The river was full of pleasure boats, and young people were speeding in the boats; the streets of Babylon, which are busy day and night, are not as noisy as usual. Because there was a wrestling match going on in the Colosseum that day, the people had gathered there.

I wondered why my enemies had made such a decision against me with the king. They were jealous of me for climbing the ladder of victory and achievement and obscuring my enemies because of will power, hard study, and above all, God's mercy. I was honored with a great position in the country for interpreting the dream and meaning to the king. God gave me the opportunity to serve as the prime minister and adviser to the king of 120 states in a historic country. Their hatred of me was blown away because I opposed superstitions, rituals, and vices without any compromise against faith. Also, we did not take part in any of the shouts or screams with them, as we would do with other teenagers enjoying sparkling drinks at night parties. They may have been annoyed by the fact that they had a better idea of what a godly life should be like and wanted to live free from all of their disguises and pretensions. A new statue was erected recently near the main gate, whose ears are deaf are blind and tongues are dumb.

Since they could not find any reason or guilt in me, it was decided that the application should not be made except to the king for thirty days. According to the king's proclamation, if anybody prayed to any other gods other than the king for thirty days, he would be thrown into the lions' den. For this reason, the great festival was organized with dazzling views. Everywhere there is ancient cultural programs, which has a great sentiment, is flowing. Sculptures of small and large versions of legendary characters, great emperors, warriors, women, kings, famous forts, palaces, mansions, temples, traditional weapons, folk culture, and unique natural forms were displayed. The views were endless to seeing all even after you have few weeks. Even after learning that the king's decree was written, I opened the window of the upper room to Jerusalem and knelt three times a day and prayed before God as usual. I spent as much time as usual in prayer after reading the book of the law, which was sweet in night's utter silence. For the devotee, prayer, renunciation, and the Spirit-filled life are essential. The joy of being in the presence of God in prayer was indescribable. All the nobles and the inmates of the Royal Court made accusations and held me accountable. I ignored their mocking looks. Appointed by the king as a diplomat in the country, the king had no qualms about throwing me into the lions' cage. I needed the breath of God-given breath to blow out those coals while filling the vast chambers of my own coworkers' jealousy with me.

Darkness began to spread as the sun had finished painting with red and yellow dyes. At sundown, they threw me into the den of lions.

As usual, the king was curled up under a velvet-colored blanket on a soft mattress; he could not sleep that whole night. When he woke up in the morning, he felt guilty, drowsy, and a zombie-like feeling after a night of minimal or no sleep. Because of the sleep deprivation, when he woke up, he had body ache, felt his eyes swollen, and feeling of heaviness in his chest. But I had a good sleep, and I snored like an elephant that was sedated with a tranquilizer gun loaded with tranquilizer agent. My enemies thought I was in the position of an ant creeping on top of a boiling stew. The next morning, the king hurried up and changed his clothes and came to the lions' den. It was not normal for looking to know what happened to the victim. But certainly the king and his other ministers too came to look for me. Almighty and glorious God kept me safe from the lions. Eventually the king realized that their intrigues were trying to trap me. But I was amazed at what the king announced publicly like this: "I issued a decree that in every part of my kingdom, people must fear and revere the God of Daniel. For He is the living God and He endures forever. His kingdom will not be destroyed. His dominion will never end."

Darius was waiting for the first glimmer of dawn so he could see how I was spared. The king was delighted to learn that I was still alive and asked me, "Did your God protect you?"

I said, "Yes, my God sent his angel, and he shut the mouths of the lions. They have not hurt me, because I was found innocent in his sight. Nor have I ever done any wrong before you, O king."

Eventually the king realized that the intrigues were trying to trap me. The king commanded to pull me out of the lions' den, and Darius put me in charge of more people in his empire. At the king's command, the men who had falsely accused me were brought in and thrown into the lions' den, along with their wives and children. And before they reached the floor of the den, the lions overpowered them and crushed all their bones.

Reporter: Explain your moral life lessons.

We should be praying in the good times as well as in the bad times, even before we face with the threat of a lions' den or in a fiery furnace. When praying about the sins of others, we should confess our own sins as well. God does not always answer all our questions. Devastating tragedies and adversity can come into our lives, but we must overcome. We should be committed to follow God's ways and righteousness. Committed to pray even the death penalty was ordered. You can be a victim or you can be a survivor. The choice is yours.

CHAPTER 2

Life Sacrificed for God in the New Testament

John the Baptist

REPORTER INTRODUCTION: BIRDS just chirping as the red rays of the rising sun are only becoming clearer. After searching for John, we set out from Nazareth about eighty miles eastward on the east bank of the Jordan River. We see there is a large crowd on the shore, and John is in their midst. John being a Nazir was wearing a camel's hair, unattractive garment with leather girdle about his loins, similar to the prophet Elijah. His food was the food of the poorest in the land; he ate locusts that were gathered in the desert and wild honey, which was scooped out of the hollow part of trees. He never cut his hair, so it grew up to the shoulder, and some of his hair was tangled in the beard. Some people were really afraid of him. I felt something appealing to him beyond the zeal and laziness of John's gaze. Let's take a closer look at his speech. What John says about Jesus is greater than him. "I am baptizing in the waters. But the messiah baptizes in the Holy Spirit and fire. He being above all" (Matthew 3:11). John said himself that he is not even worthy to take off his sandals. He said further, "I am a forerunner and prophet of the messiah who prepared people for the coming of Jesus Christ. One of the most influential men in all of history is this man who lived in the desert." You've probably heard stories of him, or know some interesting facts about his life and ministry. I still have a lot on my mind to write about him.

The one who came down from the womb of his mother with the mission of election and mission and was melted down in the rough muzzle of a very acute lifestyle. Who came with a thunderous voice to prepare the way for Jesus in the wilderness? He was the man who gave his life for Jesus. John was just as important as the call in any mission of the one who sold his life and was prepared to carry out the mission and had the courage to accept the pains and failures he faced. John broke down the barriers in front of the huge walls and the iron bars of the authorities who could not move forward. John the Baptist was a man who spoke out against injustice and stood up for the marginalized. One who sees injustice without regard for material comforts or security, does not compromise with it, and honestly sets his feet forward. John's life experiences were based on letters and words, without the formalities. John sold himself to God like a fool without paying the price for the associations of those who have earned the nickname of the winner in the vision and reckoning of time and those who wander in high places. One who keeps himself from losing his sanctity at a time when your unique skill and personality of visions are crumbling and new curves of addiction are being formed. John the Baptist was a man sent by God with a certificate of merit. Jesus declares among those born of women, there has not been raised anyone greater than John the Baptist.

Reporter: Share with us your faith journey?

John the Baptist: I was a simple man with no illusions of luxury and no appetite for any worldly pleasures. My lifestyle is living in the lap of poverty just like a mendicant. I used to walk and live like a hermit without even trying to run with the flow of other people. I was a man who willingly chose whatever suffering and sacrifice that I could to defend the truth. I heard what the people said about me that I came with Elijah's spirit. I have always sought to bring about a radical reformation in the worship of the Jewish denomination. Many called me a lunatic, and I did not care about it or pay attention to it. I had a perfect sense of what I was and what I should be. If I try to introduce myself, it will be so. I came to witness the light He must increase, I must decrease. Someone stronger than I am coming after me, the lace of whose sandals I am not worthy to stoop down and untie. I am not the Light, but a Witness to the Light. I came to give the baptism of repentance. I have come to point out the kingdom of God. I'm just a voice; I'm just giving myself the position of a shadow. I am not afraid of those who hate me or try to kill me because I have no fear of death.

Reporter: How did you become a prophet instead of a priest?

John the Baptist: Let me summarize how I came to wear the robe of a prophet though I am a son of the priest and supposed to become as a priest one day. But my calling was to go to the desert and preach. I could have chosen Jerusalem as the headquarters for my ministry, but I prefer the Judean desert near the Jordan, in the desert west of the Dead Sea, where there are snakes and foxes. I have no time to groom my hair or wear expensive cloths. My pulpit was in the thickets and mountain hills and cliffs on the shores of the Jordan. The garland-decorated auditorium had no safe pavilion on the spacious grounds. There were no extremely powerful tools for advertising with graphics posters, flyers, huge tents, invitation cards, social media graphics, banners, yet throngs of people flocked to.

Tears of joy and gratefulness of confession would roll out uncontrollably as I speak. Although I could have chosen the profession of a priest with luxurious costumes, I decided to wear a rough garments of a prophet's robe. Although I had the opportunity to live in the luxury of authority in the synagogues, I didn't hesitate to give it up. I wanted to see life as the crowning example of simplicity in everything from clothing to food. Sometime I walk through the heat of the fire and near freezing ice and fog and other times the tears of silence. The ministry of the prophets has to go through much criticism and praise that time. I am not a hypocrite or a men-pleaser with eye service, but in sincerity of heart, fearing God. I do not think the pulpit speech that pleases the sinner. I loved the sharp prophetic words that repeatedly called for uncompromising repentance. I was the one who cried out that the ax of God's wrath was about to fall on the tree. I was talking mainly about baptism of repentance and judgment. My lectures were clear and relevant on the subject. My voice may have sounded like thunder to some, like fiery words cooked in a fiery furnace, because I was someone who was melted down in the rough muse of intense life. For some conservative aspirants, I may be an allergy for them. It is natural for those who take a clear stand and try to swim against the current to get hurt.

Reporter explanations: News desk now, breaking news from the river Jordan, where a huge crowd has gathered to wait for the arrival of someone really exciting. Over to our reporter, live on the scene. I'm standing here at the river Jordan where a crowd has been gathering all morning and listening to this guy you can see behind me. His name is John the Baptist, and he's a bit strange, as far as I can tell. He's wearing bits of animal fur, and he seems to be actually living out in the desert anyway. He's telling the crowd that the person everyone is waiting for is on the way right now and that we all need to get ready. Let's stay here few hours and see if we can find out what he is preaching about. In a nut shell of his message was that God's judgment on the world was imminent and that, to prepare for this judgment, the people should repent their sins, be baptized, and produce appropriate fruits of repentance.

Reporter: Why many people are not getting the sacred calling for God's work?

John the Baptist: If we ask why the commission to proclaim the word of God does not come to most people, we are too busy, not in the wilderness, not to hear or recognize the voice of God. If we move away from the hustle and bustle and spend time alone before God, we will have the voice of God. I realized that proclaiming the Word of God was a God-ordained duty. I did not hesitate to sacrifice my life for the Lord. Sometimes life can be in danger if we stand up for the truth. The mission of the prophet's ministry was neglected by the people of that time. I am not a self-seeking man but had cut off all the selfish roots for Jesus, who was coming after me. As long as my heart beat and there's sound in my throat, I will proclaim the truth only no matter whether it is king, priest, or ruler. I choose to live by the truth; the world may find it odd and may hate it because they do not understand. My aim was to make a great movement in the spiritual realm at a time when lifeless sermons and statements for spiritual revival were pushing the mind into the midst of devastation and its resonances to be utilized for the ministry of Jesus Christ.

I wish I could mold a new generation without a mask. The content of my sermon on repentance was that salvation was not possible just because I was born a Jew. The message of the day was very simple, clear, and honest, showing the world of that time that apostolic work could be done with perfect devotion and piety without sacrificing beliefs. When the work of Jesus Christ began, I determined that my work was almost finished. What does it matter to the stars after the sun has risen?

Reporter: Why the religious world, political power, king, and queen, they all try to slay you?

John the Baptist: The Sadducees, the Pharisees, the clergy, the Sanhedrin, the religious court, the authorities, the king, and the appointed queen Herodias, all had grudges against me and wanted to kill me. I pointed my finger at Herod Antipas for repentance to escape the coming destruction of iniquity and wickedness. This is because Herod had married his borther's wife Herodias in violation of Jewish law, which forbade marriage even after divorce. He did not like my advice and intervention to push away the guilt. So the spark of alienation was kindled in their minds to me. Salome, the naive teenager, her dancing pleased Herod so much that in his drunkenness, he promised to give her anything she desired, up to half of his kingdom. Herod's future stepdaughter, Salome, performed a mesmerizing dance in his honor. She has been trained to dance provocatively to please King Herod and his guests. Even by biblical standards, Salome was a seductress of the first rank. After all, Delilah only gave Samson a haircut. Salome got my entire head served on a platter.

The event started with the audience being amazed by the ever-changing scenery. The dance of Salome tempted the crowd to violate the boundaries of decency, to evoke human sensibilities and feminine passions. She danced for Herod shamelessly and erotically. There was fire burning in Salome's eyes. The costumes of politeness and decency were loosened one by one according to the rhythm of the dance steps. The invited nobles and princes were all playing lazy and perverted steps in the dim light, accompanied by music. In the glow of the red light, the dancer's presence of mind and patience was trembling to burst at any moment. Too much consumption of alcohol may start to feel pain and tingling in the limbs and remains unbalanced. Herodias was pleased with Salome's captivating performance. She said to her, "My dear, you are brilliant not only in dance but also in diplomacy. Shall I tell the king to make you ambassador to the Roman Empire?" Herodias could not hide her joy. Herod said to Salome, "I will give you whatever you ask of me." According to Herodias's command, Salome was asked to put my head on the plate.

The king thought it was just a joke when he heard the unusual desire. "A head on a silver plate! Just a head?"

Salome sighed and said, "Yes, John's head."

"Ask for pearls, corals, and jewels, my daughter," Herod laughed.

"Not enough, King. I want his head. That is why I have done my extraordinary dance for you here today. Traitors who may incite a crowd of people behave violently."

"Yet he is a prophet. Many people still believe in him and follow him as a good prophet. People's anger may overthrow power, daughter. I doubt God will burn our country."

But Salome stands firm on her demand. By the time Herod's army commander whispers to the King's ears, "Look, my lord, there is nothing wrong with killing the leader of those rebels."

Herodias was very upset with the king's comments, and she said, "It's okay. Even the king of this country is scared of the lunatic who wore a garment of camel's hair and a leather girdle around his waist. So I withdrew my request, and I will consider the king's promise as an empty word."

Herod was addicted to the beauty of Herodias and decided to carry it out and face the consequences.

Let me share some of the bitter experiences of my suffering. Herod, who only knew how to issue stone-splitting orders, could not be deterred from my ideals by the torture chambers or the heavy boots. No enemies could contain my passion and motivation. The virtue and justice I upheld surpassed or put out any fire. The world condemned me as a scoundrel and traitor, but I did not heed any of that criticism. I pointed my finger at hypocrisy and did not kneel down or submit to anyone. I did not even respond to the allegations leveled against me. No attempt was made to prove my innocence. It's the first time in history's court room that anybody rejected even the protections afforded by law without self-loathing and stood firm in his determination. I have no qualms even about my rights. Being a true disciple, I deny myself and willingness to surrender personal hopes, dreams, and desires. What other gift can I offer to God is more precious than my head.

Herod had lain hold me and bound me and put me in prison for the sake of Herodias, his brother Philip's wife. Herod was trapped by his promise, and so he reluctantly ordered my beheading. I was brought before the king by armed royals, chained like a mighty mad-man. My mind whispered that something bad was going to happen in my life. The cavalrymen wore spears and swords and wore scarlet-colored turbans, with royal emblems on their belts and shoulders, and stars according to the rank. Both my hands were tied behind my back. A Roman soldier in a black robe immediately carried out the gruesome task and gave Herodias's daughter my head on a tray. Herod regretted having to kill me at this point. When the mother and daughter were upset under the windmill in the backyard, the soldiers came in asking permission to see them. An assigned soldier put my bloody head on a silver plate. The head looked like a bouquet on a silver plate in their hand. The plate was filled with blood. The salty smell of hot blood made Herodias hysterical. The king obeyed me finally. Salome said to her mom, "This gift is for you, Mom. There are no more enemies in your way. What more could a daughter do? Tell me! Leave me alone. I'm going to the garden in Sharon." Salome jumped up and said that someone was waiting for her there.

Herod stood before the unfading eyes of the deformed head in front of him and said, "What a miserable country man! Your eyes burn me even though you are dead. I will burn you in my oven and scatter the ashes in the olive grove. Let all worms and plants taste you. Ha, ha… It is a way of the world to constantly haunt down those who do not yield to pressure."

Upon hearing of this tragic drama performed by Herodias, the glass jar of wine fell from the king's hands and fell to the ground. He trembled with fear. Moments later, his conscious and subconscious mind pricked so badly with remorse and guilt of killing an innocent man. The misguided thoughts wandered out of control between myth and reality. Herod was filled with a terrible fear, and guilt began to haunt the rest of his life. Even the gleam in my lifeless eyes that had been cut off made Herod tremble, and his memories pierce and hurt without any pity. I was not disappointed that my ministry was completed and went to sleep peacefully on the heavenly shore where the eagle eyes of the enemies won't trouble me anymore.

Reporter explanations: Herod had been defeated in battle and was exiled by Aretas. Salome also reportedly decided to join Herod and Herodias in exile rather than be alone. They were sent to Gaul initially and then to Ilerda in Spain. Once in the winter time, as Salome had to cross on foot, as an entertainment passing over a frozen Sikoris river, the ice broke beneath her, and she sank in up to her neck. This made her dance and wriggle about with all the lower parts of her body not on land, but in the water. Her wicked head was glazed with ice, and at length severed from her body by the sharp edges, not of iron, but of the frozen water. John's beheading was swift and instant, but the woman who asked for his head suffered long before she died. Thus in the very ice, she displayed the dance of death and furnished a spectacle to all who beheld it, which brought to mind what she had done. "Herodias was bitterly crying and holding her daughter's head upon her knees in her lap and her whole house is in great sorrow" (Flavius Josephus, *The Antiquities of the Jews*, book 18, chapter 5.4). God doesn't need a sharp edge sword to cut. Even with water, he can make it sharper than sword. The Lord does not tolerate those who come against His true prophets.

Reporter: What counsels do you have for the believer's community?

John the Baptist: The gospel message is always far more important than the gospel messenger. A preacher's true spirituality is demonstrated when the crowds bypass him to hear another. God chooses and uses whomever he will, regardless of the person's natural abilities or social background. Be humble. Love for God and for others is a distinguishing mark of all true Christians. God's prophecy will surely come to pass. Even the unfulfilled prophecies will also come to pass according to God's perfect timing. God does the impossible to fulfill His purpose. We need to be zealous in doing God's work. We must always be prepared for the coming of the Messiah. It is not us who no longer live. We are supposed to be dead already, and Christ should be the one who is now alive in us. Be not afraid to stand for what's right. There's no doubt that standing on the truth can bring you into trouble. Our good deeds should point to God and Christ. Our faith will surely be put to the test. God will surely be there with us to go through trials and persecution. Let the world know that you are a devotee by life. The world is a battlefield, and not a day goes by without bloodshed. The creeds are not to burn but to glorify mankind. It is a fact that modern men, dressed in decent clothes and able to handle different languages, have a lower temperament than the cavemen of old. The caveman had to be restrained by someone like Herod, the sovereign of the kingdom. A head of state must be committed to maintaining a clear vision, action plan, and protection of values.

Stephen (AD 5–36)

Reporter introduction: It was getting dark, and we were greeted by a beautiful morning that was refreshing and bright. We got up early in the morning, took a bath, and set out on our journey freshly. The Greek Orthodox Church of Saint Stephen was built outside the eastern gate of the city. We are on our way to Jerusalem to meet Stephen. The Greek word *Stephanos* means crown who is a native of Jerusalem. He was the first Christian martyr. He dedicated his life to God at a very young age, difficult to define the thoughts of the human mind. He was one of the seven chosen to serve at the table. Stephen was a man who was like the other twelve disciples, preacher, prophet, and performed signs, wonders, and mighty works, though they were chosen to minister at the table with good witness, full of spirit and wisdom.

The seven were selected amid complaints that their widows were not being taken seriously. Stephen was full of gifts, and he proclaimed the gospel. Even some of the Jewish priests were converting to Christianity. and the number of Christians was increasing day by day. Because of this, Stephen became a headache and a most wanted fugitive for the Jewish religious sect. Stephen had ruthlessly overturned the lame excuse of their false teachings of the spiritual matters. Although Stephen's history is limited to just two chapters, he can see from his life many things that today's believers need to follow for the rest of their lives. Stephen showed no reluctance to undertake small ministries. How profound and admirable the act is of Stephen forgiving his persecutors. Stephen is a beacon of light in this crazy and frustrating world. It is not enough to find the truth; it is also necessary to have the will and courage to proclaim it. Stephen was forced to live in the fiery lava of the wrath of those who tried to blindfold him as the waves of time pounded against the black mossy walls of tradition. He worked great miracles and signs among the people and spread the gospel. The Orthodox Jews did not like the fact that so many people were so impressed with him and they always saw a crowd around Stephen. At times, he even debated in synagogues in his hometown of Cilicia. Stephen was a Greek-speaking Jew. In his private life, we have no knowledge of his father, mother, brothers, wife, children, and so on.

Reporter: How do you live out your faith in Christ?

Stephen: It all began so innocently, with my appointment as an official servant in our local church. What wondrous days followed, as God empowered both my witness and works for Him? Many new converts were added to the church, including a large number of Jewish priests. But one day, my preaching antagonized a group from the synagogue, and the battle was on! They accused me of blaspheming both Moses and God. Now here comes the pinnacle of my story. This is the part that gets me the most. I forgive my persecutors just like my master. The tortures that were given to me were difficult to forgive. May I teach you how to lean into Christ's strength and live life in such a way that Christ's love cannot help but overflow through you? The apostles must have seen something in the way that I lived my life that they didn't question me as an advocate of their mission. At the time, Christianity wasn't a popular religion, often persecuted violently, and it was a great risk to preach the gospel boldly. I show great courage in saying yes to this mission. And even greater than that, I didn't chicken out when the times got rough. When I was seized and taken before an angry council to defend myself and all my teachings, the crowd was saying my face was like the face of an angel speaking of truth. I was unafraid of what speaking the truth may elicit in my life. I saw the message of peace and love as far more important than that of political correctness. But there is so much peace in knowing that the truth never changes.

They decided to kill me anyway. So they found a way to do that. They decided to discredit me in public, arguing that I had no knowledge of Judaism and that my ideas had no value. The Jews challenged me to a public debate and set a time for it. Many people have gathered to see the learned Jewish rabbis arguing with me for a moment. It is not uncommon for them to fail at my knowledge of God's Word. All their arguments of their teachings were dashed by me. In my eloquent flow of the Spirit-filled Word of God, God caused them to break the edge of their arguments. So I was brought to the Sanhedrin, the religious court of the Jews, to be tried in the church. False witnesses testified that I preached about the temple in Jerusalem, and that Jesus Christ of Nazareth was God, and that he was correcting the laws given by Moses. The Sanhedrin, religious court, unanimously decided to charge me with blasphemy because I was making heated arguments with them. When the charge sheet was read, I remained silent without saying anything. I know I am called for to soothe the distances of hatred in the furnace of tolerance.

Reporter explanations: Welcome, ladies and gentlemen of the jury. This morning, you will be asked to render finally a judgment in the legal proceeding, which is known as The People versus Stephen, the trial that is just ending. The facts of this case are not in dispute. On a certain day, roughly thirty-six years after the Christian era started. The Jewish mob did take the defendant Stephen, out into the fields, where they willingly and knowingly stoned him to become deceased. So you are not asked to determine who killed Stephen. The Jewish mob killed Stephen. The Roman imperial clemency accused him of blasphemy, of speaking against God and Moses and causing a breach of justice. The charges inflamed the local populace, which demanded he be tried and punished. When Stephen was put on trial, several false witnesses were brought forward by the Sanhedrin to testify that he was guilty of blasphemy. He was charged with predicting that Jesus would destroy the temple and for preaching against Mosaic Law. His defense of his faith before the rabbinic court enraged his Jewish audience, and they dragged him out of the council hall and, making a sudden rush and tumult through the streets, hurried him to one of the gates of the city. He was taken out of the city and stoned to death. His final words were a prayer of forgiveness for his attackers. The Jews have no legal authority to carry out a death sentence. But Stephen is executed illegally.

Most of the time in the human courts of this world, the judgements are not always correct. This is a true story. In the twentieth century, George Stenny, a fourteen-year-old African American man, was executed by electrocution at 538 volts, but seventy years later, in 2015, Stenny's innocence was proved by a judge in South Carolina. If two people are presented with the same set of facts, they will often draw different conclusions. Human physical characteristics and their perception by the brain are under pressure by natural selection. Didn't the Sanhedrin and Pilate make a mistake in Jesus's verdict? Nicodemus was well aware of the denial of justice in the Sanhedrin, the supreme council of the Jews, so he spoke very few words.

Stephen: Before my execution, they allowed me to have a long speech. Saul and his men approached the Jewish leaders, plotted to assassinate me, and plotted against me, accusing me of blasphemy. So the Sanhedrin, the religious court of the day, sentenced me to death for their treachery. They dragged me out of town. My face felt like the light of an angel when people looked at me angrily. I prayed for them and surrendered my soul into the hands of God and gave up my soul. I saw the heavens open up for me. If the walls and stones in the history of the world had mouths, eyes, and ears, they would have told many heartbreaking stories of Christian martyrs. There are many who have melted themselves and burned their lives like a candle. Horrifying tortures of early Christians are stoning, removal of the skin, dragging to death, starved to death, boiled to death, burning at the stake, the brazen bull death, by molten metal flaying, the waist chop, buried alive, nailed into barrels, fed to wild hogs, sewn into a donkey, being flogged or beaten before being sewn into a large sack and thrown into the river or the sea. Crucified Christians on trees of the gardens, coated with wax, and set on fire to light nightly walks.

Reporter: Explain your life lessons in this crazy period of history.

Stephen: Turn any corner, and you'll see opposition somewhere. You must be brave enough to say yes despite the difficulty. You should have faith in the Holy Spirit. You should handle opposition and false accusations with grace. Do not afraid to speak the truth and share His wisdom. The core of Christian commitment is service. Nothing is more important than the Word of God. God does his greatest work through ordinary people. Christians should be confusing to the surrounding world, because they speak with both grace and truth. It may be God's will that our life isn't one that takes us from blessing to blessing. Sometimes God's will for us is martyrdom.

Andrew (Approx. AD 5–70)

Reporter introduction: Born in Bethsaida, Galilee. Bethsaida is located northwest of the Jordan River, west of the confluence with the Sea. The word *Andreas* literally means brave. Andrew was a disciple of John the Baptist, brother of Simon Peter. After the marriage, Simeon moved to Capernaum. Andrew also moved in with him. Although they were fishing, they eagerly awaited the arrival of the Messiah. Upon hearing the Baptist's sermon, these two brothers became his disciples. Andrew is one of the first two disciples who decided to follow Jesus. Jesus was looking for Simeon and Andrew, the sons of Zebedee, who were repairing the nets. Matthew was called from the toll booth. Peter's call is no different, leaving the net and the boat and followed him. It was a fact that all those who called him were afflicted with a kind of hysteria and intoxication eager to proclaim and witness to Jesus. Though he is only mentioned in the gospels a few times, he has proved himself to be a crucial figure in the New Testament. Each time Andrew appears in the gospels, it is a turning point or famous act in Jesus's ministry. The spotlight does not shine on Andrew as brightly as other apostles. Andrew, whose name means "manly," was the first apostle of Jesus Christ. He had previously been a follower of John the Baptist, but when John proclaimed Jesus "the lamb of God," Andrew went with Jesus and spent a day with him and took a "manly decision." It is not recorded in the Bible, but church tradition says Andrew was crucified as a martyr on a *crux decussata*, an X-shaped cross. The apostle Andrew is mentioned fourth in the list of disciples, indicating he stayed close to Jesus.

Reporter: How and where did Jesus meet you?

Andrew: The Sea of Galilee is a large lake, 13 miles long, 7 miles wide, 32 miles in circumference, and 130 to 157 feet deep. Josephus, the governor of the region of Galilee and a well-known Jewish historian, wrote that in his time, about 330 boats were fishing in the Sea of Galilee. There must have been a number of fishermen on each boat. Even if five people were put in a boat, there would still be about 1,650 people on the shores of Galilee, casting nets and repairing nets. Jesus called four of them. The four who were called accepted the call and left everything and went with Jesus. They were fishing, and they caught many people into the kingdom of heaven. Our life did not have to depend on the Sea of Galilee and the shores for boats, nets, and fish. God wanted us to do something greater than that. So we are called out for it. We could not even imagine such a call, the abandoned journey, and the life with Jesus. Those four were not alone on the shores of the Sea of Galilee; many others must have been on shore setting the nets and repairing the nets. But at the call of Christ, we left everything and followed him. Suddenly God's call changed our lives. That is the significance of Jesus's calling. No one can predict how or where to reach the destiny. Our names have a place in the gospel. Where many lose, some win. The lives of those who do not give up everything to God, they will disappear, and they will be forgotten. The voice of God has a thousand facets, which in a way is a careful discovery of history within history.

Galilee was where Jesus began His public ministry after His baptism by John, so it is no surprise that the first disciples He called were Galileans. What we might not have expected, however, is that these Galileans first called by our Lord were not experts in the Scriptures or renowned Jewish theologians; rather, our Savior called mere fishermen to serve Him. I immediately left John to spend the day with this sin bearer. That turned out to be the first step toward full-time service. The final step toward our new life would come on the Sea of Galilee. There we were fishing the four of us: Peter, John, James, and me. When he called out from the shoreline, calling us to follow him and saying he would show us how to fish for people, I quickly found my brother Simon and told him we have found the Messiah. I brought Simon to meet Jesus. We dropped our fishing nets and followed Jesus as He was passing by.

Reporter: What was the reason the Jewish people plotted to kill you?

Andrew: I went to Greece to spread the gospel following Jesus's death. Going out, in obedience to the command of Christ, I taught in many countries, as in Pontus, Galatia, Bithynia, as well as at Antropophages, and afterward in Scythia. I also traveled as far as into Byzantium, further in Thracia, Macedonia, Thessalian, and Achaia, everywhere preaching Christ, whereby I converted many to the Christian faith. At Patras, a city in Achaia, I converted besides many others Maximillia, the wife of Aegaeas, and the governor. She was very sick and counting her days. The governor was decided when his wife dies, then he wanted to end his life too. In such a situation, I prayed for her, and she was completely healed as soon as she and her brother decided to become a Christian. This enraged the governor against me, that he threatened me with death of the cross. But I told to governor, "Had I feared the death of the cross, I should not have preached the majesty and gloriousness of the cross of Christ." The enemies of the truth apprehended me and sentenced me to death. At night, everything is quiet. Life ends in the morning, but the universe is beautiful, with the evening sun, the night moon, the stars, and the new dawn. I was not afraid because I had the unshakable, firm, and pure faith to let the darkness thicken, and the last dim light pierced through a small hole in a dark room, even which also shut, I am not worried. I went joyfully to the place where I was to be crucified, and, having come near the cross, I said, "O beloved cross! I have greatly longed for thee. I rejoice to see thee erected here. I come to thee with a peaceful conscience and with cheerfulness, desiring that I, who am a disciple of Him who hung on the cross, may also be crucified." I said further, "The nearer I come to the cross, the nearer I come to God, and the farther I am from the cross, the farther I remain from God."

They hung me three days on the cross; I was silent, however, but as long as I could move my tongue, I instructed the people that stood by the cross, in the way of the truth, saying, among other things, "I thank my Lord Jesus Christ, that having used me for a time as an ambassador, now permits me to have this body, that I, through a good confession, may obtain everlasting grace and mercy. Remain steadfast in the word and doctrine, which you have received, instructing one another, that you may dwell with God in eternity, and receive the fruit of His promises." The Christians and other pious people besought the governor to give me unto them and take me down from the cross. I was not nailed to the cross, like Christ, but tied to it. I prayed to God like this: "O my Lord, my God! Who I have known, whom I have loved, to whom I cling, whom I desire to see, and in whom I am what I am." Finally, I spoke these words, and I committed my spirit into the hands of my heavenly Father.

Reporter: Give me your life lessons?

Andrew: No matter how little we are able to give the Lord; he can make it adequate for his purposes. Humility is needed to answer the call of God. Constantly seek God in your life. Do not delay your conversion. We should never think that there is a better time to answer God's calling than now. God can use us to call more people to His church. So continue to keep God's word, live the life He has called you to live, and let your light shine to the world. Salvation is of the Gentiles as well. Man often values his outward appearances and attitudes, but God values our inner value. One should try to find the beauty of life without ornaments or decorations. Dedicated lives are those who smile at the murderous ropes and spread their chests with flags, who do not shudder at the sight of the sword and spear, who do not retreat on the battlefields, but who illuminate the flames of fire within their chests. The world is full of empty jars. Even spirituality is declining as a kind of word that pierces the ears. Mostly Christians were considered a fool and a fanatic and were treated by others as the filth of the world and the filth of all things. Some stars are like that, shining in the dark and in the daytime. The moon will cover the whole earth. Suddenly, without telling anyone, without anyone knowing, a big question flies somewhere.

Peter (1 BC–AD 64)

Reporter introduction: We arrived in front of Saint Peter's Church in Capernaum on a very pleasant morning with a slight chill. It is a vast building complex. Most of the beautiful large sculptures are of divine men. They erect historic buildings and monuments that were built with stone concrete masonry structures. Travertine and tufa stones, along with reddish-orange Roman brick, are familiar structural ingredients, without modern technology or industrial development that time. I realized that there were some great mythologies in those sculptures on top of those beautiful buildings that stand tall, and I entered the church on a quick tour of the exterior views, such as the key to the statue of Jesus holding the key to the kingdom of heaven, which was given to Peter. I knew my heart was pounding, and I could not believe what I saw on my right side. Peter's sculpture is shown there he was crucified upside down. His father's name was John, and he was born in Bethsaida, which means Fisherman's

Paradise. The word *Peter* means rock. Peter is also known as Cephas and Simon. The apostle of hope, he who is like clay, became as strong as rock.

Peter was one of the disciples who taken the most of Jesus's rebuke. The one who proclaimed the revelation that Jesus is the Christ, the Son of God, and also he said, "Lord, to whom shall we go? Thou hast the words of eternal life." The one who walked with Jesus in the sea was the one who fell asleep when he needed to be awake. Peter has denied the Lord three times. Simon, the son of John, a native of Bethsaida, preached the kingdom of God in the streets of the land of Palestine. Peter is one of the closest to Jesus and acted as an "inner circle" to Christ. Peter is always the first to be recorded in the name of the apostles. Peter witnessed the resurrection of Jairus's daughter. The disciple who jumped into the water and who walked with Jesus on the sea, Peter wrote two letters to comfort the people of God, who were suffering under various trials during the Roman emperor Nero's persecution, and to give the Gentile believers the advice and counsel they needed to move forward without trusting in their fiery test against them.

Reporter: How and where did Jesus meet you?

Peter: The evening sun is a red shaded beach. I was sitting on a boulder that was ready to catch the waves crashing against the shore. The weak waves were competing to kiss my feet. Against the backdrop of the setting sun, boats swaying and swaying with the sea breeze seemed like tiny paper boats. The waves were crawling and gently drenching the sand. Suddenly my brother Andrew came running and said to me, "We have found Christ, that is, the Messiah. Jesus said, come to me, and I will make you fishers of men." The ordinary people were chosen to do extraordinary things. Then Jesus was walking ahead, and we followed him. Actually I just don't want to leave the Galilee shore, because all our life we spent time there. We have a strong bond and emotional connection with Galilee beach and nobody can separate. But Jesus's call has much greater attraction and divineness than Galilee. The image of the sun setting on the west side of the Sea of Tiberias spreads like a rainbow across the sky and water.

Reporter: How did your clay nature become rock?

Peter: Since you ask this question today, let's think a bit more about me, about my character. It was amazing the way I was changed from being an unreliable, impetuous hothead to become a rock. I am a man with certain glaring character faults. I was loud-mouthed and was boastful. I lacked humility and was unstable. I was devoted to Jesus. I have good qualities and bad qualities, two sides of the same coin. We all have unique personalities, and that personality will have both strengths and weaknesses. You might wonder why Jesus would want somebody like me to be chosen as a disciple. Our personalities need to be submitted to God so that the Holy Spirit can work to produce the Fruit of the Spirit in us. Then the positive aspects of our personality will show up, and we will help to build up the body of Christ, the fellowship of the church. Not all of us will have gregarious and extrovert temperament. When Jesus chose us, most of us were all young men with many of the faults of youth. Jesus, unlike other people, sees the other sides of my character, which are more positive. My tendency was to sink into the abyss of doubt one moment, and other time I am at the peak of faith. I have no diligence and patience in listening and am careless in answering. There have been many instances in my life where I accidentally threw the ball to the goal post for my own failure and bowed my head and walk away. There have been instances that I being the captain of my own ship and let unwrap the rope from the anchor shackle for a chance of sinking in the middle of the sea. The Lord did not choose angels to build the kingdom of God but the weak men, who were constantly falling apart. We see in history the names of some of the most famous and influential people in this world, but one day, where their place in the Kingdom of God is will be revealed.

Reporter: What evidence is there in your life and ministry that you are leading in the power of the Spirit?

Peter: After the Pentecost, my lifestyle changes completely. I began my speech by mocking the authorities as a challenge and an accusation that the Lord had resurrected, the man you crucified. The beginning and the heart of my first talk were meditated on a vague challenge in words. When they came together on the day of Pentecost, my speech changed significantly after the tongues that had split like fire appeared. As the fear of death left me, I boldly began to point out the sins and how to repent. So do not hesitate to challenge the whole house of Israel to know for sure that God has made this Jesus, whom you crucified to be Lord and Christ. I preached boldly that "the stone that the builder's rejected has become the cornerstone." There is no salvation in anyone else, for there is no other name under heaven given among men by which we must be saved. Within days, myself and several others were arrested and imprisoned by Jewish religious leaders. Just like a worst criminal. I was assigned a group of four soldiers to guard me as if I were a serious criminal. I was bound with two chains. A soldier grabbed me by the waist and started beating me. Each stroke was accompanied by excruciating pain. A pitiful cry could be heard rising from the adjoining lockup room. The drops of our blood were dripping and scattered all over on the black granite.

Reporter: Describe how you were persecuted for your faith and the crucifixion.

Peter: Emperor Nero assumes power at the age of sixteen. At first, he ruled for a number of years on the advice of General Lucius Anavos but later became a tyrant. Nero was a man who was bound to kill Christians anyway. On July 19, AD 64, a fire broke out in the tombs on the hills of Killian Valentine in Rome, and for nine days, the fire went out of control, blaming the Christians for it. They also arrested me. The trial site was adjacent to the palace. The spacious room, the entrance to the palace, is the entrance to the Legislature. In the middle of the back wall, you can see the secret corridor to the jail that the higher officials and in case the king had to visit. In the center of the room is a beautifully decorated pedestal for the seat for the judge. The written judgment rests on the throne in front of him. In front of the arch, guards stand guard at the huge Iron Gate, holding spears. On the back, I saw the word *justice* written above my head. "Fiatjustitia rust cactum" (Let justice be done even if the sky falls). The judge was constantly writing something behind the brass compound of the courtroom. Finally, someone came and read the charge sheet. "Do you have anything last to say in the sake of courtesy?" The answer is that you can only bind my body. My mind is still free. You will not be able to destroy my thinking, passion, and idealism.

The convicted victims who are waiting for death penalty were often agitated and quarrel all the time with the fellow prisoners and the prison guards. On the day of the execution of the judgment, I was walking calmly back and forth. You can hear the sound of the chain shaking when you walk because of the chains on your feet. One end of the chain is tied to a pole. Though the officials are set a date for my execution, I slept well, and the calmness of the last few days was a surprise to the prison inmates. Their question was how a person sentenced to death could sleep so peacefully. When the pages of human history are turned, the names of many such bloodthirsty dictators can be seen. The lavishly brutal games that took place at the Colosseum were hugely effective propaganda stunts that showcased the limitless wealth and generosity of the emperors who staged them. Wild animals of every imaginable stripe were brought to Rome from the most distant corners of the Roman Empire to feature in high profile games at the Colosseum. Wild animals like bull, lions, rhinos, crocodiles, hippos, cheetahs, monkeys, elephants, tigers, leopards, panthers. Battle between man and wild beasts at the Colosseum in Ancient Rome as a form of entertainment. Men who fight to the death for the enjoyment of others. I preached in Antioch for seven years and in Rome for twenty-three years. We continued to preach and teach the gospel, so Nero put us in the jail. After nine months of imprisonment, I was taken out, scourged, and then crucified. By my own desire, I was crucified with my head downward, considering myself as unworthy to suffer in the same posture in which my Lord had suffered for me. AD 67, on June 29, at the behest of Emperor Nero, I was crucified on Vatican Hill. Emperor Nero also executed Paul on the same day.

Reporter: Spiritual life lessons?

The more clearly we see our savior, the more clearly we see our sin. God does not need our advice or correction. It is more important to seek God's will for our own life than to be concerned about his plans for someone else. I am an eyewitness of Christ's earthly ministry, including his glorious transfiguration. When God calls us, we need to answer immediately. We must not delay any further. Let us live according to God's will and purpose in our lives. Remember, before you can be an effective preacher of the gospel, you must know first God and Jesus. You can't effectively share the gospel if you, yourself, don't know what it is all about. God's will is perfect, and if we want anything in this life, it should be His will. We must remember that the things that we don't see are more powerful than the things that we see. In this life, we need to realize that to see is not to believe, but to believe is to see. God shows no partiality on the basis of race or class, and neither should we. Satan might be powerful, but he is not as powerful as the Head of the Church.

John the Apostle (AD 6–100)

Reporter introduction: On the right slope of Golgotha Hill, the tops of the deciduous trees stood tall and raised their heads with crimson flowers. Little sparrows and doves were flying. Beetles and bees that come to suck the nectar from the fragrant flowers can occasionally be seen. Shepherds were chasing flocks of sheep under the trunks. The meaning of *John* is "Yahweh is merciful," which means the grace of the Lord. John's parents are Zebedee and Salome, and his brother is James. John's family was rich. They had their own boat and nets. The other disciple was named Jesus's beloved disciple. John is the youngest, longest living disciple who accepted the mother of Jesus as his own mother. John was the only disciple who was at the foot of the cross when Jesus was crucified. He was a witness to all the major events. These were James, Peter, and John, whom Jesus carried with him on all the important missions. The man who was called and separated by Jesus Christ also wrote three epistles, the book of Revelation, and the gospel of John. He also called the Apostle of

Love. Eternal life is the key analogy in the gospel of John. John called himself a young man in all his demeanor and speech, even though he is an old man in his late nineties. The only disciple who remained close to Jesus to the end was the gospel writer who revealed the divinity of Jesus. The one who saw the glorified Jesus at Patmos, and he whom received the revelation of the hidden past, future, and present. John was exiled to Patmos, as a prison of solitude.

Patmos was a place where many did not survive. It was a sterile place; crops could not produce. Food would have been scarce; people like John would have been left to starve to death, but he didn't! He survived. Patmos is a sterile island about thirty miles in circumference, in the Aegean Sea, southwest of Samos, and forty-five miles west of Miletus, now called Patino, or Patmos, and reckoned among the Sporades. *Patmos* means "my killing." It was a sterile island. *Sterile* means "unable to produce offspring, infertile; free from living; not producing or bearing seeds, fruit, spores, stamens, or pistils; lacking any inspiration or fruitless."

Reporter: Why were you exiled to Patmos and the eyewitness your experience?

John the Apostle: I was a prisoner on Patmos because I was preaching about Jesus and that He, Jesus, had been raised from the dead. I had the visions about AD 95. The island of Patmos is a volcanic, treeless, rocky island about nine kilometers by fifty kilometers, or six by thirty miles. It is about thirty kilometers, or twenty miles, off the west coast of modern Turkey. From here, I wrote to the seven churches. It was where the Romans put the criminals they did not want to escape. It was a lonely, isolated place. However, far from dying of loneliness, I had the company of millions of angels. Patmos is an island in the Aegean Sea. There was no sign of human habitation. I remember the nights I spent here listening to the roar of the sea and watching the waves rise and fall. The waves of the Aegean Sea caress my feet and go back. The surface temperature at land rises faster than the sea surface temperature, whereas during night time, the land surface cools faster than the sea surfaces. Patmos is a desolate, unfamiliar, and frightening place where flocks of birds fly. This is a place where boats, fishing boats, and ships are usually afraid to even look here. No human being is to be found. Rotten and decayed skeletons were scattered in many places. In the place of the eyes, only one or two days' old corpse was found, with only two pits and a tongue sticking out. The horrible sight of the body parts covered with dried and clotted human blood was mind-boggling. My whole body was sweating profusely, and the sight of the sigh of relief was rapid. Nothing alive was to be seen there. The waves crashing against the dark cliffs were like a blanket of water. Beneath the blackened sky, the wind blew in the waves unceasing.

On the day of the Lord, I receive a vision from Jesus Christ through an angel, which is the theme of the book of Revelation. I was in the spirit on the Lord's Day and was worshiping. Suddenly, I heard behind me a loud voice like a trumpet blast. For a moment, my mind began to feel restless somewhere. Fear of rejection, hurt feelings, grace denied, loneliness, the list goes on as to the number of reasons I feel alone, whether literally or figuratively. We weren't created to live alone on an abandoned island. Isolation is an enemy. It can roll in, take hold, and you never realize the riptide effect. Lies we believe breed in isolation because light can't penetrate.

I had been banished to Patmos Island. I was just a teenager when I witnessed the brutal and protracted execution of Jesus. Now I am in my nineties; I had many reasons to feel disappointed and even disillusioned with God. On this barren rocky island, I was alone. Ever since Jesus had risen bodily from dead, these lifetimes faithful Sabbath-keeping Jews now recognized that Christ had sanctified the first day of the week, Sunday, as His day. It was also on this sanctified day that Christ poured out Holy Spirit on his gathered disciples. Ever since that day, no matter how I felt or the circumstances I was in, the custom is to be in the Spirit on the Lord's Day.

The raging waves crash on the rocks and die. One of the most striking things about the rising sun is the way the color changes and the screaming waves and roaring whales. I know I'm not going to end up here in this lonely Island, but doubts began to roar in my mind like bees. Breaking of surface waves injects air from the atmosphere into the water column, leading to white bubble creation. I was in agony, and my heart pounded, and my eyes watered with an indescribable sigh. Jesus gave me an ocean of love to remember until the last hour of my life. If my memory serves me right, the seven of us, including myself, went with the boat and cast the net that day, throwing the net until dawn and returning disappointed with nothing. The dawn light was shining on the surface of the Sea of Tiberius. The fishing boat was approaching the shore, ripping through the waves. The disciples' faces were clouded with gloom, as if they had never been to a clear morning. The shore was deserted. It is unforgettable that our master lovingly waited on the shore, calling us children with food to relieve our fatigue. Anyway while thinking likes that I was in the spirit revealing to me as if on a screen what was going to happen in the future.

Reporter: Since you being the Apostle of Love, explain to me, is there a real hell, and why would a loving God send anyone to hell?

John the Apostle: Well, first, I believe in hell because Jesus talked about it. In fact, Jesus talked more about hell than He talked about heaven and described it more vividly. He said it is a real place, and it is a place of eternal torment. And I believe Jesus knows more about it than either you or I. But second, I believe in hell because logic and fairness demand it. Think of all the atrocities and evil that have been done throughout history by evildoers in this world. God allowing those crimes to go unpunished would mean that God is not worthy of our worship and love. Why would a loving God send anyone to hell? Well in a nutshell, He doesn't. God does not send anybody to hell. We choose to go there when we reject the love of God. Imagine I were to say to you, "On my right is a door heading to heaven, and on my left is a door heading to hell." If you walk out the door heading to hell, you don't have anybody to blame but yourself. In fact, the Bible tells us that God does almost everything, well everything possible, to keep us out of hell. He cared so much to keep us out of hell that He sent Jesus Christ to come to earth, to die on the cross, to pay for our sins so that we don't have to pay for them. He wants to set us free. He wants to give us forgiveness. God made us in His image, and He gave us the ultimate power to say yes or no. If we choose to reject

God here on earth, then we, at the same time, are choosing to spend eternity separated from Him. You see, there are only two kinds of people in the world. Those who say, "God, may your will be done," and those to whom God says, "Your will be done." When we say, "I want to do it my way," we essentially say to God, "I don't want you in my life while I'm here on earth." Then God says, "I do not want you in my heaven for eternity." You don't have to go to hell. In fact, Jesus Christ has made it possible for you to go to heaven. Open your heart to Him and say, "Jesus Christ, I need you, I want you, I trust you, and I ask you to forgive me." And He'll come in and save you.

Reporter: Can you explain to me the sufferings and how do you die?

John the Apostle: During Domitian's time, Christ's disciples had to go through a lot of persecution. I have always been imprisoned and subjected to severe torture. In the distance, on top of that huge wall, were sharp bottlenecks, a heavy iron gate full of hedges. Roman Emperor Domitian commanded, ordered me to be put in a boiling pot of oil, but I continued to preach from within the pot. Another time, I was forced to drink poison; it did not hurt me (Mark 16:18). Then he banished me to Patmos in AD 95. Obeying *God rather than man* may prove costly in this life, but do not trust your own strength. It was a constant struggle. When pain almost strangles us and darkness is our closest friend, what should we do? Lamenting keeps us engaged with God. When we lament, we invite God into our pain so that we can know his comfort, and others can see that our faith is real. When life falls apart, I find it almost impossible to rejoice. In my life, I had to go through so much pain and sufferings, but somehow I defeated that became a guide for many. The white snow-covered leaves of the month of Shevat, the roaring rain of the month of Nisan, and the hot winds of khamas blowing from the Arabian sand dunes of the month of Iyar. I have taken all the roughness without murmuring. Man did not weave the web of life; he is merely a strand in it. Whatever he does to the web, he does to himself. There is a beginning and end to all life and to all human endeavors. Species evolve and die off. Empires rise and then break apart. Businesses grow and then fold. There are no exceptions, but God's mercy stands forever.

Reporter: Life lessons?

John the Apostle: You must not delay answering God's calling. When God calls you, don't procrastinate. God calls the humble. No flesh should be glorified in His presence. Zeal must be tempered with love and wisdom. Seek to serve rather than be served. We must always be ready when God gives us new tasks. Christian leadership is about being a good shepherd. Discipleship touches every area of our lives.

Nicodemus (Approx. 30 BC–70 AD)

Reporter introduction: The meaning of the Greek word *Nicodemus* is conqueror. Nicodemus appears to have been a wealthy and respected figure, known for his holiness and generosity. He was an opponent of the Zealots and of the rebellion against Rome, which led to the destruction of Jerusalem. Nicodemus was a ruling Pharisee and was a member of the Sanhedrin, the Jewish ruling council. Jesus had performed many miraculous signs, so Nicodemus begins with polite reticence: "Rabbi, we know you are a teacher who has come from God. For no one could perform the miraculous signs you are doing if God were not with you." Jesus immediately brings the discussion down to a personal level: "Truly, truly, I tell you, unless a man is born again or 'from above,' he cannot see the kingdom of God."

From Wikipedia, the free encyclopedia, Nicodemus ben Gurion was a wealthy Jew who lived in Jerusalem in the first century CE. He is widely believed to be identical to the Nicodemus mentioned in the gospel of John. His real name was apparently Bunai, but he acquired the nickname Nicodemus, meaning "conqueror of the people," because of a miraculous answer to a prayer he made. Nicodemus appears to have been a wealthy and respected figure, known for his holiness and generosity. He was an opponent of the Zealots and of the rebellion against Rome, which led to the destruction of Jerusalem.

According to the Talmud, he was one of three celebrated wealthy men of Jerusalem during the last years of the Second Temple. Legendary accounts are given of his wealth and philanthropy. On his daily journey to the house of study, he had the whole way covered with woolen carpets, which he left lying there for the poor to take. Other accounts speak of his daughter's excessive use of cosmetics and his daughter-in-law's expenditure on her kitchen. He was also regarded as a wonder worker. During the siege of Jerusalem, he and his two associates promised to supply the city for twenty-one years with all necessary provisions. The Zealots, however, burned all the provisions so that need would induce the people to fight against the Romans. According to a Talmudic tradition, his proper name was not Nakdimon but Boni.

Reporter explanations about Nicodemus: Let me say a few things about Nicodemus. He was a famous Pharisee and member of the Sanhedrin, the highest religious law in the state. As per the Talmud chapter 3, Nicodemus once borrowed twelve wells of water from a wealthy Roman official on condition that by a certain day, he would either return the cisterns full of water or pay 12 silver talents. Nicodemus did this for the pilgrims in a dry year, promising 297 kilograms of silver if the wells weren't filled. On the day for repayment, he went to the temple and prayed. "O God and Creator of the universe, it is known to thee that not for the sake of glory for me, but for the glory of thy name, that the pilgrims in Jerusalem might have water, did I borrow those wells." Rain fell, the twelve wells refilled, but the sun had already set, and the master demanded payment. So Nicodemus returned and prayed in the temple, and the sun reappeared.

Nicodemus was named as the teacher of Israel who came to Jesus by night to discuss his teaching with him. He defended Jesus before the Sanhedrin, and he assisted at Jesus's burial. Nicodemus was a Pharisee, and he was known as a friend of Joseph of Arimathea. They both belonged to the Sanhedrin, which dealt with legal matters of a religious nature. Insurrectionists later burned his granaries. The Talmud also tells us that once when the celebrated Rabbi Johanan ben Zakkai was riding out of Jerusalem on a donkey, he saw at the roadside a poor woman who looked familiar to him. "Whose daughter are you?" the Rabbi asked.

"I am the daughter of Nicodemus, son of Gurion," she replied.

"My daughter," the Rabbi enquired, "what has happened to the riches of your father's house?"

"Melah mammon haser (the salt of mammon is want)," the woman answered, adapting a Hebrew proverb. She then told the rabbi that her father had lost his fortune and asked him if he remembered when he had signed her marriage agreement. The rabbi turned to his disciples and told them of the dowry mentioned in the agreement: "A million gold dinars from her father's home." At that, the disciples reminded him that Nicodemus had not practiced deeds of charity, because the correct form of the proverb is "Melah mammon hesed" (the salt of mammon is charity;)! (In the Hebrew, the two sayings differ from each other by the mere stroke of a letter.)

According to this, Nicodemus was by nature niggard and canny in both spiritual and monetary matters. The historian Josephus in his *The Wars of the Jews* mentions several of Nicodemus's relatives. His son Gurion entered negotiations with the Roman garrisons at the beginning of the revolt, which ended in the destruction of Jerusalem, negotiations that resulted in these garrisons' surrender. Gurion's son Joseph was chosen as the leader of the defenders of Jerusalem, along with the Sadducee high priest Animus, the same who had James, the Lord's brother, put to death in AD 62, a deed that Josephus considered one of the causes of the city's destruction. Nicodemus's family was so distinguished that the longstanding prime minister of modern Israel David Ben-Gurion took his Hebrew name from them. His former name, Gurion (green), would not have been very appropriate for someone constantly in the public eye.

Reporter: Do all regions lead to God?

Nicodemus: The truth is, all roads don't lead to Rome, and all religions don't lead to God. You see, it all depends on which direction you take. Jesus said this: "I am the way and the truth and the life. No one comes to the Father except through me." I'm betting my life on the fact that He was right because I figured Jesus knows more about it than I did. The Bible tells us that on the road to heaven, there are only two directions: toward Christ or away from Him. You can accept Him or you can reject Him; it's your choice. You know a lot of people sincerely believe that even though they've broken God's rules that they can earn God's forgiveness by doing good works. But I don't get it. How will doing some good works, that we should have done all our lives, make up for all the countless times we failed? You see, heaven is a perfect place, and that means only perfect people get to go there. If imperfect people were allowed in, it wouldn't be perfect anymore. God came to earth in human form, Jesus Christ, and He lived a perfect life, and now He offers to let us go to heaven on His ticket. And I pray that you will trust Jesus Christ and stop trying to bat a thousand because you end up not doing that a long time ago. Accept God's free ticket through Jesus Christ.

Reporter: Based on your life experience, can you give your life lessons?

Nicodemus: God, in His infinite power and divine wisdom, is often shrouded in mystery beyond the scope of human understanding. Born of flesh, the human mind cannot grasp the mysteries of the kingdom of God or understand the fullness of God. This level of understanding can only come from a spiritual transformation and re-forging of a mind that is made new, or "born again," through Christ. The Spirit of God performs His unseen work in each person. In some, salvation is to our limited vision immediate. In others, it is a matter of months, years, even decades. Even the most religious and legalistic person needs the new birth. God may use a convert in an unexpected act that would bring glory to Christ in a most unique way. God's way of salvation is not reformation, or religion, but regeneration. The new birth is absolutely imperative. No one is too old to be born again.

Paul (AD 5–67)

Reporter introduction: Situated on the coast of Cilicia, with its majestic mountains to the west, fertile crucifixes to the east, and scenic views. Olive trees, cotton fields, and vegetable gardens lined both sides of the streets in tarsus, about 16 kilometers on the right bank of the Tarsus River. This town is located in the distance 245 kilometers from Antioch to Tarsus. Cilicia is a region on the Mediterranean coast southeast of Asia Minor. Tarsus, a city in present-day Turkey, Asia Minor, was surrounded on three sides by the sea. Paul was born in one of the most fascinating and culturally rich cities of the ancient world. It is said that Tarsus was home to a large audience of Greek scholars of the time, who were considered to be the cradle of true wisdom, and the official grandeur of the Roman bureaucracy, as well as philosophical schools and colleges. The fame of Athens spread throughout the world, with many eminent poets, artists, thinkers, and philosophers. The beauty of the slow-flowing Seyhan River and its rich cultural richness were another. Tarsus was the capital city of Cilicia and was at the forefront of trade and industry. But Tarsus, who lived two thousand years ago, does not have that pride today. Damascus is about 150 miles from Jerusalem, about 461 miles from Tarsus to Patmos (Greece). It is about 300 miles from Jerusalem. Antioch is north.

Born in the tribe of Benjamin in Tarsus, Cilicia, Paul was a Roman citizen, a man of extraordinary erudition in the Hebrew and Aramaic languages and in the law. He was deserving of the title of apostle of the Gentiles. Paul is believed to have been born when Jesus was about five years old. Paul's life was lain down for Christ, and his life is dedicated to Christ. The mastery of the language of the apostle Paul, in the language of the apostle Paul, who carried the message of the Kingdom of God through the shores of the Mediterranean in Asia Minor, was an asset to the Christian church. The pearls of speech falling from the lips were the lightning bolts of wisdom and the drizzling rain of honey of spiritual joy. With the gospel of Jesus's salvation, he crossed valleys, oceans, peaks and valleys, and in many respects completed the tasks of hard study day and night. Paul was a wise man who has conquered the mountains of spiritual knowledge and acquired the knowledge of physical science. He was a brilliant orator. Those who are condemned destined to receive consequences, beatings and blows, victims of threats, control, tyranny, pride of power, and victims, Paul stood by them during the times when heart-breaking tragedies were added to trampled lives. When you unfold Paul's life, he sacrificed his life to Jesus Christ. Paul's sermons continue even after midnight and were gladly accepted by the crowds. It was possible to remove the mental cataract of the people by seizing the large audience. Hebrew, Aramaic, Greek, and Latin languages, with an intelligible incessant vocabulary, amazed the people with his skillful promise. The sermon was as spiritual as a holy penance for him. The aroma, the tenderness, and the joy of those words were fragrant breeze, soft and pleasant.

Saul may have received such a name because Paul was a Roman citizen. His father was a Pharisee and merchant of Roman faith who believed in God. Paul was born into a rich, traditional family. Paul was a Jew. Paul was circumcised on the eighth day. He was well-known as a wealthy, educated man, a member of the Sanhedrin group, and a Roman citizen. A short man with a smile on his face and an ocean of scriptural knowledge and love for Jesus in his eyes. Paul was a man of little stature, vigorous physique, with a thick hair and unibrows. He had a long curved nose and slightly curved legs and was a fanatic among the Jewish Pharisees. The story of a ravenous wolf that turns into an innocent lamb. Paul knew that he would be imprisoned and killed on his way to Jerusalem, and the story of Jesus Christ's intervention in life led to a radical transformation. The apostle of faith, rose up to the third heaven, a vessel chosen by God, the greatest missionary hero the world has ever seen. He was a person with a great deal of ability to handle language fluently with sincerity that touches the heart.

Reporter: Describe your childhood, education, and ambitions.

Paul: My childhood was a remarkable one. I was born in a Gentile country to Jewish parents. While learning Judaism from my parents, I lived in close proximity to pagan culture. My youth was spent in the cradle of prosperity. Educated in Jerusalem, I became a Jewish rabbi. I learned to build tents because it was the custom among the ancient Jews to learn a trade in addition to their studies. Growing up in Greek culture, I also learned the Greek language. I do not like to brag about myself. But in my father's opinion, I am sharp and intelligent, so they want to send me to a law school. At my father's compulsion, I completed four years of study with Gamaliel and returned to Tarsus. Later, I decided to spend the rest of my life as a theologian, so my marriage was called off. As the years passed, I came to know, as many have known, a Jesus of Nazareth who challenged the doctrines of Judaism. Everything I heard about Jesus made sense to me. People talking about Jesus, a new young rabbi came to the synagogue. Even though he had no religious or intellectual education, still people feel and see that glow in his face. Although the art of speech was not scientifically studied, it would captivate the listener as if it were some kind of magic. So I knew how to take people by the hand and understand them well. I believed that words and deeds should be one and acted accordingly. Then one day, I found out that Jesus had been crucified, and that incident did make me so happy.

A few days later, I heard some disturbing news. A group of so-called disciples of Jesus are working against the Jews, and every day, the proselytes become their followers. It bothered me a lot. Lectures evaluated in cultural context. Stories that are intertwined with myths and traditions without being subjected to the destructive processes of time as they escape through the dark passages of the centuries can sometimes be a substitute for fidelity. But we should not give too much importance to them, and they insist that we adjust our lives according to what the Scriptures say. I could see that they were touching the hearts of the hypocritical Pharisees, Sadducees, and scribes, who were disguised as pious ones, and that they were influencing the people. I decided I wanted to put a stop to this. I dreamed that I would be able to get them on the floor with the discussion, as I had learned the silly buses that contained scholarly and wise teachers' commentary on the Scriptures and the sayings of the wise. The course given by the rabbis of that time was such an in-depth and painstaking study. You do not have to answer here what happened next.

Reporter: Explain to me, how did you convert to Christianity?

Paul: I swear I have no rest until the Christians have been hunted down and wiped out from their homeland. So the days when I considered it my mission to go from house to house and drag out converts to Christianity. The persecution of innocent Christians created an atmosphere of terror in Jerusalem. I was overjoyed to have Stephen, a disciple of Christ, killed. After four centuries of experience, I was impressed with myself as an undefeated and perfect man. I walked with the impression that I was a strong guardian of Judaism. The news that Damascus was becoming a major center of Christian power reached in my ears. This made me very upset and then unknowingly came out with the authority to arrest and imprisons the Christians in Damascus. The arrogance was going away. I tied the knot to bring all the Christians to Jerusalem by hand. God send a direct and immediate intervention on the way to Damascus. The one who was afflicted with religious fanaticism and became arrogant was thrown out of it and became blind. We can live with the loss of an arm, a leg, a hearing, or any other organ, but all of a sudden, when we wake up in the morning, our vision is lost, and if it is dark all around, how can we face it? God helped the light to come in by removing the veil of darkness and showing the golden ray of hope. After three days of blindness, God intervened vigorously, spreading the spring of vision. The hysterical power of destruction was burning in my mind, which was bound to end the way of Christ anyway. So I rode on horseback with great pride and authority. One afternoon, as I was about to approach the city, a light from the sky suddenly fell on me, and I became blind. I fell as if someone was pulling me off the horse. If the power of God works in anyone, they will be knocked down like me, no matter how high they are. I was terrified. Just before leaving the middle of this unexpected event, a thunderous sound came to my ears. "Saul, Saul," I heard a voice saying to me. "Why are you bothering me?"

As soon as I heard this, I trembled and asked, "Who are you, Lord?"

"I am Jesus, whom you are persecuting," Jesus replied.

What happened after that, I said to Lord, "What shall I do?"

"Arise, and go into Damascus, and there I will tell you what to do."

My vision was completely destroyed, and I could not see anything. The attendants took me to the house of a man named Judas in the city. Ananias, a disciple of Christ, prayed, and I regained my sight. My repentance spread like wildfire, and I was branded a treacherous soldier and guardian of Judaism. I stayed with the disciples in Damascus for a few days, preaching that Jesus himself was the Son of God. The Jews had to contend with the Scriptures about the Messiah they had been waiting for centuries, and in the spirit of a little wisdom for their foolish and cruel nature. People were excited to hear my heartfelt sermon. I was soon expelled from the synagogues because they were afraid that this would uproot Judaism. When I went to Jerusalem, the Christians did not accept me either, because I am not surprised that they could not so quickly believe Saul, the persecutor of the Christians. I answered with my life to those who doubted me. They later accepted me, as his disciple Barnabas had said. Soon the Jews decided to hold another secret meeting to eliminate me. They guarded the city day and night to prevent me from escaping. Believers in Damascus learned of this and hid me in a house on the outskirts of the city. One night, they put me in a basket and tied me with a rope and lowered me against the wall. So I went to Jerusalem, but unexpectedly, the Christians there refused to accept me. After this, I surrendered all my strength to Jesus and started working.

Reporter: Briefly narrate your role of sufferings taken for spreading the gospel.

Paul: Let me start with a word that I am not at all sad that I have gone through some "light affliction, which is but for a moment" only. I am now rejoicing in my sufferings for Christ's sake, and in my flesh, I am completing what is lacking in Christ's afflictions for the sake of His body, that is, the church. I became its servant according to God's commission that was given to me for you, to make the Word of God fully known. There was lot of terrible trials and sufferings I went through. Here is a list that still falls short of all suffered.

Hellenists seek to kill me in Jerusalem, so I had to flee to Caesarea. I was persecuted and ran out of Antioch in Pisidia. Facing likely arrest and stoning at Iconium, I flee to Lustra and Debra. I was stoned, dragged out of Lustra, and left for dead. I was opposed by elders and others in Jerusalem. I was arrested as a disturber of the peace, beaten with rods, and imprisoned at Philippi. I was ordered by Roman officials to leave Philippi. Attacked where I lodged in Thessalonica, I was forced out of Beroea and must flee to Athens. I was mocked in Athens for teaching about the resurrection. I was opposed by the silversmiths in Ephesus, who riot against me. I was plotted against by the Jews in Greece. I was apprehended by the mob in Jerusalem. I am arrested and detained by the Romans. I barely escape being scourged. I was rescued from the Sanhedrin and Pharisees during their violent uprising in Jerusalem. Assassination plots are made against me by fellow Jews, who swear an oath to find and kill me, and I endure a two-year imprisonment in Caesarea. I was shipwrecked on the island of Malta. I was bitten by a snake. I was imprisoned in Rome.

I do not think you have time to listen to even a brief description of the suffering I have experienced. In short, it will take a few days. Here I will try to draw a small picture of the great suffering I experienced. The Jews unleashed a great deal of persecution against me; they portrayed us as traitors and sorcerers and threw stones at us, knocking us unconscious. They thought I was dead and dragged me out of the city. I was given thirty-nine lashes with a stick five times. The Jewish extremists abandoned me, thinking I had been stoned to death. The Jews brought me before the Sanhedrin. I was handcuffed and could not even wipe away the tears. But I did not hesitate to sing praises to God. Little did I know that I was a slender man with a blackened face disfigured by blood clots? Nothing could stop me from the love of Christ, the paralysis of an aging body with gray hair. When Agabus took my belt and bound my own feet and hands and said, "This is what the Holy Spirit says." I said to him that I am ready, not only to be bound but also to die. The Roman emperors Nero, Domitian, Vespasian, Hadrian, Trojan, and Licinius, Marcos, Arila Jesus, Sevastopol, Perpechua, Agapets, and Valerian Diocletian—they all try to kill all the Christians and wanted to abolish Christianity.

The sidewalks were rough and dangerous. It is one that stretches across the gorges formed by the Kaiser River and beyond the heights of the Psidia Plateau. These gorges are located at an elevation of about three thousand feet above sea level. It was surrounded by snow-capped mountains, desolate wastelands, dense forests, and many streams, large and small, flowing through gorges. The journey through the landslide-stricken areas was unbearable. The voyage was truly horrific, with daytime commuters and night owls lying on the roadside listening to the roar of wolves roaring through the woods and the cold of the woods, robbing passersby. I was persecuted several times by Jewish leaders. Three times during a missionary voyage, I was hit by a shipwreck and starved to death. I came to Corinth by this sea, which is surrounded by mountains and hills. Hundreds of small islands full of rocks. My efforts to bring Corinth back to true worship, full of Greek myths, superstitions, and idolatry, are indescribable.

Corinth was at that time a colony of the Roman Empire, a major port city, a prosperous trading center, and a place of great historical heritage. I longed to work anything for Jesus even as little as possible. I have tried to mark for the future generations the travelogues that have been utilized during the favorable monsoon seasons on the ships, when favorable travel conditions were found, which may have been able to inspire the followers. The days of the year were not as systematic as they are today. On another occasion, the soldiers stripped me of my clothes, whipped, bound me with my legs, and were carefully guarded inside the prison. We did not interrupt the prayers even as we lay on the cold floor of the prison with our wounded bodies. When we were praying, suddenly there was an earthquake. The foundations of the prison shook, all the doors were opened, and all our chains came loose and fell down. We were in "double cell" solitary, housed with another prisoner in cells as small as six feet by ten. Leg irons are widely referred to as shackles, foot cuffs, a mechanism of physical restraint used on the feet or ankles to allow walking but prevent running. The excruciating pain caused by the deep wounds all over my body. But for us, the foundations of the prison were shaken, the closed doors were opened, and the chains and shackles of the foot were loosened.

I had been beaten as if the flesh were being ripped from the bone that causes chest pain. The lockup rooms, heavy boots and cufflinks, or tortures do not dampen our spirits. In addition to the bruises inflicted on the body, the lack of sleep due to fatigue weighed heavily on the eyelids. The voice of Jesus spoken to me at the gates of Damascus was enough for me to have the strength to overcome any terrible suffering. I was surrounded by those invisible chains of love and the bonds of love of Christ. That's why I wrote, "Who shall separate us from the love of Christ? Shall trouble or hardship or persecution or famine or nakedness or danger or sword? No, in all these things we are more than conquerors through him who loved us. For I am convinced that neither death nor life, neither angels nor demons, neither the present nor the future, nor any powers, neither height nor depth, nor anything else in all creation, will be able to separate us from the love of God that is in Christ Jesus our Lord."

Reporter: What you have to say about your missionary journeys?

Paul: People used to say that I am one of the greatest missionary of all time; I went to the ends of the known world, heart set ablaze, to bring the gospel message to all the lost people groups of the earth. I took four main long missionary journals through the Mediterranean and even went as far as Spain. Crete is one of the largest islands two hundred miles south of mainland Greece, located in the southeastern side of Mediterranean. After I was freed from a Roman prison, I traveled to the island of Crete for my fourth missionary trip. Crete is a blend of three principal regions: Lowland Hills to the east, High Mountains to the west, and the central Messara Valley. The island is a source of ancient culture and refinement, and it is a beautiful island where the four snow-capped peaks always radiate white mist. I have made many missionary journeys because of the gospel. During those times, I faced many challenges. Festus sent me, a Roman citizen, to

Caesar for trial. The sea voyage was in danger as the summer was coming to an end. The roar of the rain in the hills closed all means of escape in that terrible atmosphere. Also, I was strictly warned not to travel, but despite all that, I started the journey thinking that it was only a short distance.

I was traveling with a group of prisoners on a cargo ship carrying wheat from Egypt to Rome. The atmosphere changed quickly, and a strong wind blew against the ship, forming a storm. Unable to resist, the cargo was thrown into the sea, but the madness of the waves deepened their endurance. They thought that the ship could capsize at any moment as the storm intensified, extinguishing the last straw of hope in the minds of the ship's passengers. The shore returns to receive the soft touches of the raindrops, which are like a jug of drops, with the occasional rising of the horizon. Babylon, Turkey, and Greece are the three most important nations in Scripture that are intertwined with history. Antiquities are the mirror of time, and they have a story to tell to anyone who studies them. There are hundreds of rocky islands in the Mediterranean Sea, many of which are uninhabited. In Greece, beautiful temples with special marble carvings could be seen. Greece is home to many myths and legends surrounding the temples of Apollo, Venus, Heracles, Poseidon, Tyke, the goddess of fortune, and Aphrodite, the goddess of love. Some of those who had been scattered by the persecution of Stephen came to Antioch, where they became known as Christians. The gospel has been passed from one person to another and from one country to another by word of mouth.

Reporter: What caused your shipwreck at Malta?

Paul: I was on a ship carrying 276 prisoners, and I can tell you about that shipwreck. I was also a chained prisoner on the lower orlop deck of that wide ship. In that room where the light is reluctant to pass, they lie flat and curved. It was a journey with many who had been sentenced for years. I knew the helpless and pathetic look in their eyes, which makes my heart saddened by the cruel struggle they faced in their life. One of the soldiers picked me up and tied one end of the chain to one of the iron rings fastened to the bottom of the cup. Everyone there is bounded in such rings. He pulled the chain that locked me, and after they made sure, the four of them left the orlop deck. Behind them, with a roar, the arch door closed, and for days passed, a group of men without any contact with each other. They were at the bottom of that ship, in spite of their inevitable fate.

We're on a voyage aboard to Asia. The next day, we arrived at Sidon. I was told by God there would be adverse winds and that the voyage would be difficult and there would be a great deal of misery. I had communicated this message to the centurion. But they didn't heed my advice, and they decided to go, because they think that the south wind was blowing, which is a good sign to travel. The speed of the westerly wind increased gradually and constantly. If the wind direction is different, the ship may have a longer delay in arriving. Clouds gathered in the northeast corner of the sky and clashed. The sky was overcast. Even though it was noon, it was like evening. Heavy rain shook the sky and the earth. The colossal wave and gusty wind created terror in everybody. The captain of the ship guessed any time the ship can sink because the ship contains lot of cargo inside. So he decided to toss all the cargo into the sea. On the third day, the water came inside the ship and started drowning. No one thought there would be any more escape from the endless expanse of sea. The people on board were in dire straits, with no place to go, no food, and no fresh water. With the words of hope, I encouraged travelers who could not even stand up straight due to the exhaustion and of not being able to eat during the fourteen nights of the sleepless and horrific life-and-death struggle.

In that situation, what I reassured them was that the ship would crash, and no one would be killed; it was just a meaningless lament. It was as if the body was wrinkling in the cold wind, listening to the roar and music of the waves. Darkness lay like a cloud over the rock below. Outside, darkness and light are still intertwined, despite the throbbing and rhythmic heartbeat. The rooms are in pitch dark where daylight does not penetrate. I was aware of the presence of flocks of sea crows near the shore. I put my hands over my eyes and looked deeply around through the small glass window, and my guess was not wrong. Something like a dot in the distance, yes, it must be land. I became energetic. The other prisoners were also awakened by the sound of seabirds chirping. As they slowly opened their eyes, they saw that the vast ocean was calmly spread out like a blue crystal ball, and the golden rays of the rising sun shine like crystal.

The bright sun that brings back, not light alone, but new life and hope and freshness to all. The rocks are protruding into the sea on one side and mountains hiding them in the lap. I could see a variety of unnamed fish leaping out of the sea. It felt like the sun had accumulated some water on the horizon in the rain of last night. By noon, we saw a sandy bay, cut anchors, raised their mats in the wind, and made their way to the shore. The trembling of their many nights, which had passed through the bridge between life and death with a frozen mind, had not yet left. Passengers who were swayed by the trapeze of life were taking deep breaths of relief. The magic that the Creator has hidden in our fingertips is immense.

Reporter explanations: Ocean traveling is an amazing adventuring experience, especially the cool breeze touching to your nose. Also smell the sea. Listening to the waves is fun. Waves can suddenly turn and become unmanageably big. It may appear that the ocean is a stagnant place. But this is far from the truth—the ocean is constantly in motion. Water is propelled around the globe in sweeping currents, waves transfer energy across entire ocean basins, and tides reliably flood and ebb every single day. The moon's gravitational pull causes water to bulge on both the side of earth closest to the moon and on the opposite side of the planet. The moon's gravity has a stronger pull on the side of earth that is closest to it, which makes the ocean bulge on that side, while on the opposite side of the planet, the centrifugal force created by the moon and earth orbiting around one another pulls the ocean water out.

Ocean waves can be terrifying in size and strength. The sailors estimated that some waves could reach 60 feet higher than large buildings. In 1933, a 112-foot-high surge hit the navy's oil tanker *Ramapo*. On a stormy night, a huge wave of 135 pounds slammed into a lighthouse called Tillamuk Rock off the coast of Oregon and slammed into a lamppost 100 feet above the water level. An unusual sight is seen in the Gulf of Fundy on the east coast of Canada. The tides in the Gulf of Fundy are much higher than anywhere else. During low tide, the river overflows its banks with a thunderous sound and occasional waterfalls. However, during high tide, the river's streams and waterfalls flow in opposite directions, upward through the river. The river is as calm as a pool when the sea and river water levels are the same between the two. These are called reversing falls / reversing rapids. It occurs at the point where the Saint John's River flows into the bay. Ships are always imaginative constructions. How many ships ended up in the depths of the sea, which did not reach the port they had hoped for on their voyages in search of harbors at the mercy of the roaring waves when they reached the deep sea, which looked like a gigantic fortress? How many faithful captains were there who finally let everyone safely out of the sinking ship and made the final voyage with his ship to the depths of the sea? But God is worthy of believing in all of them.

Reporter: Your convictions on the use of alcoholic beverages and drugs?

Paul: A conviction is a belief or value we embrace as a crucial part of what we stand for and who we are. It is very different from a preference or merely assenting to a belief or value. Our biblical convictions should be first and foremost. Where the Bible is emphatic, we must be clear and take a firm stand. We certainly must urge fellow believers to follow what the Word actually says. Many Christians suggest that the Bible teaches moderation in drinking, while many others have concluded that the Bible teaches total abstinence. Like it or not, many young people are now drinkers, at least on occasion. Many Christians believe drinking alcohol is wrong, even in moderation.

Drunkenness is a sin. Ephesians 5:18 says, "And do not get drunk with wine, for that is dissipation, but be filled with the Spirit." The problem, though, is that most alcoholics live in denial. Sometimes the best way to overcome sin is to focus upon loving God and loving others. He calls us to one service His own. He has bought us with a price, even His own precious blood, and therefore we are Christ's bond servants. Drinking is a filthy habit, as its most inveterate users will admit. But God exhorts us to "cleanse ourselves from all defilement of flesh and spirit, perfecting holiness in the fear of God" (2 Corinthians 7:1–2). "Know you not that your body is a temple of the Holy Spirit which is in you, which ye have from God? And ye are not your own; for ye were bought with a price: glorify God therefore in your body" (1 Corinthians 6:19–20). But physicians—the best of them—tell us that some of the worst forms of disease of heart and eye and brain come from the use of alcohol. It poisons the one who uses it and his breath and exhalations poison his wife and children, who are closely associated with him. Of course, this defaces, defiles, mars, destroys the temple of God, but God says, "If any man destroyed the temple of God, him shall God destroy; for the temple of God is holy, and such are ye" (1 Corinthians 3:16–17). Is it right to indulge in any habit that will destroy God's temple? And if not right, is it not sin? (1 John 5:1). Is it glorifying to God to use it? "Whether therefore ye eat, or drink, or whatsoever ye do, do all to the glory of God" (1 Corinthians 10:31). Is it to God's glory to defile His temple?

He calls us to one service—His own. He has bought us with a price, even His own precious blood, and therefore we are Christ's bond servants. Tobacco is a filthy habit, as its most inveterate users will admit. But God exhorts us to "cleanse ourselves from all defilement of flesh and spirit, perfecting holiness in the fear of God." Tobacco is a narcotic, benumbing all the finer sensibilities of soul and body. Is it to God's glory to defile His temple? Or to destroy His temple? Then think of the expense to you every year. How will you give an account to God of how you have used this means? Much more might be said. As to the first question: "Is there a remedy?" There is. Some men are strong enough or the habit weak enough so they can quit themselves. Some have been helped to break the habit by drugs. But these are uncertain cures. There is one infallible remedy, Jesus Christ. If He cannot save you from tobacco, He cannot save you at all. But He can save. He was anointed "to proclaim release to the captives," "to set at liberty them that are bruised." "Thou shalt call His name Jesus [Savior] for He shall save His people from their sins" (Matthew 1:21).

Reporter: Can you briefly explain your personal life?

Paul: I was executed by decapitation in AD 68 July by Emperor Nero who persecuted Christians mercilessly after the fire in Rome. The pollinators of the lies invented by Nero quickly spread to other lands and became part of history. During the reign of Emperor Nero, Christians were brutally crucified, thrown in boiling oil, beheaded, skinned, or thrown in front of hungry lions. Nero locked me in a stone cage, and in the narrow cells, chains, locks, and shackles could be seen everywhere. The brutal and inhumane treatment of flogging, the wounds have a substantial damage to the skin and body. In rare cases, the death penalty is imposed for very serious offenses, and such persons are given special imprisonment. I did not go to any legal battles, appeals, or petitions. My trial took place in Rome, and I was acquitted because things were favorable. The muggy weather was warm in an unpleasant way because the air feels wet in that evening. Clouds dipped in crimson in the sky. A panicked voice rang in his ears. Nero was sending me as a prisoner to Rome to be tried before Caesar. I was sure I was in the role of the last scene of my life drama. That beautiful face of death gave me hope. It would be utter nonsense if my enemies thought that blowing out my kerosene lamp like light would darken the whole world. They take me five kilometers outside the city of Rome at Three Founds on the road to Austria. Before the execution, I was stripped of my clothes and flogged. I walked barefoot, with shackled feet and hands cuffed behind the back, led by a soldier. My eyes are covered and are blindfolded. The executioner is handed the sword and raises the gleaming scimitar, often swinging it two or three times in the air to warm up his arm muscles, before approaching me from behind and jabbing him in the back with the tip of the blade causing the person to raise my head. Then with a single swing of the sword, the prisoner is decapitated.

Reporter: Give us your spiritual lessons.

Paul: We should not blame ourselves when people aren't open to the gospel. This is a spiritual battle. We do our part, and God does his. But people still want to resist God. We must not be afraid of persecution and hardship to follow Christ in this. We must fight the good fight, finish the race, and keep the faith. We must move our eyes from the pain to the promise. We will all stand before the "judgment seat of Christ" and give an account of our lives. To mistreat another Christian is to mistreat Christ himself. Christ identifies with his disciples. No matter how unresponsive people may be when we present the gospel. While some may scoff, there are many others whose hearts prepared to hear. God can use and change anyone for His glory; no one is beyond the saving grace, or outside of God's reach. Our past or achievements doesn't define us. Be content in any situation, and stand firm in Christ.

CHAPTER 3

Called to Sacrifice Their Life but Not Loyal

SCRIPTURE ALSO SHOWS that those who receive the call will be mercilessly rejected from God when they fail to live faithfully to it and do not live according to God's will. Among these are Lot, Saul, Samson, Gehazi, Solomon, Jonah, and Judah. Dedicated lives are those called by God and entrusted with a special mission. This reminds us of the holiness that those who are called to have in their area of life and the need for them to grow in choice through the life that is called. God gives each one the grace they need to survive and grow in the calling. But sometimes in the paths of life, when we live according to our freedom, we begin to deviate from our calling. Perhaps we do not recognize it at first. We can understand this from our attitude toward the living conditions we are in. Whatever the call, it has its own set of problems and crisis. We can see this in any end of life. Scripture also warns that "there will be troubles in this world (John 16:33), and there will be thorns and thistles, and we will have to sit on scorpions" (Ezekiel 2:6). Our response to such situations reveals an attitude toward calling. Perhaps momentary carelessness and decision-making will cause us to become unworthy of God's choice, as did Esau.

Lot (Approx. 2055–1930 BCE)

Reporter introduction: Before introducing Lot, a little flashback is needed. Ur was a place of immense civilization and a place of indelible memories of the history of ancient art, with many pottery sculptures, stupas, and ancient inscriptions shedding light on the ancient culture. Thus, his nephew Abraham set out from Mesopotamia, the cradle of historic world culture, to a land where he could not be found together. He chose the riverside area that was as beautiful as Jehovah's garden and settled there. As for the city of Sodom, there is no need for further description of its mayor, Lot, whose name is so familiar. Lot was a colorful presence in the country. Sodom, the city of Lot, is on the southwest coast of the Dead Sea. There are large pillars of salt. One of the pillars is named after Lot's wife. It was located in the northern part of the Lisan Peninsula on the east coast of the Dead Sea. The city of Sodom was located in an area rich in tar. Everyone is familiar with the history of the Dead Sea. It is a beautiful view of the setting sun over the Dead Sea. The Dead Sea is the world's shallowest ocean. Even those who do not know how to swim can simply float in the water, where historical truths, geographical features, and geological truths converge. The depth of those roots that penetrate into the history of the country is unknown.

The Dead Sea is forty-five miles below sea level, about seven miles wide, and is isolated, with no flow to the outside world. The journey to Lot, with his ears pricked up to hear the trumpet of a new dawn as the water began to recede east. We spent some time at the shade of big tree to escape the extreme heat of the summer sun. Because of fatigue and thirst, we couldn't walk any further. By the time, we saw from far a large signboard Bethel Lot Villa outside a heavy duty security gate. Let us go down to the old settlements where many historical stories lie. In the distance, in the valleys, there are clusters of sugarcane towering along the road, and the history of the place is drenched in red sandstone-colored soil. On the way, we saw ruined forts, churches covered with shrines, stone pillars, and gates without doors. Suddenly the sound of someone walking by, a bearded man with all his beard and mustache and dangling clothes was walking toward me. Abraham didn't care about the wealth of Sodom that was going to be consumed by the fire of God's wrath. The devil will bring many such offers before us as well.

The most important thing for a God-fearing person is to live a life pleasing to God. After few years, Lot was promoted to mayor.

In the cradle of power, he fainted at the position that the inhabitants of Sodom held against Lot. Lot held an honorary figure for the rest of his life. Its inhabitants were shamefully degraded spiritually and morally. There are major occasions of celebrations. Lot, as a prominent figure, gets to inaugurate cultural programs and dedicating government buildings, etc. Lot even thinks about sometime that if he follows Abraham, then he would not have reached the present status. But God did not allow us to enjoy the pleasures of prosperity and luxury for too long. The dream land of the desert has become a Dead Sea, spreading its enchanting richness and aroma of gold mines and inland streams. God told Abraham that He was determined to destroy the entire city. But Lot did not want to leave the place, so he asked God through Abraham for some more time.

Reporter: Can you describe what happened when the angel's appearance?

Lot: Let me tell you the story that actually happened. Abraham and I were happily traveling together. When I arrived at Sodom, I was fascinated by a beautiful, waterfront, fertile area, like Jehovah's garden. I was saddened to lose the vast protection of God's presence and to become an elder at the city gates of an enemy camp. The life of one who is not dedicated to God is like a broken earthen vessel; no matter how much water is poured into it, it disappears in a short time. They have only this fleeting worldly life, but God, the Creator, will not abandon these vessels but will do great works with those who dedicate their lives to Him. When God intervenes in a way that is too simple for us to understand, we are misunderstood and miss God. The secret behind the humiliating disintegration of my family, which was supposed to live a life of perfect devotion, was greed and greed for money. It takes a lot of patience not to be distracted by the fleeting pleasures and achievements of an instantaneous world. The outside world should not be compromised by innovations, celebrations, and pageants. Until now, I was proud to have achieved everything in life. How quickly everything turned upside down. Whether happy or sad, one should know that none of this wills last forever.

One evening, two angels came to my doorstep. I was sitting at the town gate as usual. It was a day when I was very tired than usual and had to deal with a lot of problems. When I saw the angels, I bowed down to the ground and washed their feet and invited them to stay over and dine with us. But the angels said, "No, but we will spend the night in the open square." When the men of Sodom heard the guests in house, they came out of every man's house and besieged the house roundabout. As I was blocking the door, they pushed hard and came closer to break down the door. At that moment, the angels blinded them. The angels told me to flee from this place as soon as possible and not to look back. My wife was not at all happy about this and reluctantly decided to leave Sodom with me. But my wife disobeyed the angels, looked back, and was left as a pillar of salt. In a world where the grounds for knowledge seem so shifting and uncertain, characters rightly mistrust what they see and hear.

My wife looked back as if she had lost something of value to her and became a pillar of salt. Although she didn't take serious about God's words, my disobedient wife's separation saddened me a lot. I felt lonely. I was sitting on a stone bench when my body began to tingle as I ran, and the angels agreed to let me go to Zoar, a small town near here. The sight of the flames engulfing Sodom Gomorrah and the surrounding cities of Adama and Sebaim before long is indelible. A whirlwind of wind swept through the area. It was as intense as a blazing fire. The horizon shuddered at the experience of lightning scattering. I will never forget the bridge of God's grace between me and death. I was shocked to see this horrible scene. The shock was reversed, and after a moment of stunning, it felt like an earthquake. He saw the sky swell with fire and the smoke spread like a terrifying demon. It was not a wildfire or a deliberate fire. This sulfur burning fire cannot be extinguished by firefighters. Neither water nor gases could be extinguished. Abraham and I went down to Canaan together, but the difference between us was, I exchanged a candlelight for bright sun. I'm in a dilemma of not knowing the true meaning of the events that unfolded unexpectedly in the late afternoon of the holiday Sabbath day. The cities of Sodom and Gomorrah were engulfed in flames, and the Dead Sea was filled with a storehouse of mineral salts. I'm able to tell about the sight I saw. The sighs of Sodom will not stop, the tears will not stop, and the trembling will not end. Even today, it seems to be overwhelmed by the dust that swirls in the fire. The lust of life, the helplessness of those whose wisdom is frozen in not knowing what to do.

Reporter: What is the problem in terms of your destiny?

Lot: Even though I choose Sodom irrespective of my backsliding in my life, God had declared me to be positional righteous. Based on what has happened in my life, it was not a righteous person does. I was leading a life in a sinful nature. As I became a man of authority, I sat at the city gate. In fact, sitting in the gate meant that I had so entered into the society of Sodom that I was a judge there (Genesis 19:9). In spite of my position, the men of Sodom had no respect for me. It was wealth and excitement that attracted me to city life. I was foolish enough to choose the most depraved place around. Never move your tents to a place near Sodom. Don't seek the company of ungodly people. When you are delivered from Sodom, don't return. Spiritual compromise can injure your own soul. Invite the contempt of nonbelievers and even bring immorality and death to your own family. Our modern sensibilities, it's hard to understand why God would allow these two terrible incidents to occur.

Reporter explanations: A recent study by two British geologists, Graham Harris and Anthony Bordeaux, found that salinity made human habitation impossible and that drinking water was scarce. There will always be an earthquake in the area where the Dead Sea is located. Such an earthquake would be enough to destroy the city of Sodom. In addition, the tar may have exploded and caused the fire to burn. Magical archeological excavations, Dead Sea Scrolls, Qumran scrolls, and historians' writings and references are some of the materials used to write later Jewish history. The history of the Old Testament period is very important and necessary, all of which mark their cultures. These bastions have stories to tell of the sandstorms and storms of the underworld. Three months of severe winter and nine months of hot dry weather, sometimes up to fifty degrees.

Reporter: Give us your life lessons.

Lot: God gives us the whole truth about biblical characters, their sin, their failures, their victories and good deeds, and we are to learn from their example what to do and what not to do. In fact, this is one of the ways God teaches us what we need to know in order to make good choices as believers. We can learn the easy way by knowing and obeying God's Word. We can learn the hard way by suffering the consequences of our mistakes, or we can learn by watching others and "taking heed" from their experiences. Don't draw by the appearance of things, if things looked good, if the area looked better than where you were. For every major decision, you have to consult the Lord. Give honor where honor is due. Choose your new associations wisely. Your direction, not your intention, determines your destination. What you set your eyes on, you begin to value. Live by faith, not by sight. Sin always has your "best interests" at heart; sin is incredibly deceptive. Don't find justification and rationalization for your decision to live in Sodom. Don't wait until the fire starts raining, and run away from Sodom. Your choices will directly impact those you love and the future generations. All that glitters is not gold, but we, are often shortsighted. Stay in the will of God. Do not be moved by the appearance of things. Choose wisely, walk in honor, listen to the Lord, and safeguard your destiny. Look before you leap.

Samson (Approx. 1118–1078 BCE)

Reporter introduction: The history of Samson underscores the fact that the ups and downs of the mind come at a great price in life. Samson was God's chosen man to deliver the Israelites from the Philistines and to execute judgment on Israel. Samson's father was Manoah. He was a Nazirite to the LORD from his mother's womb. Some give Samson the resemblance to Hercules, the mythological Greek super hero famous for his incredible strength, courage, and intelligence. Despite being a young man with a strong body and a steel-like mind, he tossed his life for cheap physical pleasures. We should not forget Satan is a schemer. Foolishness is best described by the lack of connecting consequence with compromise. In the course of time, the most powerful judge in Israel, like an ordinary man, sold his heart to Delilah, forgetting the sanctity of life and his vow. In Samson's life, we are going to see the pitiful fall of a brave man who was called and chosen by God. Our purpose was to visit the place where Samson, who had forsaken his precious faith jewels thrown before the idolaters and uncircumcised Philistines, had made him a slave in their hands.

Reporter explanations: Before modern archaeological excavations, scholars had little evidence of the construction of Philistine religion and temples, building their hypotheses on hints in the Old Testament such as accounts found in Judges 16. The term refers to an architectural form consisting of an open porch, or more correctly, portico, which is a main hall whose roof is supported by columns. This would allow Samson to rest on the pillars, in the shade, at a respectful distance from the Philistine leaders. The temple had two main parts, an antechamber and a main hall; the building measures twenty-six feet wide by forty-seven feet long. The antechamber is entered through a wide opening taking up the entire width of its north wall.

The altar served as the focal point in the temple ritual. Its location, exactly opposite the center of the entranceway, appears to have been carefully chosen. Both the altar and the entranceway lie on a line north of the central axis so that the visitor had an unobstructed view of the altar from the entrance to the main hall. Then the Philistines seized him, gouged out his eyes, and took him down to Gaza. Binding him with bronze shackles, they set him to grinding grain in the prison. Therefore, when Samson dislodged the pillars from their bases, the portico, and the main hall of the temple would collapse, followed by the rest of the structure being brought down. The Dagon temple is built of sun-dried mudbricks lain on stone foundations and plastered over with a light-brown plaster. Its walls, whose average width is about four feet, have been preserved to a height of approximately two and one half feet.

The city wall is made of a single stone and is interlocked between these large layers of granite using a ball and lock mechanism. When you reach the high canopy approaching the tower, these layers of granite merge to form a single ridge. The protruding parts can be seen by looking at this stone wall. The symmetry, which evokes the excellence of ancient architecture repeated at regular intervals, is the temple and halls of the temple, which are the main towers in the middle of the spacious rectangular courtyard that passes through these two towers. Apart from the hundreds of priests for daily worship, thousands of temple ladies (Devadasis), hundreds of musicians, clerks, dancers, sculptors, artisans, florists, and animal sellers, a large number of people depended on the temple for their livelihood. It is dedicated to Dagon, the god of the Philistines.

Reporter: Tell us about your divine calling and childhood days.

Samson: An angel told my father and mother that they were going to have a special baby. My parents took a vow that their son will promise to serve God even before I was born. God helped me to grow up very strong. My great strength was to be used to serve God my whole life. I was a Nazirite. Nazirites make certain vows that are like very special promises. One of the vows of a Nazirite is that they must never cut their hair. A Nazirite set apart to God since birth. If my head were shaved, my strength would leave me, and I would become as weak as any other man. When I became an adult, I told my parents I wanted to marry a Philistine woman. They told me that I should choose a wife from the Israelite, not a girl from their enemies. God's plan was for His people to be set apart from sin so that those who do not believe in the One True God could see His greatness through His people. Through Moses, God gave His people laws and instructions how to live a life set apart for Him. He told them to drive out the enemies living in the land He promised them and not to make any covenants with them or to be married to them. God loves His people and always knows what is best for them. He knew that if His people married His enemies, they would turn their hearts away from Him. The trouble started from this because of my rebellious nature.

Reporter: What are the responsibilities of a Nazarite, and how did you break the vow?

Samson: Actually, I didn't mean to break the Nazarite vow; because of my impulsive lifestyle, I break the laws. A Nazarite vow is taken by individuals who have voluntarily dedicated themselves to God. The vow is a decision, action, and desire on the part of people whose desire is to yield them to God completely (Numbers 6:1–21). *Nazir* means "consecrated" or "separated." This vow required the man or woman to abstain from wine, wine vinegar, grapes and raisins, intoxicating liquors, vinegar distilled from such substances, and eating or drinking any substance that contains any trace of grapes. Refrain from cutting the hair on one's head, but to allow the locks of the head's hair to grow. Not to become impure by corpses or graves, even those of family members After following these requirements for a designated period of time, the person would immerse in a mikveh and make three offerings: a lamb as a burnt offering, a ewe as a sin offering, and a ram as a peace offering, in addition to a basket of unleavened bread, grain offerings, and drink offerings, which accompanied the peace offering. They would also shave their head in the outer courtyard of the temple and then place the hair on the same fire as the peace offering. It has a specific time frame, has specific requirements and restrictions, and at its conclusion, a sacrifice is offered. Nazir was separated by strict restrictions not only on diet but also on thoughts. Spiritually, I grew up controlling bad habits and cultivating good feelings and good intentions. The Nazirites were people with a different outlook on life who were strict and tolerant of life, resisting temptations, and not indulging in luxuries. I was a healthy person, sturdy muscles like they were about to explode, a total heroic atmosphere. Sunlit face, I used to go to the place where the arts were taught daily and perform sports. The spirit I gained from it was reflected in my field of work.

I went to Timnath and came to the vineyards, and a young lion roared against me, and I killed it. After sometime to see the carcass of the lion and found honey and ate. I went down to Ashkelon and slew thirty men and took their clothes. I drank wine (Judges 10–17). I was near the bodies of 1,000 dead men (Judges 15:14–16). Touched the jawbone of a donkey (Judges 15:15–17). I went to Gaza to a Harlot, which is forbidden (Judges 16:1). I went and married a philistine woman; intermarriages are forbidden for a Nazarite (Judges 14:1–3). I failed all five requirements. I was impetuous and impulsive, and I went down into ignominious defeat, and this is a solemn warning of the pitfalls into which any.

It is my experience that prayer has been a source of inner conflict and emotional turmoil for the uplifted the spiritual man. But the Nazirite age and the chosen caste were all shattered, and Delilah stole my heart, which defeated me. My love for Delilah is like a fiery furnace that can't be extinguished or slowed down. Delilah laughed heartily as the glass fell on to the floor and made my mind addicted. She was very attractive, her hair scattered like a black cloud. My mind wandered in the dream world like two flamingos swimming in the moonlight. Delilah subdued me because of my weakness and the mental disability. I became a slave to sin because my ungodly thoughts enslaved me. So I had to go through many hardships; sin had a special attraction than works of righteousness.

Reporter: What sin do you struggle with the most?

Samson: The three women in my life were all Gentiles. The first was the woman from Timnah whom I married, the second was the whore from Gaza, and the third was the only woman mentioned by name, Delilah, with whom I "fell in love." The relations with these women were a means to be revenged upon the Philistines. My parents were trying to convince me not to marry a Philistine woman. "You shall not intermarry with them," in order to forbid intermarriage with all the seven nations that inhabited Canaan, including the Philistines. However, I did not heed my parents, preferring instead what my eyes saw (Judges 14:3): "But I asked my father, 'Get me that one, for she is the one that pleases me.' This was the Lord's doing" (Judges 14:4). Marriage to the woman from Timnah was part of the divine plan to take revenge on the Philistines for their dominating and harassing of Israel. This weakness would reveal itself again in my liaisons with the woman from Gaza and with Delilah, and I consequently was punished even for the first relationship, which was a formal marriage, because of this proclivity. I have many liaisons with foreign women from my end. When I was imprisoned in Gaza, I was a "mill slave in the prison" (Judges 16:21).

Reporter: How do you fell into what was the root cause of your fall?

Samson: What a solemn warning against playing with sin in any form! It is a shame that a judge of Israel in the lap of Delilah, lulled by the Devil, defeated and defiled, with his strength depleted and his sight gone! I tried to follow God without being willing to turn from sin. Ultimately I was defeated because of lack of determination to follow God. My love for Delilah proved greater than my love for God. Here are some basic principles that can cause failure in the Christian life. I went where I should not have gone! (Judges 14:1). Timnah was a Philistine town just a few miles from my home. The Philistines did not love God. Israelites were forbidden to go to the land of the Philistines. I involved others! (14:5). I involved my parents with the Philistine woman. I partook of the forbidden! (14:8–9). As I continue my downward slide, I went "down" to Timnah and came to the spot where I had previously killed a lion. I couldn't resist looking to see if the carcass was still there, which was expressly forbidden (Leviticus 11:27). I should not think of this as a skeleton of the lion but the carcass. In hot dry climates, all the moisture in a body evaporates sometimes in less than twenty-four hours following death without passing into a state of decomposition. The body remains for a long time like a mummy without change or stench. This is why bees often live in carcasses. I followed the pattern of the world and did the customary thing! (14:10). My life had been consecrated to God.

After my wedding, I held a feast that lasted for a week. One favorite way of entertaining guests in those days was posing riddles hard questions with tricky answers. I became a party boy! (14:11–12). I enjoyed being in the limelight as the life of the party. It wasn't long before trouble developed between me and my Philistine wife (14:20). Things continued in a downward spiral, and my wife and father-in-law were burned to death (15:6). I began to play the field! For the second time, I went back to Gaza, a Philistine city, to see a woman. Once again, I was flirting with disaster. I met my match! (16:4). Delilah was a Philistine woman whom I took into my confidence. She was not the first Philistine woman I saw. Sin has a way of allowing the sinner to appear to get away with sin at first. I lost my source of power! (16:4–19). Three times Delilah tried to deliver me to the Philistines. By now, my sins had desensitized me to the danger to which I had become accustomed. I was bound! Delilah most likely urged me to take a nap customary for men during the hottest part of the day. Delilah made me sleep upon her knees, and she called for a man, and she caused him to shave off the seven locks of my head, and she began to afflict me, and my strength went from me. I was in the habit of trusting the wrong people. I died in disgrace! (16:31). My strength had been in the Lord, not in my hair. God used me mightily because of my Nazarite vows. But I continued in my own way until enough was enough! God humbled me. My life warns me of the high cost of sin and encourages me to trust the Lord and to resist Satan's subtle temptations. "…truly, as the Lord lives and as your soul lives, there is but a step between me and death" (1 Samuel 20:3).

Reporter: What happened to your life, and how did you take revenge to the Philistines?

Samson: I wonder how many people are out there at the temple. Though I could not see anybody, but by the volume of laughter, there must be thousands. What a pathetic sight about me half dressed, dirty, totally blinded. A life of sin does not exactly produce a glorious rainbow at the end of the trail. I'm sure it all began with uncontrolled lust. Not even my Nazirite vow or the mighty power on me could save me from myself. Once again, I turned to God. I realized I had been wrong, and after a while, my hair began to grow again. They have taken me as captive (16:21). I no longer have the strength to resist. The Philistines gouge out my eyes; a tragedy happened to a person who did everything what was right in my eyes. The Philistines also brought me to Gaza and bound me with bronze shackles. I was made to ground at the mill in prison. I had lost everything my strength, family, confidence, and sight. "The hair begins to grow again after it had been shaved." You know that my power did not lay my hair, but because God was with me, and this hints at how God was still using me on in this narrative. One day the rulers of the Philistines had a big celebration to honor their false god. Their pagan temple was crowded with thousands of people. During their party, they brought out me so they could laugh at my weakness. But this is no time for thinking and debates the plans again. So I prayed to Lord God, "Strengthen me just this once that I may with one blow take vengeance on Philistines for my two eyes." I stood between two stone pillars that held up the roof. I prayed to God for strength one last time. Then I pushed on the pillars with all my might, and the temple crashed down, killing me and all the Philistines. God had helped me avenge myself.

The Dagon temple, which stands tall as a reminder of the past, is also home to remnants of ancient civilization. It bothered me so much that the memories of the past in my life flickered one by one. Tears welled up in my eyes. The goal was the same, even as we crawled through the dark abyss of despair and perseverance. The mind was tense, and the chest was burning. I realized that I had to take revenge against the Philistines. I have decided to ask for the power that God has poured out on me once more and to reveal the power of the Lord God before them. When I finally cried out to God with great repentance, God strengthened me and enabled me to do greater works than I had ever lived in my life. My life remains a testament to the fact that overcoming human weaknesses can sometimes demonstrate the power of the Spirit of God. No blindness could touch my fighter or fighting spirit.

Reporter: Give us your life lessons.

Samson: The spirit of God can use us mightily in spite of our human failings and our wrong choices. Casting the pearls of our faith before godless people can lead to our own spiritual blindness and slavery. God has given us a free will and moral agency to choose the right thing. This means that we have the freedom to do whatever we like. God has set in motion the immutable spiritual law in the universe. If you choose to break the law of God, bad consequences will follow. Though God can forgive you, the consequences of your actions will continue to haunt you. Satan's chief aim is to cause the faith of the child of God to collapse. The collapse of faith does not take place suddenly but gradually. The collapse of faith is bound to follow the deliberate breaking of God's commandments. We are called to live a holy life; God has set us apart, for a higher calling. God can use bad situations to fulfill His purposes. You can still correct your mistake. God's purpose is way greater than our biggest mistakes. You are free to choose, but you are not free from the consequence of your choice. Every action you make will either bring closer or farther to God. Always choose a partner within your faith that should not be based on your impulse. Use our strength for God's work; it is our duty to use our strength for the glory of God. God's love for His people is greater than we can ever understand. Despite the rebellion, finally I wanted to admonish you that if God has given you a mission to accomplish, do not let anything in the world distract you from it.

Solomon (1015–975 BCE)

Reporter introduction: Solomon wasn't born with wisdom, nor did him study or search for it. God graciously give to him power, fortune, fame, and honor. We should pray for godly wisdom. God gives his best to those who allow him to make the choice. Because we are fallen human beings, even the wisest among us can ignore the best advice. He changed the face of Israel and became the first man in history to be described as a milestone in history. He holds an honor that no one else has. Solomon possessed the brightest personality.

Let us begin to take a closer look at what the people of Israel were like four thousand years ago. Along the road, we saw a shepherd girl has a basket made of papyrus vines in her hand. An old man dressed in a dull white Arabic robe as one suited to the *climate*, serving as a protection against heat, dust, and blazing sunshine and also wore a kefiyeh on his head. Next is a rural farmer plowing the field with yoke of oxen's? He also wears an ancient Arabic robe and a sunscreen. A man pushes water into his backyard using a sturdy trough tied to a rope at the end of a bamboo pole lowered into the water. Someone sits on the ground and prepares mud for building. He is holding on to a bamboo stand made by another person and mixing something brown with his feet and treading on the mud. Some are trying to build a wall as part of his housework with unbaked clay bricks. The shepherds were grazing the sheep, herding them to areas of good forage and keeping a watchful eye out for poisonous plants. Some flocks may include as many as one thousand sheep. Everywhere you go; people talk about Solomon who was anointed as king a few days ago. People say about Solomon that you can ask about anything under and above the sun, and he will give you answers to even the most illogical and ambiguous questions. Tradition says Solomon wrote three books and may have been written in three periods: in youth the Song of Songs, the Proverbs in middle age, and the Ecclesiastes in his old age.

To the best of my knowledge, it is impossible to say the beauty of Solomon's palace and Jerusalem temple. Only those who see it in person can give the details of the expound beauty in architecture. We will ask Solomon questions about the temple of Jerusalem. Its stained glass window was magnificent. The view inside when the sun was shining outside was colorful and indescribable elegance. The arches are broad and square with arches and are full of carvings. You will forget to blink your eyes in amazement at the wonders of the extraordinary remnants of an ancient empire. The majestic structures of the cave temples and the beautiful sculptures carved in the rock evoke the skill of the sculptors. The granite pillars sparkle when the sun hit. The royal secrets and tactics must have been discussed in this secret chamber. Everything is guaranteed national security, the integrity of the country, the prevention of foreign invasion threats, the intrusion, and the lives and property of the people.

Solomon had chariots with 4,000 stalls and 12,000 horsemen (1 Kings 4:26). Normally horses need 18 pounds of Bermuda grass hay and 40 liters of fresh water per day for those long granite tracks where horses drank water and granite vessels to store the water for horses. The foundation of the palaces and other buildings were attacked by enemies and plowed few times in the past. The remains of the canal still found that carry the blood of the sacrificial animals eventually fall into the Kedron River. Pictures of the warriors were

145

painted on the stone walls of the legislature buildings, office complexes, and also held political prisoners in the basements. History tells the story of King Solomon and his entourage, who flourished at the height of their luxury. The estimated value of the gold is about $1,867,722,380. Solomon's provisions for a single day estimated $731,320.

Reporter: Explain your achievements as a king.

Solomon: Successful merchant built professional army, had government officials to assist in ruling. Diplomatic relations by me had married daughters of foreign kings in order to maintain the diplomatic relations. I bring wise men, artisans, architects, craftsmen, builders, and building material especially wood and precious metals to build a temple and palace. The best known and most gifted people from Phoenicians. A team of architects and masons from Tyre was also present for the construction of the temple. I built the temple for the worship of Yahweh, established trade links with neighboring nations, built many cities in Israel, infrastructure, organized the central government and improved tax collection, established a strong army to maintain peace, established diplomatic links with other countries and nations, built a magnificent palace, settled disputes wisely, installed the Ark of the Covenant in the temple, and dedicated the temple of God.

Reporter: Why did God reject you as a king and a political leader?

Solomon: The probable reasons for the failure of my life, I first wanted to admit that my achievements are not achievements in the sight of God. There are so many reasons God was displeased in me. I married many foreign wives who brought with them the worship of foreign gods to Israel (Exodus 34:16). I allowed my foreign wives to worship their gods in Israel. I built high places of worship/temples for the gods of my wives (Exodus 20:4–5). I worshipped the gods of my wives alongside the God of Israel, thus broke the covenant with God. I imposed heavy taxation on my subjects and the districts in order to raise part of the government revenue. I overspent and misused the wealth of the kingdom by building a huge palace. I overtaxed my subjects to maintain my extravagant and high standard of living in my royal court. I introduced forced labor to carry on the building programs (i.e., palace and temple), therefore breaking the covenant rule of brotherhood. I gave King Hiram of Tyre an area of Israel's land to pay off my debts, thus treating the nation's land as my own personal property. I killed my brother Adonijah (1 Kings 2) because I suspected that Adonijah could be my rival to the throne, thus committing murder. I practiced nepotism by exempting my own people from taxation and forced labor (i.e., tribes of Judah and Benjamin exempted from forced labor and payment of taxes). I hired the skills of pagan craftsmen in the construction of the temple and his palace. I made treaties with foreign nations, neighboring nations against the covenant requirement.

Improper decisions were made for momentary pleasures and subject pleasures. I built temples/shrines for idols. I was unfaithful and dishonest. I did not tell or teach people who God was. I was disobedient to God. I did not rule according to the Law of Moses. I did not listen to the prophets. I broke the covenant with God by disobeying his commands not to worship foreign gods. I worshiped both God and idols, syncretism, worshiped idols. I sought alliances with neighboring states instead of relying on God. I did not pray for God's wisdom and guidance, get drunk with power and enforce labor on others. I should avoid immoral marriages. I must maintain faith in God, not to be influenced into evil practices to develop nation's economics. Although I was noted for my wisdom, I made some very foolish decisions. Some of my lapses in judgment would even have to be categorized as dumb mistakes and fatal sins. The nation began to come apart as a spirit of rebellion spread throughout my kingdom.

Reporter: Please explain the history of the beautiful Jerusalem temple.

Solomon: Today, the day when the blazing sun ended, the sun went down with enchanting beauty. The sky painted with a mixture of red and saffron. The golden crowns stand tall in the aurora borealis of the setting sun. You can see the towering fountains rising high, accepting the adornments of the setting sun. The large bungalows with colorful lanterns created an atmosphere of ecstasy. I'm sure that no one will stop and marvel at the beautiful sight of the temple. When you see the Temple of Jerusalem hanging in awe before your eyes, you will be amazed by the surroundings and the innumerable historical wonders. According to the Tanach, the Holy Temple was approximately 180 feet long, 90 feet wide and 50 feet high. Massive amounts of cedar wood imported from the kingdom of Tyre were used in its construction. I also had enormous blocks of fine stone quarried and hauled to Jerusalem, where they served as the foundation of the temple. Pure gold was used as an overlay in some parts of the temple. Garnished with precious stones, surrounded by spacious courts with magnificent approaches, and lined with carved cedar and burnished gold, the temple structure, with its broidered hangings and rich furnishings, was a fit emblem of the living church of God on earth, which through the ages has been building in accordance with the divine pattern, with materials that have been likened to "gold, silver, precious stones," polished after the similitude of a palace.

The first temple is one of the most famous buildings of the ancient world and also one of the most mysterious. The Jerusalem temple is the sanctuary of Yahweh, the God of Israel. The temple is built in 950 BCE. The construction of this temple, God had enlightened the sculptors with their vast knowledge, creativity, and unique architectural skills. The spacious, cold, and dark interiors seem to invite us into the mysteries of the divine. When you get inside of the temple, your body feels a sharp tingling sensation. Its construction and design are beautiful, indigenous architecture, serene atmosphere, and indescribable and eye-popping views. The sculptural beauty of the facade carvings is beautiful and glamorous. The masculine splendor of the fine arts shines through; the curiosity those dawns in the eyes when one looks at the colorful new sights evokes a sense of wonder.

Reporter: How does the religion conflict with science?

Solomon: There is much debate in our culture between science and the Bible. Religious teachings tend to focus on how people can live alongside each other with love, understanding, and compassion. The present is not the key to understanding the past. Rather, the Bible is the key to understanding both the past and the present because it gives us the key events in history to understand both! Science and the Bible work together to help us understand the world around us better. To be very clear, there is no conflict between evolution and religion. The truth is, the Bible and science is completely compatible! Science is a gift from God who is the Source of all good things (James 1:17). The fact that we can use our intellect to explore the physical world and make discoveries that improve our living conditions is not only wonderful; it's also biblical! I believe that all truth is God's truth. I believe that God is the creator of science. He created molecules, atoms, everything. I think that even a scientist doesn't have all the explanations and has to take a leap of faith. I think the theory of evolution is a leap of faith as well, because it can't be proven. I believe that God created the world and that Christianity doesn't go against science.

Reporter: Would you please give your life lessons?

Solomon: Prayer can bring forth the answer or enlighten that you need. Whatever you do must be done to the best of your ability. God wants you to give your all because you are honoring God by your excellence. True wisdom comes from God and glorifies Him. Stay humble. When you pray to God for success, make sure you ask for the character to withstand the prosperity. Bad company influence and corrupts good character. Do not allow jealousy to take over your thoughts because it can become toxic. Always serve the Lord with a loyal heart. Never allow vanity to consume your life because things that are vane will not last and have no real value. Administrative skill is a sign of wisdom. If God doesn't lay the foundation, your home will collapse. Our labor cannot replace God's sovereign provision. When we rest and listen to God, His Word helps us to understand who we are in Him.

Jonah (Approx. 960–740 BCE)

Reporter introduction: Nineveh was the famous capital of ancient Assyria. Nineveh was one of the largest cities in the world at that time, with a population of over one hundred thousand much larger than its rival, the city of Babylon. Geographically, Assyria occupied the middle and northern part of Mesopotamia. It was situated between the Euphrates and Tigris Rivers, and its major cities were Calah, Zab, Ashur, and the capital, Nineveh. Nineveh, the oldest city of the ancient Assyrian empire, situated on the east bank of the Tigris River and encircled by the modern city of Mosul, Iraq. Nineveh was located at the intersection of important north-south and east-west trade routes, and its proximity to a tributary of the Tigris, the Khawṣar River, added to the value of the fertile agricultural and pastoral lands in the district. Assyria is chiefly remembered for its military prowess, advances in weaponry, and meticulously recorded conquests.

In Nineveh, there were indescribable experiences that descended into the spirit of an ancient people beyond the mere sight of the eyes. The sun was beginning to set. The cupolas glistening in the golden glow of the sunset. The sea that hides unknown wonders is always a great phenomenon. The glittering beauty of the sunset was thrilling. We stood in awe, wondering at the infinity of the vast ocean that swelled in the waves. The heartwarming sunset was pleasing. As the sun prepares for sunset by bathing in the ocean of pleasure, it seems as if that the sun is in a hurry to receive his beloved as he approaches the sea.

Jonah was the son of Amittai of the tribe of Benjamin, who lived during the reign of Jeroboam II. *Jonah* literally means dove, the only prophet in the Gentile world. Who was sent by God to Nineveh? When Jonah was moved to tell Nineveh of the Word of the LORD, which he had spoken concerning the great city of Nineveh, he first departed from the counsel of God, but God did the work by himself. Before the interview with Jonah, I want to tell you a little bit about the ocean and the depths of the sea. The oceans are a treasure trove of resources for future life on earth. The cool breeze cools the air, and the atmosphere is refreshing and enticing. It creates dull and lazy waves and battering the shore with white milk foam. Sometimes all of a sudden, the sea is mad, the screams are deafening to the tumultuous waves. The ship is shaking in the dark sky, and the passengers are terrified of the unexpected change and are wandering without knowing what to do. We have heard so much news that the raging oceans of blessings are making waves on the shore, killing millions of people in an instant.

The Qur'an considers Prophet Yunus to be a very true prophet. Gathhefer lived north of Nazareth. Jonah, who had disobeyed God's command, was thrown into the sea by a shipwreck and swallowed up by a huge fish and was eventually brought ashore at Ashdod. To this day, a mountain in Ashdod is still called Hebrew Givath Jonah. Nineveh is an ancient Assyrian city near the Tigris River in Mesopotamia. The name *Nineveh* literally means the place of the fish. The river Ghoshar has two sand dunes on either side. The small sand dune on the south side is called Tel Nabi Yunus. It means the sand dune of the Prophet Jonah. Archaeological, geographical, historical, religious, and philosophical research has shown that the flood caused great changes, not just on earth, but throughout the universe.

Reporter: Why did you disobey the Lord? What happened when you disobeyed God?

Jonah: I was told by God to go to the great city of Nineveh and shout against it. "The wickedness of Nineveh has come before me. Nineveh will be destroyed." But I disobeyed and ran away from God. I need to introduce myself here. I am a very conservative Jewish prophet. Nineveh has long been one of Israel's most important enemy nations, and I was glad to see them fall. I did not want the Lord God to always save someone from the calamity that the merciful God would bring to them if they repented and returned. That is why I disobey God's command. But I ran away from the Lord and headed for Tarshish. I went down to Joppa, where I found a ship bound for that port. After paying the fare, I went aboard and sailed for Tarshish to flee from the LORD. Then the LORD sent a great wind on the sea, and such a violent storm arose that the ship threatened to break up. All the sailors were afraid, and each cried out to his own god. And they threw the cargo into the sea to lighten the ship. But I had gone below deck, where I lay down and fell into a deep sleep. The captain came to me and asks, "How can you sleep? Get up and call on your god! Maybe he will take notice of us so that we will not perish."

Then the sailors said to each other, "Come and let us cast lots to find out who is responsible for this calamity."

They cast lots, and the lot fell on me. So they asked me, "Tell us, who are responsible for making all this trouble for us? What kind of work do you do? Where do you come from? What is your country? From what people are you?"

I said to them, "I am a Hebrew, and I fear the LORD, the God of heaven, which hath made the sea and the dry land."

This terrified them, and they asked, "What have you done?"

They knew I was running away from the Lord, because I had already told them so. The sea was getting rougher and rougher. So they asked me, "What should we do to you to make the sea calm down for us?"

I replied, "Pick me up and throw me into the sea, and it will become calm. I know that it is my fault that this great storm has come upon you."

Instead, the men did their best to row back to land. But they could not, for the sea grew even wilder than before. Then they cried out to the Lord, "Please, Lord, do not let us die for taking this man's life. Do not hold us accountable for killing an innocent man, for you, Lord, have done as you pleased."

Then they took me and threw me overboard, and the raging sea grew calm.

They threw me into the sea and fell into the mouth of a whale! God sent a big fish to swallow me. The whale was overjoyed to find an unexpectedly large prey without any labor. But from the moment he swallowed me, the whale started having stomachaches. The whale wandered in circles and lengths through the water for three days and nights with excruciating abdominal pain. Sea creatures are more ubiquitous than land creatures. Because the land is a dynamic area, terrestrial organisms can only travel in length or breadth. But sea creatures can move very comfortably up and down, not just in length and breadth. Finally, when I was suffering, the whale threw me to the beach. From there, I walked for three days and came to Nineveh, and called out to them. At the end of forty days, Nineveh will be destroyed. The people of Nineveh repented of their evil ways, and God repented of their sins. The evil that he said he would send was not sent upon Nineveh.

Reporter: What is one of the main themes in your story?

Jonah: My life story shows that God is omnipotent over all human activity and nature. The seven things in nature are found in obedience to God's command. Sea swell, violent storm, huge fish, heat waves, castor, worm, east wind. I cried out to God, "You hurled me into the depths, into the very heart of the seas, and the currents swirled about me; all your waves and breakers swept over me." Let me explain the impossibility of light in the deep sea. The light falling on the ocean surface is absorbed by each color according to its depth. It should be noted that the average depth of the sea is 2,500 meters. He threw me into the depths, into the middle of the sea. The currents surrounded me. The waves passed over me. The depths around me are covered with moss, and my head is tightened. Floating plants are microscopic plants that cannot be seen with the naked eye.

Reporter explanations: These microscopic plants' growth and multiplication is unimaginable. In three days, a floating plant grows to thirty-five million. We must also know that God has taken care of the microorganisms in the ocean, a few millimeters long copepods, to prevent this astonishing increase. The growth of the copepod is also unprecedented. They feed on marine life, from small fish to giant whales. Coral reefs are made by marine corals. The Great Barrier Reef, a coral reef in the Pacific Ocean east of Australia, is 2,000 kilometers long and 150 kilometers wide. It is said that the Great Barrier Reef would not be as large as all the man-made buildings and structures in the world today. Jonah might have gone down to the bottom of the ocean, where the mountains are rooted. The Mariana Trench in the Pacific Ocean, known as the deepest point, is two kilometers below the ocean, two kilometers below sea level to see its highest peak, nine kilometers high, and the pressure is a thousand times greater than our atmospheric pressure. In addition, the ocean is an inexhaustible source of minerals and gasoline. The sea has more minerals and organisms than land. We are reluctant to praise God's omnipotence because man has no proper knowledge. When we look at the vastness of the universe or the vast expanse of the ocean, their size reminds us of our nothingness. There is not a single centimeter of air or a gram of soil on earth without water. The temperature of seawater plays a major role in regulating internal temperature and climate. Land and sea receive the same amount of sunlight, but the land cools down quickly when the sun sets. After the environment cools down, the oceans slowly release the heat stored by the seawater during the day, thus regulating the atmospheric temperature along the coast. The sea seems to be stagnant if you keep an eye on the still sea, but it is dynamic. Salt and heat are the main motives behind the sea. Nature teaches that there is a God, that he is worthy of worship, and that he has given us a basic moral order, the sum of which is equivalent to the moral content of the Ten Commandments. Nature testifies to God's existence.

Reporter: What is the message of your life experience?

Jonah: Actually, I had hoped that the people of Nineveh would just ignore my preaching so that God would rain down his fire on them just as he did on Sodom. But the people of Nineveh repent, and the city was saved by God. God's mercy is wider and God's grace is greater than all of our sins. God uses all means to extend his grace to all kinds of people. God's mercy is motivated by God's love for his own creation, and he doesn't play favoritism.

You cannot hide from God, both believers and unbelievers. Sometimes the disobedience and sin of a believer brings suffering upon unbelievers. Disobedience will create turmoil in your life. Keep your vows to God so that he won't find it necessary to bring a whale experience into your life. Repentance must produce obedience. Our God is the God of second chance. God has mercy on every part of his creation, including nonhuman creatures. When God speak to you, make yourself available. You are created with a mission and specific purpose. You are called by God to do something very meaningful in life; never lose sight of that meaning. Don't run from your purpose, and don't waste your resources. Your choices will dictate the life you live. God will always provide a way; God will never call you to something you can't accomplish. God has no problem removing you from your comfort zone. Don't live a life of complaining. Even in our failures, God can use it for good. Some blessings are like coals covered in ashes; just blow it once, and you can see that it glows red again.

CHAPTER 4

Elected People but Sold Out Their Life to the Enemy

WIND IS A great phenomenon of nature. It is not possible for human beings to control it, and some uncontrollable storms can arise in life as well. But life's success lies in being able to take advantage of that wind. The gardenia flowers attract everyone, spreading its fragrance in the air when darkness spreads. These flowers are generally white and are often much more fragrant than their day-blooming counterparts. One of the reasons the white flowers that bloom at night are often more aromatic is that they need to attract nocturnal pollinators that must find them in the dark. The night expands its petals and helps to spread the fragrance. In human life too, when there are often depressing experiences, they arouse our consciousness instead of discouraging us. Sometimes we have to travel over steep cliffs and other times over rough surfaces. Sometime through the jungles, sometime with the desert. Sometime through the mountains, and other times through the valleys. That is life.

The true disciple is one who breaks down in front of people and pretends to be anything, but serves silently without reward, without making a fuss, without wanting to show anyone back where no one is looking, and without paying attention to anyone's attention. Those who blow the coals inside despite the darkness around them. Those who abandon worldly desires and lead a righteous and godly life. Yesterday's riots and anxieties, tomorrow's worries and distress, shady living environments where not even a single ray of bright light can radiate into the present, burning living conditions but a departure from tradition.

Cain (3927–3797 BCE)

Reporter introduction: The eldest son of Adam, Cain was a tiller of the ground. Cain's offering was rejected by God. We don't know for sure why Abel's offering was accepted and Cain's rejected. The reversal, the ascent of the youngest is a frequent motif in the Bible, particularly in Genesis, where the younger child is consistently raised above his or her siblings. Isaac over Ishmael, Jacob over Esau, Rachel over Leah, Joseph over his brothers, and Ephraim over Manasseh. The ascent of David over his brothers is a later repetition of this same motif. God's preference of Abel's offering over Cain's is simply the first in this series, but Cain's response makes it the deadliest. Cain's faulty character may have rendered his sacrifice meaningless. The word meaning of *Cain* is "to acquire" or "I," but when you examine his life, he didn't acquire anything. With a lot of good expectations, Eve named Cain and said that she had received a man from God. He was a man who was angry with God, who did not want to do well, who killed his brother, who was cursed, who lied, who disobeyed God, and who was displeased with God and so on.

If we look at Cain's character, his disobedience to things, his worship of God according to his views without looking at his will. The answer to why Cain did not offer the sacrifice of faith like Abel tells us in 1 John 3. Cain is a prototypical unbeliever, unregenerate, and wicked. He became angry at God for rejecting worship that did not conform to God's commandments and killed the one who worshiped rightly out of revenge. Anger is just one letter of danger. As per the New Testament teachings, "Do not be angry until the sun goes down." God was trying to unfold the mystery from Cain, but he refused to reveal and didn't have any remorse. There are many different opinions about sin. We were created with the faculty of conscience, of distinguishing between right and wrong, and so are accountable to God the Creator for our actions. Cain had no right to be upset when Abel gave a superior gift.

157

The second sign in the Bible is the sign that Jehovah gave to Cain so that he could run to the land of Nod, east of Eden. And so we see that when Adam and Eve sinned, the Lord God appeared to them. When Cain did wrong, Jehovah appeared to him, but Cain did not admit that he killed his brother. God being the All-Wise knew everything, but he still hides the truth from God. After flipping the first few chapters of the book of Genesis, you can see that hatred, negation and forsaking, decorativeness of God, and shedding innocent blood. An atmosphere of full of excitements of dripping blood to the ground can be seen in the history of men. When you carefully examine the Cain's sacrifice, there was not even a drop of blood from the heart of his sacrifice. If your sacrifice is not from the heart, there is no value, and God will not bless you. What Jesus did in Golgotha was the epitome of the supreme sacrifice of bloodshed. The marks of that sacrifice are deeply etched in the hearts of people all over the universe.

Reporter briefing about Cain and Abel Case HSC # 2:

Prosecutor: There were no eyewitnesses when Abel was killed. Neither the parents nor anyone else was present to file the case in court. But Almighty God himself took up the case. It does not take months to prosecute without losing evidence. The case is being heard on the same day as the FIR registered. There is no need to look for prominent police officers to crack down on unproven cases. The iron gates, which are locked with huge walls, chains, will automatically open in front of this investigation team. Welcome to today's news hour. The main defendant, Cain, was under the watchful eye of Jehovah God. He was arrested in the courtyard of the house in the evening. Today, the Caucasus is analyzing the news related to this. In this discussion, some trees and stones from the vicinity of Eden join us. The archangel Michael and the representative of the heavenly court join us. The false prophet has come from hell to plead for the accused. Satan has agreed to join the phone line from hell if necessary. The audience is also free to participate in this live discussion, given the severity of this unprecedented and rare event in world history. Chief angel Michael archangel is investigating the case. Assumptions, theories, and witnesses are very important in criminal investigation. The village where the murder took place is in the throes of noon.

Reporter explanations: Abel's murder is the one that shook the whole world and created the whole of Eden. Time changes everything. People's hair turns white as they grow older, but one thing always stays the same, the feathers of the crow that never change its color. I am aware that the crow's black color irritates people, but they are oblivious to the fact that even the blackest feather on the crow's body is nothing compared to the human heart when it grows black because of sin. How strange the species called *humans* and how grave his contradictions are! How great God's mercy and forgiveness is to man! Excuse my language for I am a little bit angry. Although he received a rare sentence from the heavenly court, Jehovah God did not allow him to be imprisoned in an iron cage. Human justice systems will always have cruel faces and dark hands. There will be humanitarian interventions to convict the accused. There will be a tendency to look for positive evidence and deliberate moves to avoid looking for negative ones. Assumptions, theories, and witnesses are very important in criminal investigation.

There are some differences between the first two trials. The case of Adam and Eve concerns a transgression against God, the non-fulfillment of a divine command. The case of Cain deals with the highest crime among humans: the willful ending of another's life. Adam and Eve confess taking the fruit while assigning the blame to one another, Adam by denouncing his wife, and Eve by blaming the serpent. Cain, on the other hand, denies outright the murder of his brother. Humans have little role in these trials other than to stand as the accused and give their testimonies. The proceedings of the trials follow an inherent biblical logic; since there was no one around to investigate, prosecute, or judge Adam and Eve, they being the sole inhabitants of the garden of Eden, God must fill all these functions. The second trial was the murder of Abel by his brother Cain. It certainly would have been difficult for Adam and Eve to avenge one dead son by punishing the other; therefore, God must conduct the trial. After these trials, the roles of investigator, prosecutor, and judge passed into human hands.

Before I proceed further, I will give some comparison what is the difference between divine judgement and human judgement. God's standard of judgment is defined by his holy character. God judges perfectly and totally. His judgment is eternally significant. But God judges the heart and all humans according to the highest and purest standard, his perfect and holy character. Rightfully, God is concerned with the hallowing of his glory; His judgments are true. Hidden things of darkness will be brought into the light. Nothing will be hidden from him; he sees all. No darkness can hide from him; no hiding can baffle him. When God is the judge, the result will be an absolute condemnation. There will be praise as well as blame. Judge of the earth, Psalm 94:1: In God's judgements, the defendant is entitled to a fair trial. So earthly justice and divine justice are incomparable. Human judgment of each other is often superficial. We judge our neighbor according to outward markers (i.e., wealth, social etiquette, health, intellect, influence, eloquence, pedigree, and beauty). Our judgment is often self-centered. We accept people who will increase our glory and praise. Human judgement is fallible. Do not forget that human powers are limited, information is often very defective, and the minds very subject to bias. Human judgments affect the providence and dealings of God. So fallible is human judgment that often the best men have been counted the worst, and the worst the best, and also ours are faulty and self-centered. So much is hidden from us; we judge from part. Judges are subject to bribery and corruption. Earthly justice is all about this balancing of the scales.

A heartwarming principle has been written to prevent this tragedy. Even if a thousand criminals escape, not a single innocent person should be punished unjustly. Therefore, humane judicial minds try to maximize the benefit of the doubt to the accused. It is enough to have strong evidence and reason before the human court. There is no need to zoom in on the visuals on the divine court ruling monitor. There is no need to go to the source of the crime scene by collecting footprints, circumstantial evidence, speculation or forensic report, no matter if the body is decomposed. There is no need for petitions, picketing, protesting, or nonviolent assembly to reveal the mystery of death. There is no need to stick any note tape to protect the X-crime scene evidence from being lost. The whole world is in a celestial observatory and station boundary. God's judgment will be blameless, true, and impartial, and there is no end twist in the case. I welcome the plaintiff and the defendant to this episode separately. Let's start with the first tricky question.

Plaintiff Jehovah: "Where is your brother, Abel?"

Defendant Cain denies the murder, stating, "Am I my brother's keeper?"

Plaintiff Jehovah: The Almighty, knowing all the facts, informs Cain, "Your brother's blood is crying out to me from the ground!"

Court angel: The court angel clerk asked the defendant if you are ready for trial. Then the angel clerk called jury panel numbers and the juror goes to the jury box and gives the oath like this. I do swear in the name of God solemnly affirm that what I shall state the truth, the whole truth, and nothing but the truth. So help me God.

Plaintiff: I wanted to hear your versions why God rejected your offering? It is your chance to present your version of the case. I am not going to interrupt you anytime. When you finish it, I will interrogate you.

Defendant: My Lord, my offering was not accompanied by faith; everything was all about me. I worshipped according to sight—according to what my own senses and wisdom dictated would be an honorable gift unto the Lord. I waited until I was sure that there would be enough of my crop for myself. Then and only then, I did bring my offering to the Lord. No faith was involved on my part. Enough time had passed that my crop was now sure and certain. My crop was most likely already in the barn. I thought to myself, *I've now got plenty for myself. I'll take a little to the Lord as an offering*. I thought that I could earn salvation and please God through the work of my hands. My parents had made sacrifices for their redemption and return to paradise. We were also trained to do that. Abel's sacrifice was a sin offering, and my sacrifice was a meal offering. "Rules must be obeyed." The sacrifice I made to God was not in faith. God gave me a second round, but I missed that opportunity. The world of hatred, when God asked me, "Where is your brother?" I was angry with God. Sin comes to you for the fulfillment of its desires, because you did not do well. You must conquer sin. I did not like this command of God. The goal was not to let God know, but to tell me what I was selling. The story would have changed if my heart had been plowed at that time and tears had flowed. I was a very strategically planned assassin. And I went out from before the Lord and dwelt in the land of Nod, east of Eden. Every tragic hero has his own reasons, and I'm not an exception. Life's voyages are shattered by a moment's emotional turmoil.

Plaintiff: Did you premeditate to kill your brother and why?

Defendant: I committed by premeditating to kill my brother Abel. But this murder was motivated by a collection of other sins: jealousy, anger, hatred, and resentment. I murdered Abel "because my own actions were evil and my brothers were righteous." From the beginning of time, those who reject God have hated those who love Him. So we went into the field, and I said to Abel that my offering was not accepted with favor by God. So I felt very bad because of my brother's rejection as well as the rejection by an unfair God. My fortunate brother put me down and refuses to take my bitter experience seriously or sympathetically. This made my frustration mount to the point that I come to a conclusion that there is no justice at all on earth or in heaven. We had a heated argument and finally I killed my brother.

Plaintiff: Can you explain me your life after you killed your brother?

Defendant: There was anxiety and excitement in that run. How many times I washed my hand to take away but in vain. The sights of losses passing through the steps of the past were scattering my vision. It does not matter if I search for the key to peace that I have never been able to find it. There was not a single ray of light left in

162

the sky to penetrate the clotted darkness in my life. The beetles were disturbing the silence of the night. When Jehovah God asked that unexpected question, of where my brother Abel was, burned me to ashes. I had to work hard to get the words out of my throat. I felt a trembling spread from my thumb to my whole body. I was punished for being addicted to childish prejudices, insane education, and blind imagination. Feelings of emptiness, desolation, and loneliness were felt in those moments when the foot was burning and the upright body was swollen. The court convinced me that the accused should be given the maximum punishment prescribed by law and that the accused had committed the crime. The archangel Michael argued that since my brother had been brutally murdered without provocation, the accused should be punished accordingly for continuing to spread the wrong message in the community. God mercifully punished me for my wrongdoing, and I have no complaints about it. I made an unforgivable mistake.

Plaintiff: Did God address your concern about your punishment?

Defendant: My respond to God was a lie. Obviously God knew where Abel was exactly in that field. It was merely the instinctual response of a guilty man. I knew that the Almighty God knows everything and what I did. When God let me run to Nod, I had an obvious worriment "My punishment is more than I can bear. I will be a restless wanderer on the earth, and whoever finds me will kill me." God, however, placed a "mark" on me so that no one who found me would kill me. This might seem odd, for why should God care about preserving the life of a murderer? Ever since sin entered the world, there has existed a causal relationship between murder and revenge, but it was not revealed until I killed Abel. This decree suggests that when someone has been killed, an avenger of blood will almost certainly arise.

It demonstrates that murder, whether accidental or intentional has the effect of creating in others a desire for revenge. It was, in fact, merciful especially compared to the death sentence that I would have received under the Law. "Now you are under a curse and driven from the ground, which opened its mouth to receive your brother's blood from your hand. When you work the ground, it will no longer yield its crops for you." The result of this curse was that it transformed me from a farmer into a nomad: "You will be a restless wanderer on the earth." I was forced to abandon my vocation as a farmer and instead had to find other means to feed myself and my family. Thus, in time, as I wandered in the land of Nod, I naturally began hunting and gathering. Unlike my brother, I had ignored my parents' instruction regarding sacrifices and presented to God an unacceptable offering. I had ignored God when I said, "If you do what is right, will your offering not be accepted?" and I had ignored God when he warned me to "master" my emotions. In all likelihood, I never asked for forgiveness.

Reporter: Give me your life lessons.

Cain: God's words still haunt me. "You will be accepted if you respond in the right way." I must admit, though, that during some of those sleepless nights, I have secretly wondered if offering a lamb would have changed everything after all. Obedience is important in our relationship with God. Envy can lead to more outward sins, even murder. We must exercise willpower in our fight against sin. Sin can have lifelong consequences. Life without God is a lonely existence. God cares about and protects even those who sin against him. Forgiveness brings more peace than revenge. The strength of the human will to be unbroken. If you can take it, you can make it. Never assume things; never burn bridges. Life without God is lonely, tiring, and frustrating. Obedience strengthens our fellowship with God. My experience is that if hatred is carried inside, it will not hesitate to kill anyone. The consequence of sin is that it lasts a lifetime and lasts forever.

Ahab/Jezebel

Reporter introduction: It was a journey in search of Ahab. Beyond the vast cornfields, a glorious sunbeam was slowly rising from the back slope, slowly bathing in the red. The melodious music of the drizzle in the cool, lush dawn, bouncing off the flowers and leaves. A faint musk from the ripe wheat fields lingered in the air. Ahab, the son of Omri, was wicked than all the kings who had ruled Israel before, with Jezebel, who was the daughter of King Etbal, the king of Sidon. She was the wickedest of women and has been denounced as a murderer, prostitute, and enemy of God. The characteristics of Ahab are as follows. Ahab led a carefree life, handing over power and responsibilities to Jezebel. Ahab was a man of masculinity and leadership who was incapable of responding to specific life circumstances. Fearing Jezebel, he was bound by her invisible chains, and things were handled by Jezebel without preference to his will. Ahab was the one who pushed his life away like a puppet because all the powers were in Jezebel's hands. Ahab lived a life of ignorance of light and darkness. Ahab was the one who dedicated his life to God and sold his people Israel to Jezebel instead of living in obedience to God's counsel. Ahab was not interested in the welfare of the people and ruled with the jealousy of Jezebel. A king should always be idealistic and socially conscious. It is desirable to have a life partner who knows and obeys God more than anything else in the world (Proverb 31:10). Life that opposes God brings disgrace, shame, and death. What Ahab did was put into practice the erroneous ideas that had passed through Jezebel's mind. It is a meaningful folk saying extracted from agricultural life. "The bird may have flown over our heads, but we must not allow it to nest in our heads."

Let me give some of Jezebel's descriptions of the heroine so that it will shorten the distance to know her. Her eyes that illuminate the undulating blue sea. She focused only on her own life and comfort. Jezebel conquered the world by applying lipstick, black eyelash tinted, carnation adorned with pins, and a special face powder on her face. Her lips, nails, and face were painted in all sorts of ornaments, and the beauty was artificial (makeup) (2 King 9:30–33). She has a way of being active not only in action but also in nature and speech. She walked with a sharp sword to cut through with her poisonous tongue and intrigues. How to make a good sword out of bad iron? The nature of rain does not change. It grows flowers in the garden and thorns in the swamps. The rainy season of the creative process spreads roses in some human hearts. Jezebel was to set new standards of patriotism, so many pious people were imprisoned and killed for treason, abusing the unlawful activities.

Reporter: What can we learn from Ahab and Jezebel about authority, responsibility, and humility?

Ahab/Jezebel: The marble wall has indelible black marks that were painted in Ahab's palace. Chariots, gardens, swimming pools, and gymnasiums, all seem to be the last word in luxury. The interior is more beautiful than the exterior, and a lot of woodwork enriches the hall. Malicious people say that my tongue is a little too long, and my words are arrogant, and I am a born criminal. My enemies say that in my eyes, they could see the coals of anger burning. There are those who say that my tongue has a furlong length. There is no need for revolution to overthrow a bloody tyrannical imperialism and monarchy. Elijah was being pursued by my spy eyes. The pillars, the armories, the chariots, the silver lights of the swords, and the power that came to my hand were like a wreath in the monkey's hand. The strongholds of sin built up in the tears and blood of many saints were torn down. The eyebrows on the glowing face were so cruel that even the wind was afraid to enter the palace courtyard. The cruel mind could not be shaken as nature stood still without even a hint. My mind was like an invisible deep sea. I issued a lookout notice to imprison and kill so many prophets that didn't do any crime. Ahab's palace was like a slaughterhouse where the lives of many were wiped out. Pride is the first step toward a man's failure; that was my problem. Finally, God planned to end my dictatorship. When God have an action plan whether it is a shrub or a big tree blocking His way, He will cut it down. It is a pitiful scene where my body and the head lie apart like a spaceship that has slipped out of its intended orbit. My brain and blood were scattered on the ground. This brutal massacre took place during the heyday of the emperor's dictatorship.

Ahab: Life lessons?

God is not rushed, but justice will ultimately serve. God's laws and precepts are specific and purposeful. Good people suffer and even die due to the evil intentions of others. In God's omnipotence and omniscience, He doesn't necessarily save us all from early death. Evil people seem to get away with it. Whether it's lying, cheating, stealing, hurting, or even killing, it seems that sometimes the bad guys get away with it. It's not for us to judge how God will deal with wrongdoings. We can trust, however, that God sees all wrongdoings. God deals with evil and disobedience. All evil and disobedience is ultimately dealt with by God. There's no getting around it. He has the final say.

Judas Iscariot (Approx. 2 BCE–33 AD)

Reporter introduction: *Judas*, son of Simeon of Kirith in Judea, literally means praise. Judas is the only disciple from outside Galilee. Although the Bible mentions seven first-century Jews living in Judah, the image of Judas Iscariot, a disciple of Jesus, comes to mind when we hear of Judas. He walked and slept with Jesus and traveled together. He was a disciple also in charge of finance. Although the other disciples in the crowd could not understand Judas, the all-knowing Lord gave some hints and warnings. Judas, in the face of hypocrisy, became an unnecessary character who had little to contribute to the world. Judging from the Scriptures, Judas was the one who invented the word *greed* and registered its patent. Our protagonist is the number 1 penny-pinching person. The ten disciples that the Lord first chose were all but martyrs, except John. Judas alone was hated by all and lost. Judas called Jesus Lord and Master, and for three years, he was a constant companion. Any doctrine that is not revealed by life is of no value. Judas walked into the darkness with a burning kiss to his master. Only the Antichrist and Judas are mentioned as the Son of Destruction. Judas, who betrayed Jesus, is a symbol of deceit and scorn. Jude is the most misunderstood disciple (John 12:6). The man with the shimmering coins drew new figures into the pages of his life.

A chief administrative officer, during the British rule in India who brought home government papers with his workload, studied and took notes, used accounted candles in the government treasury to read it. When he wanted to his personal reading of a book, he lit up his own candle. The honesty and integrity of this person is commendable. One cannot measure one's life background by look-ing at the exteriors. The life of Judas reminds us that the purity of one's heart cannot be measured by outward appearances. Without rethinking and caring about tomorrow, money is the standard by which everything is miscalculated. Such people are like those who leave their lives in the lurch. It is true that everyone's accounts are kept very accurate by God. Reap what we sow. Whatever we sow, we get back a hundredfold.

One day, Luqman al-Hakeem's master ordered him to slaughter a goat and bring him the most pleasant and delicious two parts from it. Luqman brought him the tongue and heart. The master asked, "Didn't you find anything more pleasant than these?"

Luqman said, "No!" After a while, the master ordered him to slaughter a goat and to bring two of the most malignant parts. Luqman slaughtered the goat and brought the tongue and heart.

The master exclaimed and said, "I ordered you to bring me the most delicious parts, and you brought me the tongue and heart, and I ordered you to bring the most malignant parts, and you brought the tongue and heart. How can this be?"

Luqman said, "Nothing can be more pleasing than these if they are good, and nothing can be more malicious than these if they are malignant." the Story of Luqman Al-Hakim-zahrt ash shams.

One of the most learned and intelligent of the disciples could have reached a higher level in life than the other disciples, but he went astray. He was chosen as one of the twelve. Called for great-ness, but became a spy, and the end of Judas was tragic. The name Judas may be synonymous with the most heinous of traitors and a maligned biblical character.

Reporter: How did you meet Jesus, and who brought you to Jesus?

Judas Iscariot: I was born in Kerioth, a small town in southern Judea. When I was a lad, my parents moved to Jericho, where I lived and had been employed in my father's various business enterprises until I became interested in the preaching and work of John the Baptist. I was an only son in my family, and my parents are wealthy

Jewish parents living in Jericho. I had become the disciple of John the Baptist, so my Sadducee parents had disowned me. My previous experience was with finances. Nathaniel invited me to join with the twelve apostles. I was thirty years of age and unmarried when I joined the apostles. I was a good thinker but not always a truly honest thinker. I was a good matchless treasurer, a learned man. Money could never have been the motive for my betrayal of the Master.

Shortly after I was expelled from my home for going down with John the Baptist's disciples, I arrived at Jesus's camp. The first time I saw Jesus was on a rainy day. Most of the disciples had given up their lives, family, and security for the Master. Back of their minds, they thought when Jesus gets the political power; with high hopes they would be able to play a leading role. But the thoughts that had been built up collapsed like a castle on the very first day. They are still sitting by the ashes where the nightmares have burned, but I was worried when I saw the course of things, and then the invitation to betray the high priest came. My dreams were shattered when I later found out about the secret plans of the Jewish Roman Empire. But what I wished was that I had calculated that even if they caught Jesus, who had the solution to all the problems and miracles, he would escape.

When I realized my mistake, I tried to repay the bribe I had received from the high priest, but they did not accept and threw me away. It seemed to me that it was very sad that the world did not forgive me, who had atoned for my wrongdoing with my own life, without waiting for anyone's trial or judgment. But later I realized that the delayed remorse was irrelevant. There is no honesty in that remorse. I was saddened by Jesus's betrayal. Jesus gathered his disciples around the Lord's Table for the unleavened bread cutting ceremony, which is part of the Passover. A thousand thoughts came into my mind. The horrible suffering that Jesus was going to endure the next day, dragging the innocent Master down the street like a great criminal, the nails piercing his body, and finally hanging on the cross. Jesus didn't complain because He knew that only through this could the atonement of mankind be possible. On the night of the betrayal, I could not find a mountain or ocean to hide in, but one

place that came to my mind was only in the darkness of the valley of
Ben Hinnom, which ordinary human beings do not hesitate to cross.

Reporter: What was the story behind the betrayal of Jesus?
Iscariot Jude: While we were eating, Jesus said, "Truly I tell you,
one of you will betray me." But woe to that man who betrays the Son
of Man! It would be better for him if he had not been born.

Then I was pretending that I don't know anything and ask Jesus,
"Surely you don't mean me, Rabbi?"

Jesus answered, "You have said so."

I went on thinking that it would have been better if I had not
been born. For some time, my eyes were filled with guilt as it hit
my chest. I had decided to execute myself for my crime, and there
was no time to wait any longer. I had learned that death is not the
answer to anything and that it is just an escape from life. I ran down
the street like crazy. The gale blows at night on the head of the outer
cane. It was a terrifying sight to see its black shadows leaping in the
wind. That voice woke me up from my thoughts. I now preferred
darkness to light. The nymphs hanging upside down on the branches
of the trees had my eyes glazed over at night. Nature covered with a
blanket of darkness outside. It felt like a thousand volcanoes erupting together in my mind. It took moments to regain consciousness.
I hope the end of a human being does not become so terrible. The
other end of the rope was tied to a tree branch, and the nerves in my
neck tightened. The betrayal money I threw in the church courtyard,
they bought a piece of land with that money. This place is known as
Akkaldama, near Entrobale in the Hinnon Valley. It means the land
of blood, the potter's field.

Reporter: Is suicide a sin according to the scripture?
Iscariot Jude: At least I didn't go down without explaining
myself first. My death was just an escape from reality. Many seek
refuge in suicide to escape the clutches and clutter of life. Life is a gift
that is given as a gift, a blessing that the giver should experience with
gratitude until it is added to eternity, and the arrogance of rejecting
the gift extended by the eternal and giving it back to him is ungrate-

ful. A devotee should always see life as a precious gift from God. We do not have to destroy or annihilate, as we please. Suicide is unpardonable sin. Suicidal attempt is a criminal offence Heaven Penal Code 1 Corinthians 3:16–17. As per the Justice Paul, and even as per the human court system IPC 309, US suicide Act 1961 section 2, Section 309 states, "Whoever attempts to commit suicide and does any act towards the commission of such offence, shall be punished with simple imprisonment for a term which may extend to one year or with fine, or with both." God is the one who knew and loved me before I was born in my mother's womb. Although theology can be interpreted as a sin of suicide, I thought for a moment that there was no better way to sacrifice my life for the felonious action committed by me.

Reporter: Life lessons?

Iscariot Jude: You can't serve God and mammon. God gives us a chance to repent. Being a disciple of Jesus Christ is not a guarantee of salvation. People in rebellion against God prefer darkness to the light, the better to hide their sin. God gives us a chance to repent; remorse without true repentance is worthless. Unconfessed sin always opens the door to Satan's power. Money of itself is not bad. However, the love of money is. Don't give Satan a foothold. Never be double-minded, and you will reap your sowing. Choice brings life or death. Truth will one day come out on who you truly are.

CHAPTER 5

The Creation

THERE ARE MANY questions associated with the creation and evolution of the major constituents of the cosmos. A basic question astronomers must address is, how did the universe create its first stars and galaxies? Once these entities were created, how did they influence subsequent galaxy, star and planet formation? This is an important question, because these later objects are made of elements that can only have been created by the first generation of stars. Scientists believe that our universe began with one enormous explosion of energy and light, which we now call the big bang. Creation is a subject matter that has many implications. One of them is that the universe formed by an explosion is out of the infinite number of celestial bodies and earth is one. The scientists believe that carbon, hydrogen, oxygen, phosphorus, and sulfur are said to combine to form amino acids, sugars, and fats, from which life is said to have evolved. The first single-celled organism came into being through the unique combination of inorganic matter and the history of life, organisms, and man, which modern man dug out of the depths of time. Cells doubled and more complex organisms emerged in the ocean. All living things contain 113 different elements, all of which are on earth and in the atmosphere, and the atmosphere is made up of a combination of these elements without the hands of an external being. Life that we see today has evolved into the millions of species as a result of the combination of free elements in the atmosphere due to different climates and especially heat from the sun during different periods of time.

Millions of years ago, the monkeys who came down from the tree seeking for food for survival, and at some point in the steady flow of time, they learned how to stand on two legs. He hunted with stones as weapons and became a jungle dweller, became a country dweller. These scientists believe that the tree-dwelling monkeys are the ancestors of humans, moved from trees to land that are like acrobats. Did humans change their habits from four legs of almost equal length to two legs? Humans have relatively large brains for judgment, and their legs are longer than their arms. At what point in evolution this change occurred, scientists have no idea. It is foolishness to think that billions of people are born and die, eat and drink, and strive to satisfy their hunger. Man is a very, very late newcomer to the long history of the earth, almost as long as the history of life. At any stage of human history, this alienation can be seen as his rebirth.

In the eyes of the early proponents of Babylonian culture, the earth was like a flat plate. The sky is a folded vessel that covers the ocean and the earth and the ocean around that plate. The stars are the gems encrusted in that vessel. Although all the stars were motionless, they thought that the sun, moon, and five other planets were orbiting stars. Those concepts may seem strange today, but we must remember that these were the deliberate thoughts of the brilliant people of the day. We live in a constantly evolving universe, and galaxies and other objects are constantly disappearing from our horizons due to the process of evolution. In a very distant future, would not all galaxies be gone, and the entire universe would be utterly empty? Then all the galaxies will stop moving, and they will not become dead matter. Will that be the end of the universe? We don't have a definite answer to such questions that arise from the theory of explosion. In our quest for the universe, we come across many contradictory questions and answers. We have not been able to reach a final decision. If this theory proves to be true, many of the basic laws of physics will have to be refuted especially the law of conservation of matter. New laws will have to be enacted that can accommodate this new counter-concept. Anyway, one thing is clear: the threads of many complex cosmic problems are still untied. Epicurus states that the elements in this physical universe, made up of atoms, the smallest particles of matter, are infinite and eternal. Epicurus was Darwin's philosopher who began the theory of evolution about 2200 years ago.

The mysteries of the universe are something that man can never comprehend, and I can only briefly describe what we see when we look at this cosmic beauty of God's creation. If you look at the wonders of nature, you can see God hidden in every sprout of flowers and grass. In autumn, trees have yellow, red, and brown colors. Spring tulip fields, loneliness and darkness leaf litters of full of vivid bright colors on the streets. Overlook a space of flowers, and the silent isle embowers. Isn't it interesting to see the fascinating waterways of nature painted with dark colors crashing into the black rock formations and falling steeply to a deep depth? At the time, when the mind-blowing golden moon rises, the solitude experienced in the blue sky of the moon flower bathed in the golden moon is exhilarating. The rustle of the tree branches and the chirping birds jumping from the twigs of the birds chirping are like the background music of a pure sweet song is euphoric. Nightingales perfect pitch helps to control the emotions. You can see the moon falling through the trees where the shadow and the moon have been painted. Butterflies and yellow parrots, flocks of crows fly through the sky, feasting the eyes. Those who travel only on the path of reason will not understand that a person who looks at nature sees God in it. Go to the edge of the sea, and sit idle for a while, or in the coolness of the shade tree, or in the silvery drizzling rain, and the mind will find a place to lie down and gaze at the glory. When you walk enjoying the beauty of nature that God has prepared, all the sadness in your mind will be removed, and you will get good energy. The solitude of nature! It's beautiful, mind-blowing, and intoxicating.

The morning sun shines as the rain clouds change and the sky turns blue. Watch the rainbow intertwine with the combination of drizzle and light sun. There are 750 million species of living things on earth, on land and at sea, and most of the species have many similarities, with only man being created from the soil by the physical body. Our gross body (earth = soil). According to the Hindu religion, everything in nature is made up of five elements such as earth, water, fire, air, and space. The principle of earthly in humans, the principle of air in birds, the principle of water in aquatic beings, the principle of fire in angels, and the principle of darkness in the devil are all over. When you think about the truth of God: (1) Cosmological arguments intelligent (Isaiah 40), the Omnipotent and Almighty creator (Romans 1:20–21). (2) Teleological argument intelligent designer (3) Ontological argument finite human versus infinite God. (4) Moral argument (Romans 2:15), right and wrong.

How does man recognize oxygen from the atmosphere and absorb it and emit carbon dioxide? The body only separates oxygen from the many gases in the atmosphere. We inhale all the atmospheric air through our noses. God's finger touches green lives. The Creator is not inferior to anything in creation. Creation does not exist without a Creator, and the cause of creation is the Creator. In the early days, there was no ocean or desert (Ezekiel 28:12–19; Isaiah 14:11–12). These passages make sense.

The famous scientist Stephen Hawking's book says that God has no place in the existence of the universe. But if we read its contents, we will unknowingly glorify God. Remember the grand design of this universe. The very name given to his book by the brilliant scientist is a paradox of his own idea. We need to think a little backward to know the truth of this. His words are proof that even Einstein, the originator of the great theory of relativity, revered God in all its meanings. "Science without religion is lame and religion without science is blind." Do not limit yourself to God and just be foolish! Who can change the orbit of the moon or the rotation of the earth? The enchantment of nature scenes is evocative. At the beginning of this chapter, some attempts have been made to present the mysteries of the universe in a way that strikes the mind with the backing of philosophical realism. Attempts have been made to honestly present the true and unpleasant truths in the social mind. I have tried to write in it to explain many of the elements that astonish the reader and open the eyes. Bible proclaims that there is only one solitary being created in the universe and all that is therein without assistance from anyone else. One question that atheists ask is, if God created man and all life on earth, how could God not create the best of human beings on earthlike planets and all that man needs? It is foolish to try to measure and analyze this vast universe and its Creator with the wisdom that God Himself has given us just to live sixty or seventy years. Man admits that he is incapable of giving a definition when it comes to things that are beyond his comprehension and beyond his power. If science is truth-seeking, then spirituality is the realization of that truth.

There is one thing that evolutionists, knowingly or unknowingly, acknowledge that there was something in the beginning. They have no explanation for how life-giving objects came to be. They do not acknowledge that there is a Creator and Owner of this universe because of their fistfight. God is transcendent, causal, and real. In this universe of billions of living things, every atom has its own place. The Creator has authority over creation. Creation does not exist without the Creator. The cause of creation is the Creator. A creator is hidden behind the creation of a substance, but a substance does not create a creator. A sculptor by his imaginary address never happens to mesmerize a sculpture. Distorted knowledge and despair of God can blind our spiritual eyes (Ezekiel 3:26, 12:2; Psalm 10:4; Acts 17:26). Who taught us to breathe? Who gave us eyes, ears, speech, and voice recognition? Many of the discoveries made by science were later refuted as hollow. We must have the wisdom not to say that everything we do not see, experience, and know is a fabrication. When logic says that everything is in the brain, it is the urge in the heart.

Since the creation of this universe, century's people tried to solve the riddle of the purpose of creation. The Creator created mankind and wishes to raise human beings to the highest possible degree. God created man for one of the reason is to know Him and love Him and have fellowship with Him. But God created them with a free will that is, with the ability to either love Him or reject Him. God wanted communion with man, fellowship with man. This is key purpose for which God made man. In our life, there is nothing greater or more important than knowing God and being in relationship with Him. In creation, we see God's lordship on display in his control over all things, his authority over the entire universe, and his presence in every part of creation. Creation establishes God's ownership of all things in heaven and earth (Exodus 20:11). Because all things are his, there is no limitation to his controlling power. It also establishes his authority, his right to tell all creatures what to do. He commands and things obediently come into being (Colossians 1:15–16). Creation is also the basis of God's presence in all places of the universe.

Robert Genti's book *Creation's Tiny Mystery* has nullified almost all the arguments of evolutionists by providing ample evidence of creation. The theory is that God created man in the image of God. This is a denial of the existence of God and a rejection of the Bible. It is an insult to the fact that there is an eternal home in heaven. Its purpose is to undermine the credibility of salvation. Even atheists and scientists who taught that there is no God are now studying the truths of the Bible in detail. Michio Kaku, professor of theoretical physics at the City College of New York and CUNY Graduate Center leading physicist, concluded that the universe was created by an intelligent scientist and that the scientist is God. It is said that God is the best mathematician and that we all live by such a precise matrix. The realization of space travel transcends the human dream of conquering new spheres. As time goes on for world science and other theories, mistakes can be made and corrected, but not a single word in the Bible can go wrong. The people of the world who are only believe in seeing and hearing. It is a journey through the straight line of facts on the opposite ground of logic. God created us in His image and made us on earth. We did not come from somewhere by chance. We are sons and daughters of Almighty God (Galatians 3:26).

CHAPTER 6

Why God Created Man, and
What Is His Motives?

WHAT IS THE meaning of human life? Where is man's journey? What is the purpose of human creation? These are some of the many questions that have arisen in the human mind. Eternity is a mystery that is completely incomprehensible to the whole mind. The most complex and profound question man has ever asked. The problem that has been plaguing the human mind from time to time is what the purpose of human creation is. The purpose of human creation is to know and worship God. Worship is the act of bowing down to the Creator. Reality and unreality are inextricably linked. Everyone believes that there is a force of nature behind this universe that cannot be explained by man. I do not mention them all here for fear of adding more pages.

Why do I exist? One of the most common questions people ask is, why do I exist in this world? That's the most fundamental question of life. Everything around us has a purpose. But when it comes to explaining our own purpose, for many, it is a difficult task. From our childhood on, we are taught that everything exists merely because of countless accidental evolutionary changes. So we live in a culture that has been greatly influenced by the consequences of evolutionary thought. Evolution denies a purpose greater than self. Where there is no purpose greater than self, we are forced to live only for ourselves. We're not just a collection of atoms, proteins, and molecules spinning like planets around the sun. It's true that the laws of chemistry can tackle the rudimentary biology of living systems. But there's more than the sum of our biochemical functions. Science has failed to recognize those properties of life that make it fundamental to our existence. Have you ever thought why do you exist in this world? In fact, Jeremiah answered this question over 2,600 years ago (Jeremiah 20:18). "Why was I born? Was it only to have trouble and sorrow, to end my life in disgrace?" There have probably been times in your life when you have felt that way.

Was I born just to have a bunch or problems? Was I put on this planet just to have heartache and grief and stress? If God is to be glorified in our lives and in the church, knowing Him must become our life's pursuit. Because Scripture tells us "You were bought with a price" (1 Corinthians 7:23), "and you are not your own." God has a wonderful purpose for your life. We exist to proclaim God's word and reason out that to everyone. We exist to glorify God and praise Him and to do good works to others. According to 1 Peter 2:9–10, you are a chosen people, a royal priesthood, a holy nation, God's special possession, that you may declare the praises of him who called you out of darkness into his wonderful light. Once you were not a people, but now you are the people of God; once you had not received mercy, but now you have received mercy. The Bible says, "God made you to love you." You were created as an object of God's love. He put you here on earth to know Him and love Him. That's why you exist.

Who is man? (Psalms 8: 4–5). What was God's purpose for mankind? Where is he going? These questions are still big questions in front of mankind. Let's see if we can find the answer to this ancient question. It is a fact that there is still no satisfactory solution to this problem on the basis of existing psychological theories. In a word, man is an intelligent being. Man is a combination of the three elements of body, soul, and spirit. The *I* am the main character in all the experiences related to the five senses. I see; I hear; I taste; I smell; I'm touching. In the same way, I am the Lord of all voluntary deeds. The truth is that no one can say that anything is theirs, even though they say many things that are mine. We spend a lot of time in this earthly inn, the land, like a wayfarer. Human life is a mystery that no one has ever been able to fully analyze. Man has so far been able to discover only a limited amount of knowledge about man. Life is not a phenomenon that returns to the five elements return to the earth. There are so many things in this universe that man does not know, but they think they conquered everything and that everything is in their hands. Man's knowledge is like an iceberg in the ocean (Isaiah 43:7; Psalm 100:2–3; John 17:4; Romans 3:23–24; Hebrew 2:6–8).

Every human being should be aware that if the creative power that sustains our body and soul is withdrawn for a short time, we will end up in emptiness and acknowledge our nothingness as creation. We must acknowledge our emptiness before God and acknowledge that all of man's natural abilities are gifts from God to a person who is utterly unworthy. The fact is that in this universe, man, who is not even the size of a speck of dust invisible to the naked eye, is only here, blinking for a moment. Even our vision has limitations, and we can't see in the darkness, and no matter how insignificant our gaze, it is impossible to see without the help of the light that God has given us. We can't hear sounds less or more than a certain decibel. The deepest desire to be what we are is dormant in all human beings, and it should not be labeled as exaggeration or delusion, but on the other hand, it is the nature of the unknown that dwells within us. We must use the gifts God has given us according to God's will, not to glorify Himself. We need to take into account our insignificance and be well aware of it.

What is the best creation of God? If this world and the stars, the planets, and the mountains had the power of sight, they would look down and marvel at man. When you examine the scripture, God wants man to worship the Lord his God for life like Adam (Genesis 4:25–26). Abraham proves, there's no greater faith than believing what God says (Genesis 15:6). Joseph proves there's no greater trust than the assurance of God's guiding hand on your life no matter what happens (Genesis 50:19–20). A man should the Holy Spirit like Moses (Numbers 11:29). A man experiences God's power like Joshua (Joshua 10:12–14). A man should pray like Samuel (1 Samuel

12:23). A man worships God exuberantly like David (2 Samuel 6:14–15). Solomon was given enough wisdom, but he didn't follow God. A man should ask wisdom and walks in God's wisdom (Proverbs 1:1–7). True heroes of the faith stay faithful to God to the end, whether we die or meet the Lord in the air (2 Kings 2:1–11). Men of God have faith and courage like Daniel (Daniel 12:3–4). Man of God should be devoted himself to the study and observance of the Law of the Lord (Scriptures) and to teaching its decrees and laws in Israel like Ezra (Ezra 7:9–10). A man does great works like Nehemiah (Nehemiah 6:15–16). A man follows the Messiah no matter what like John the Baptist. A man lives as a gospel worker like Paul (1 Timothy 3:1–13). A man should have admitted his mistakes and repent like Peter. A man looks forward to eternity no matter how much struggles he have faced to be with Jesus like John.

Does my life really matter? Well, it's a good question. Yes! Because he made you. And this is true regardless of what you do, or what you achieve. It is true regardless of your own opinion of yourself or other people's opinions of you. Your life matters to God because you are made in his image, and so you have inherent and inestimable worth. Isaiah says, "My work all seems so useless. I have spent my strength for nothing and for no purpose at all." This was said in one of his weaker moments, but if that is what anybody believes on a continuous basis, then life doesn't seem to matter at all. Sometimes people in great distress and pessimism tend to ask, do I really matter to God? In 1905, a box was shipped from South Africa to England. There was nothing special looking about this box. It was just an ordinary shipping box. And inside the box was a rock, but it was no ordinary rock. The rock was a diamond, the Cullinan Diamond, the world's largest diamond, weighing 3,106 carats! It was a present for King Edward VII on his sixty-sixth birthday. Well, we may look ordinary on the outside, and you may feel very ordinary today. But your life is incredibly valuable to the King of Kings! Your life is more valuable to God than a diamond as big as the sun! The truth is, if there is no God, your life doesn't matter. But because there is a God, and He had a specific purpose in mind when He created you, you do matter.

You matter because God created you. You matter because He sent His Son, Jesus Christ, to die on the cross. If you want to know how much you matter, think of Jesus Christ with His arms outstretched, saying, "I love you this much." Personal relationships to God and to other people are the most important thing in life. God wants you to know Him, and He wants you to have a relationship with Him because you're worth so much in God's eyes that He sent His Son to die for you.

One day, we will have to stand before God and give an account of what we have done with our lives for him. Make each day count. Live it for the glory of God. Live your life well. In life, there are two ways to choose from: an easy way or a hard way. A single decision can determine your destiny, shape your life, and transform your future. But it is tough decisions. Which do you choose? Sometime ago, I read an illustration about Buridan's Bridge. The fourteenth-century French philosopher Jean Buridan stated that Buridan's donkey was a philosophical concept that symbolized the inability to make decisions. The idea is that if a very hungry and thirsty donkey were placed between a bundle of hay and water of the same size, there would be no logical reason to choose one instead of the other, so Buridan imagined that the donkey would starve to death without deciding which to eat from. Likewise, it is hard to take to the decision to follow Jesus. Trust God completely. When you follow Jesus, you are swimming upstream, going against the current of popular culture. You are marching to a different drummer. You are willing to be different, not just go along with the crowd. But you are not alone. You travel the hard road in the company of Jesus and of others who have chosen to follow him.

CHAPTER 7

Is Man a Robot or Slave of God?

WE SHOULD NOT be upset if a slave of God does not receive praise or reward when he does a good deed. One who is devoted to God must show immediate obedience without neglecting any mission from God, which we must understand as man's obedience to God. A slave is a slave to his master. It is the duty of the slave to act without questioning what the master says. The master has the right to kill and bless the slave. Sovereignty over the slave belongs only to the master. The slave always waits to find out what his master wants. A true slave is one who is completely submissive to a master. The yoke that connects the oxen is tied to the oxen until the end of the journey. The five special qualities of a slave are that he must first be willing to do whatever work he receives, one after the other, without any consideration. Second, do not expect any honor for doing the ministry. Third, do not ever blame or to call the master selfish. Fourthly, must be admitted that he is not worthy of anything and say that he is a slave with any kind of consideration, and there is no place for pride or boasting. Fifthly, be humble, meek, and tolerant, admit that he simply say that he did nothing special but only duty. The disciple is the one who keeps whatever God commands to do and tried to be like the master. He who has the attitude of Jesus, who gives up that entire he sees as profit, should fear and love only the Master.

The one who is dedicated to God will be the one who knows about our worthlessness before God. We should only reveal in our words and deeds that the glory of God should be revealed, not to our benefit. The dedicated person should know that he is inadequate for a superior thought, for a fair trial or a just judgment, or for a just act.

We are becoming prisoners of pride in the pursuit of self-justification. We can understand God only if our humility in us disappears and a process of purification begin in us. We are not our own, they belong to Jesus Christ, we are bought (2 Corinthians 6:19; Colossians 1:16). We are indebted to the Lord for the love God has poured out on us. You can see the guard responsibilities in Ezekiel 33:2–9. The prophet must be the ones who make the people of the world aware of the impending doom and tell them the way to salvation. They are accountable to God for the number of people who perish. The term servant of Jesus Christ means slave of Jesus Christ. The qualities of a true servant are humility and self-sacrifice. We are useless slaves who say that we have done what we should have done.

Let us examine the response of some who are called to be a slave. Moses left when he was living in all the comforts and splendor of a royal palace. Isaiah was called to the temple during worship in front of the altar. God called Samuel was sleeping in the temple with Eli, the priest. Abraham was engaged in a good business in the highest city of the ancient world. It was when David was in the wilderness with his own flocks and herds. Paul is called when he was determined to wipe out the Christians traveling on a horseback with pride, with the authority of the Sanhedrin court. We do not just obey this call; there is something rewarding and inspiring about it. They are God's love, His kindness, His compassion, His grace, His Kingdom, His promises, all of which motivate us to obey. The call is look like very simple with a covenant of God.

Those who have lost their lives are those who have faded in the flames of failure while alive. Failure was their choice. There are oppressive defeats and elective defeats, and those who are dedicated to God are the ones who accept defeat. The guilt of not being able to succeed will be the ones who walk away unscathed. Isaiah was one of those who saw it with his own eyes. A flock of migratory birds prepares to fly ahead along with other birds first to face the consequences. It is a bird that may sacrifice her life for the cause of the birds flying behind them. There may be ample of chances the first bird to disappear from a hunter's trap, sling, or may be electrocuted by the power line. When it is in danger, the rest of the birds change their direction and fly away from danger. When these birds flew hours and hours and finally they take rest in a tree branch, none of the birds sit on the main branch. It has already assigned and emptied the space for the first flying bird. Even those little birds know that it has a place in the twigs, just as we owe it to ourselves, but the so-called smart man does not know or to give up that space. No winner has the strength to usurp that space. Those who are sacrificing their life are like trees that shade in the summer and absorb radiant heat from the sun (Jose Capuchin).

In April 1806, while sailing in the harbor of Calcutta, Henry Martin, a young soldier, uttered very passionately these words, "Let me burn for God now." Six years later, at the age of thirty-one, when he returned to the heavenly abode at the end of his ministry. Martin was able to accomplish all the work that should be done during a lifetime in that short time. He considered many of the gains in his life to be detrimental. As a missionary, he made history by exposing the dark continent of Africa to the silver lining of the gospel. David Livingston had a brother, John Livingston, whose only desire was to make a lot of money in life and become famous. But his brother Martin wanted to be a missionary. David was departed forever from the world while he was praying in the hut like a fool without acquiring anything in this world. But even after centuries, he is still being preached throughout the world. Hudson Taylor once said if I had one thousand pound, I would give it to China. If I have a thousand lives, I will gladly give it to China. Hudson Taylor was a missionary hero who dedicated his life to the evangelization of China.

Those who work as a carpenter know the pith or the heartwood lays at the center of the tree the strongest part. Such trees found on the top of the mountains because those trees that survive all weather like wind and rain. Devotees want to be on top of the mountain in the face of the worst weather. I have heard of some seeds of the crust are very hard and the soil can't dissolve. Wildfire is only way to break that shell. The crust breaks in the fire. Some people will reveal their inner core only on the extreme trials. Dedicated people allow their lives to pass through the fire. With the extinction of the dodo birds in Mauritius, the special deciduous tree also became extinct. It was too late for researchers to find that they were connected. The seeds of this weed tree were exchanged by a small bird called the dodo, which causes the seeds to fall off as they go through its digestive process. There are very few missionaries in Christendom today who are dedicated to going through the chemical process and becoming a sacrifice. It is a paradox that some people are addicted to the taste of blood when they eat a lot of thorns and cut their lips and tongue and bleed. Even though there is only one sun but will be reflected in thousand bowls. Likewise, there is only one God, but whoever has a deep desire to see Him, God will give them His appearance. It's a shame when in childhood; we want to have that which is glitter. Adolescence is an innate chaplaincy, youth is called pride, and old age is called charisma. This greed makes the adult man a beast. It is a life lesson that we get everything when we have no desire, and nothing will be lost in our hands. All the addictions and desires in this worldly life will ultimately lead to sorrow.

As Paul says, if we remember the weight of eternity, all our worldly pleasures and luxuries are momentarily decaying and falling apart. A contract is not for a fixed period of time but for a period of time that serves the master until death (Exodus 21:1–6). Paul says that Moses was a servant of the Lord (Numbers 12:7), David a servant of God (Psalm 119:125). Mary, the mother of Jesus, says that "I am the handmaid of the Lord." In Luke 1:38, the word *servant* is used 112 times in the New Testament itself. One of the main criteria for discipleship is to hate life itself. One must know that one can do without God is very limited. Looking at a masterpiece, it is true that it is not the paint and the brush but the artist's hands that work behind it. A servant who is dedicated to God must give a lot of things, actions, arrangements, internal conflicts, and concerns for God. Because they will bravely say that my God bought me at such a high price. I do not know what to do. Dedicated people are those who try to satisfy the hunger of others even when they are hungry. Those who wipe away the tears of others even though their life is in tears.

Every person in the world one way is a slave. To be slave of another means two things. First, it means that you do not have rights over yourself any longer. Second, it means that ultimately you are not in control of your own life any longer. You have a mind, and you have a will, but your mind is conformed to the mind of the master, and your will actively coincides with the will of the master. A slave is not just one who serves and then goes home, but one who is completely owned by the master, body, mind, and soul. In fact, a slave is who no longer lives for himself but lives for the master, though you are living in a free country with freedom of speech and liberty to pursue happiness. Here we are discussing about the slavery is not a political or economic slavery. This slavery is a spiritual bondage, either to sin or to Jesus Christ. All live in slavery to one of two masters, either to sin or to the Savior. You decide whose slave are you? You are a slave if you are prisoner of your own beliefs and if you let others decide of your beliefs limited by the world reality you create and live in. At the slave stage, we feel pain because we become our own warden every day; we create the prison we live in. We sin because we are not under law but under grace. When you present yourselves to someone as slaves for obedience, you are slaves of the one whom you obey. Sin resulting in death, and obedience resulting in righteousness (Romans 6:15–19).

The key word in Romans 6:15–19 is *slave*, which is found five times in these five verses. It is translated from the Greek word *doulas*, which means "one who gives himself up completely to a master." This word for slave is different from the word for servant. A slave is much lower than a servant. A servant was someone who still had some degree of freedom. He could choose to accept a job or not to accept it. He still could own property, receive wages, and go home at the end of the day. He could do his own thing, go his own way. He could return the next day, if he chose, or he could let someone else be hired to work in his place. But this word for *slave* (doulos) is totally different. It represented someone who had no personal freedom to do as he pleased. His entire life was to be given in servitude to his master, who had paid a price to purchase him from another owner. A servant is hired; a slave is owned. A slave has no independence, no self-autonomy, and no personal rights. In fact, a slave was a piece of property that was owned by someone else. When a person was owned as a slave, it meant that he was a possession of his master, bound to obey him. There was no negotiation by a slave with his master regarding what he could decide to do or not do. He was bought and owned by his master, and so there could be no hesitation or argument to obey him. To be a slave meant complete submission and total obedience to a master. It is difficult for us to fully grasp what it meant to be a slave, because a slave has a master, who has the power of life and death over him. The master, who has the right to issue commands without any explanation and expects obedience immediately and completely. The master has bought the slave at a price, and the slave now belongs to him. A true Christian is a slave.

Paul began the book of Romans by identifying himself as a slave and sovereign lordship of Jesus Christ. Paul devoted himself completely to the Lord Jesus Christ and submitted himself entirely to His divine will. Paul's will have been given up to the service of Jesus Christ. The same is true for every follower of Jesus Christ. As a slave of Christ, the existence on this earth is lived in submission, surrender, compliance, and obedience to the supreme authority. As believers, we recognize that we have been redeemed and ransomed by Jesus Christ. We were once in the slave market and in bondage to sin, self, and Satan (John 8:34; Ephesians 2:2–3). One day, however, there came into the slave market and paid the last penny for you and bought you to set you free. Jesus paid the price of our redemption with His own blood (1 Peter 1:18–19); He bought our redemption on Calvary because He wanted to make us His own forever (1 Corinthians 6:19–20). The Lord never forces anyone to serve Him. The cry goes out, "Choose for yourselves this day whom you will serve" (Joshua 24:15). Here was slavery that was not the result of war, or even debt, but a voluntary slavery by choice.

CHAPTER 8

God's Expectations and Qualities of the Elected One

GOD EXPECTS MAN to fear Him and obey Him (Ecclesiastes 12:13). God expects man to place his trust in Him (Psalm 4:5). God expects man to love Him (1 John 4:19). God expects man to be obedient to His will (Revelation 22:14). God expects man to desire Him (Psalm 27:4). God expects man's exclusive devotion (Matthew 4:10). God expects man's praise and devotion (Psalm 100:4). God expects man to worship Him (John 4:21–24). God expects man to be His servant (Roman 6:16–18, 22). God expects man's prayers to be addressed to Him (Matthew 6:9).

In this chapter, we will examine what it means to be a dedicated person to God and what their characteristics are. The word *sacrifice* has various meanings in the modern context. *Sacrifice* is defined in the Old Testament as the ritual slaughtering of animals and offering them to God. The word is derived from a Latin word meaning sanctify. The concept of sacrifice is as old as humankind. Leviticus chapters 1–7 describe the various sacrifices that the people of Israel had to offer. The sacrificial laws of the New Testament church are quite different from the old ones. It is not the quality of the sacrifice, but the condition of the whole heart of the sacrifice. In the Old Testament, sacrifices were often performed as an atonement, thanksgiving, or ordination. The basic sacrifices are offered to Jehovah God. Different words were used in the Old Testament to refer to sacrifice. The Hebrew word for sacrifice is a combination of two words *hikrib* and *korban*. *Hikrib* means "cooked." Many kinds of sacrifices are mandated in the Hebrew Bible of which one type is animal sacrifice. The Hebrew term usually translated as "sacrifice" is *korban*. *Korban* literally means "drawing near." Just as in the Latin term, then sacrifices of all kinds are linked with an approach to divinity. The word seba (Leviticus 3:1) is used in connection with the sacrifice of peace.

Sacrifice is a term closely related to the divine covenant or relationship established by God. The book of Genesis shows that sacrifices were made to atone for sins. And the divine blessing is embedded in the sacrifice. The first animal sacrifice is recorded in Scripture (Genesis 4:1–5). After the flood, Noah offered a burnt offering to God (Genesis 8:20). Blood-drinking and the shedding of human blood are forbidden in the Mosaic Law (Leviticus 3:17), and God requires Abraham to offer His Son as a sacrifice (Genesis 22:28) in order to test Abraham's obedience. After the setting up of the tabernacle, the animal sacrifice and the meal offering were offered on the altar. Occasionally altars are built and sacrifices are offered as part of the calling on God's name (Gideon in Judges 6:24–27). Sacrifices were performed on various occasions. Some offerings were made daily, morning, and evening (Exodus 29:38–42), while others were offered on the Sabbath (Numbers 28:9–10). It was celebrated at the beginning of the month (Numbers 28:11), the Passover, the Feast of Tabernacles (Numbers 28:16–17), and the full moon (Numbers 29:6).

Let me write a few simple things without expressive preparation and language that is difficult for humans to understand. It is a title that does not require much explanation, but let us briefly examine it. Let us see what the New Testament interpretation about the sacrifice. Jesus once became the sacrifice for us. Therefore, New Testament believers should never sacrifice sheep or other animals, but rather offer sacrifices of praise and good works. We don't need to sacrifice daily for our sins like those high priests did. Jesus did it once, offering himself. Therefore, as New Testament Israel, we do not need to literally make sacrifices. In ancient times, divine contact was possible through the tabernacle or through the priests. But today, we can always draw closer to God through Jesus Christ. The various meanings of the Old Testament sacrifices can be understood in relation to the New Testament.

Sacrifices with animal sacrifices recorded in the Holy Bible appear to be as ancient as man. Jesus Christ, the true sacrificial object incarnated to redeem mankind in order to receive God's favor, was the Lamb who was slaughtered before the foundation of the world. All the early fathers from Adam were saints who made sacrifices and made a covenant with God. The sacrifices made by all of them are generally considered to be burnt offerings. The sacrificial animals were the young bull, the male sheep, the male goat, the ram, and the pigeon. All these sacrificial objects were in harmony with man and of a calm nature. Those who have devoted their lives to God must be like the obedient, tolerant, gentle beast that plows, threshes, and bears burdens for his masters. The best grain is to be offered to God. The devotee is willing to give up all that he has his rights, and influence and surrender completely to God. The burnt offering on the altar on the wood all night means that we must be in the fire of the presence of God on the worst nights of this world, but one morning will dawn for us. Next, the fire in the altar must always be kept burning. The essence is that all the success and pride of the soul should be humbly submit and consecrated as a burnt offering.

As David said to Araunah "No, I insist on paying you for it. I will not sacrifice to the Lord my God burnt offerings that cost me nothing" (2 Samuel 24:24). Believers in communist countries and orthodox Muslim countries love the Lord dearly. The whole burnt offering was burned with fire (Leviticus 1:9). It signifies complete submission. Items that are offered once will not be returned, just as items that are offered in a fire are completely reduced to ashes. *Holocaust* is the Greek word for sacrifice. Its Latin form, *holocaust*, and means complete digestion (Ephesian 5:2; Hebrew 10:5; Mark 12:33). The aroma emanates from the sacrifice, which shows a broken heart. Thus divine fellowship and connection are obtained, which creates an inspired church. It is an interesting fact that the head of the sacrificial object is not cleansed. But the whole body is cleansed. This indicates that the Lord, the head of the church, does not need to be cleansed, but the church needs to be cleansed by the Word of God. Jesus comes second to unite the pure and undefiled church. Are we ready for that? (1 Peter 1:19). For you know that through the precious blood of Christ, who was worthy of eternal death, who made me heir to everlasting life. Therefore, glorify God in your own body.

The following are the differences in the lives of those who are dedicated to God. When you see the greatness of God, the greater the depth of their worthlessness revealed (Exodus 33:19; 1 Peter 1:24), and as they understood the wisdom of God, their foolishness was made manifested clearly (Jeremiah 10:12; 1 Corinthians 11:33). The more they see the abyss of holiness of God, the more their defilement becomes more visible (Isaiah 43:15; Exodus 15:11). The more they see the light of God, the more their darkness is revealed (1 John 1:5; Psalm 36:9). The more they see the goodness of God, the depth of their evilness will be revealed (Psalm 145:17; Isaiah 64: 6). When God girded the mountains with strength, whoever seen the power of God, their weakness is revealed so profoundly (Romans 7:18; Number 1:5; Isaiah 64:6). When they see the glory of God, their shame is made manifest (Ezra 9:6), and when they see the perfection of God, their imperfection is revealed (Matthew 5:48; Psalm 19:7–11). The more they see the humility of God, the more their false pride is revealed (Romans 2:4; Titus 3:4–7; Proverb 16:18). Their bitterness will be revealed as they taste the sweetness of God. The more they see God, the more their true self will be revealed.

All of us are stewards. A steward is someone that has been entrusted with various responsibilities. The faithful steward is rewarded for his good work, and the unfaithful steward is punished for his negligence. Pay day is both now and futuristic. The Lord blesses us now because we are doers of the Word. But He will also pay us at judgment (Revelation 22:12). "And behold, I come quickly; and my reward is with me, to give every man according as his work shall be." Not every saint will hear the Lord say, "Well done." The main objectives of our work are to promote God by promoting and exalting Christ.

Let us examine the character traits of a person who has devoted himself to God:

1. One who is faithful and obligated to spread the gospel.
2. Is willing to do anything for the gospel.

3. Do not shy away from small problems or be afraid.
4. He will not give in to the will and desires of the heart.
5. Those who have given up their lives to keep themselves holy. He will be a hard worker.
6. Those who have given up life will see themselves as empty.
7. Those who gave up their lives tied up everything they had with the Kingdom of God. He will be a seller for work and for God.
8. He is not interested in amassing wealth on earth.
9. They will not serve two masters.
10. Those who throw everything into the abyss.
11. They will not be reluctant to count all the gains as losses.
12. Those who offer their life as a sacrifice.
13. They do not conform to the world and worldly pleasures.
14. They are not servants of men, but of God alone.
15. They do not walk like other gentile nations.
16. Those who try to walk in obedience to Jesus as Jesus did.
17. Intolerance when insulted by others. He is the one who accepts those insults without saying a word.
18. Forget self without being dependent on or praising your own power. Because the say themselves that they do not deserve any praises in their life. Be aware that opinion about oneself is irrelevant.
19. Be humble. The English word for humility is derived from the Latin word humus. It means fertile land. The land is trampled by all, unnecessary rubbish. Accept it all quietly despite being sidetracked or neglected. But it accepts any seed that was sown to germinate. Transforms something good and gives it back.
20. Knowing the presence of God and embracing the truth.
21. Even calling them at the eleven hour to work in the garden, where they were standing idle by the roadside. That the wages were not of great merit, and that the master gives them equally. The only thing is that they have been called in, and all of them should be treated with due respect. Depend on the harvest and the knowledge of the harvest

in the field of the good Boaz. That he is not fit to pick up even the plucked ears to be recognized.

22. The devotee that admits that he deserved only the worst part of anything and the lowest step.
23. Accept exceptions and accusations without murmuring while innocent.
24. Those who are hated by others will be the ones who accept it.
25. They do not want to receive special care, love, and respect.
26. They are patient with their own emotions.
27. Those that do nothing with the aim of attracting others.
28. Be restrained in speech and do not exaggerate.
29. Those that do not run away from everyday life.
30. Be considerate of others more than yourself.
31. They consider themselves to be the poorest of all. One cannot serve two masters at the same time. It is not possible to set foot in two boats. Everything that is evil to God belongs to those who have sacrificed their lives for Satan.

The man, who was speeding to board the train parked on the platform, did not see the blind boy and the apple basket he was carrying. He could not even pass the scattered apples. When he came back and put apples in the basket, then he gave the cost of the basket full of apple. So the boy asked the stranger, "Are you Jesus Christ?" Even a blind person can see some people with the face of God. This is a short picture of what it was like to be the one who actually sacrificed his life for God, the one who sacrificed himself for God (*Assisi*, March 2018). The person who has dedicated their life to Jesus is the one who resists temptations. Those people who survived the scorching heat of the desert and the freezing cold of the woods, melting and freezing to the point of extinction. Those who stand with a helping hand with a relentless mind to give a new color to many lives that have faded. Those who can guide the hearts of the people through creative preaching activities. Those who pass by leaving some trail for those who come after. Those who laugh at the faces of those who need to be demolished and show the courage to call out that they should be torn down.

Those who have sacrificed their lives will not pass by without seeing those who come for a moment of comfort with their cheeks drooping with tears. It may not be forgotten that the Lord's men comforted the widow of Nain by telling her, "Do not weep for your son." Those who dedicated their lives are the ones who have ruined their lives for God. Dedicated people, who comfort those who cry, share their sorrows with those who grieve and laugh with those who laugh. Dedicated are those who know that there is nothing of their own and who realize that even the body is not their own. They will remember that everything they received was given and that they themselves were bought. When one empties oneself with nothing and nothing, one will be aware that God will open the treasury of grace and pour out blessings to give to the people. Hagiography is the biography of the saints described in Christian contexts. Such people will be different and walk differently (Fr. Jose Capuchin). Everyone knows what the reaction would be if somebody tried to snatch its fledgling from its nest. But if you take its chicks from a pigeon's cage, it will not try to attack you like other birds but will stare at you sadly and fly away to another place. This is the path of a real life giver.

There is still much to be written about those who have dedicated their lives to God. They are the ones who come up with words of consolation in times of distress. Good people who walk hand in hand will be the ones who stand by the side of the road, waving flags, and promoting small victories. The sun is generous, giving light to the moon, as well as those who give light to others, even when the sun is burning. Dedicated will be those who are in a state of mind detached from worldly pleasures. Discernment and innocence will adorn them. They are the ones who please God through selfless deeds. Even when life is fraught with violence, occupation, and conflict, these dedicated souls will rain cold. The sign of the devotee is that he becomes a watering can for the weary stranger who walks in the summer, a beacon to keep from escaping at night, and a good crutch for the blind. The thread of love is made of gold thread. There are silver linings even among the clouds. Calmness is to come after storms. Spring does not come after winter. There are also intervals between waves. The mornings bring the evenings, and the midsummers carry the pregnancies of the new dawns. Separations give strength to the encounter.

An Old Testament ritual was never complete without sacrifice. Sacrifice is a process that God has ordained to lead people to purification. But later sacrifices became a mere ritual (Job 1:18, 2:3; Daniel 6:4–5). Those who have sacrificed their lives have seen a beautiful life that is blameless and sinless. To walk with God means to stand alone, even though the whole world opposes God. The Old Testament sacrifices all point to the crucifixion of Christ. At this point, we need to ask some questions. Is my life a living and acceptable sacrifice to God? Am I willing to spend my whole life for God? It is recorded in the tomb of William Carey, the father of the modern mission, "The helpless and miserable worm falls into His hands." What a meaningful statement this is. It is a sacrifice acceptable to God. Those who claim to have won a lot end up with the only human life on this dusty threshold of lost glory. We may be a harpist and possess a harp, yet the rhythms and pitches do not produce until the fingers touch the strings of the harp, which is dusty and useless and silent.

III

CHAPTER 9

IIIIIIIIIIIIIIIIIIIIIIIIIIIIIIIIIIIIIIIIIIIIIIIIIIIIIIIIIIIIIIIIIIIIIIIIIIIIIIIIIIIIIIIIIIIIIIIIIIIIIII

How to Become an Elected Person for God

ANYONE WHO IS not born again is outside the kingdom of God. Satan is the one who thwarts God's plan and his plan of salvation through Christ. The process of rebirth is made possible by the chemistry of life that transforms momentum into inevitability. One who is born again must be able to resist the glare of this magical world. Simply put, it is a life of surrender to Christ without the desire for anything in return, without expecting anything in return. He who serves men for God, like Moses, every disciple is called to see a life burning for God and for God's people. The social order around us should not be limited to sermons but should portray our lives as a model. Those who have called to be sacrificed for the abandoned, the exiled, the destitute, rejected, hated, and the captives. Those who are willing to lay down their lives for Christ. Those who uphold Jesus in any crisis more than the gift of life and life itself. Like wheat grains called to fall to the ground, they may recognize the call of life and enter into God's choice. The called are many, but the elect are few (Matthew 22:11–12).

We should present our entire lives as living sacrifices to Him because of all He has done for us. Because God has already provided for us a dying sacrifice the death of Jesus His Son. How can I know that I am one of God's elect? All of those who were chosen by the Father were redeemed by the Son and shall be regenerated and called by the Spirit. God's elect shall be eternally saved. God's elect one will never contradict Scripture. God's callings for us will always draw us closer to Him, not pull us away from Him (2 Corinthians 10:4–6). All who are chosen of God will hear the gospel of God's free and sovereign grace. God's elect one will always be accompanied by His peace, as well as anything else we need. God's elect one becomes followers of Christ. God's elect one will often be accompanied by confirmation. Many times God will confirm what He's asking us to do through situations and even through other people. (1 Thessalonians 5:16–21; James 1:5) God's elect are a people committed to the gospel. God's elect one will always result in His being glorified. If your calling seems to be all about your happiness and success with no thought, thanks, or credit being given to God, it probably isn't from Him (1 Corinthians 10:31; 2 Thessalonians 1:11–12). Those who are born of God live in the anticipation of Christ's glorious advent. God's elect one experience genuine conversion and the most important thing to remember when figuring out your calling is obedience to God.

Every elected one of God has a mission to accomplish. He has chosen us in him before the creation of the world to be holy and blameless in his sight (Ephesian 1:4). Who will bring any charge against those whom God has chosen? (Romans 8:33). In our chaotic and unsettling world, it is sometimes hard to understand how God's purposes are being worked out in our lives. Whatever the case, in the midst of the confusion, fears, anxieties, and distractions of this present world, all of us can benefit from a firmer confidence that God is indeed working out His plans in our lives. The God of the Bible is a God of purpose, and not just general purposes but specific ones. He is the supreme, long-term strategic planner of the universe. He does nothing in a random or haphazard manner. And His purposes extend from eternity past to eternity future, encompassing not only the ultimate destiny of His creation but our personal lives as well. Every person who has been born again has been given a least one special enablement by the Holy Spirit (1 Corinthians 12:7). The Spirit's gifts equip us to glorify the Father and the Son through serving our brothers and sisters in the church and, in some cases, serving people outside the church in mission. Serving God in His church is a major part of His plan for our lives and also a great source of satisfaction and fulfillment in our life on earth. In conclusion, if we truly want to do God's will and fulfill His plans in our lives, and if we ask Him, He will lead and empower us to do so, for He knows our hearts.

Some are called on a special mission. However, we can experience the fullness of God's call only when we strive to understand and live by God's call. That perfection will qualify us to be chosen. Throughout Scripture, we find descriptions of such called and chosen persons. This history begins with the special calling of Abraham (Genesis 12). When we look at the history of all the ancestors, we see that they were all faithful to their calling and were therefore chosen. The Word also testifies that not everyone who receives a call is chosen. In the seventh chapter of the book of Judges, Gideon describes how the people of Israel go to war with the Midianites. God chooses only three hundred of those who went to war with thirty-two thousand warriors. To put an end to the arrogance of the Israelites, they go to war and win with those three hundred chosen ones. This verse also reminds us of the trials that befall those who receive the call. Being a Christian is a calling. Through the church, God also gives us the gifts to live in it. Everyone has a duty and a right to cooperate with it and to obey the church. When a person clings to the church as a Christian, God will exalt him in that way and bring up many in a way that draws them closer to God. It is the fulfillment of God's plan to be chosen through him. Otherwise, they will have hatred and animosity toward the church and the church authorities, living as nominal Christians and eventually moving to other branches. Those in the ministry are no different. God uses that person strongly when he clings to the anointing of the Spirit of God. But with this growth, the weeds of pride will begin to grow. Unaware of these weeds being sown by the enemy, the weeds eventually grow and cover the paddy seeds, which are supposed to be fruitful for many. Those who are 100 percent faithful to the call will enter into God's choice.

The life of one who is not dedicated to God is like a broken earthen vessel; no matter how full it may be, it will vanish from the pot in a short time. When God intervenes in a way that is too simple for us to understand, we are misunderstood and miss God. There are some other aspects that we need to consider. What should the life of a saved person be like? With these in mind, let us conclude this chapter. "For to me, to live is Christ and to die is gain" (Philippians 1:21). This is a word that should be read with a lot of concern. I live in the world now, but I live by faith in the Son of God, who loved me and gave himself for me. What more can you say about life. A person who has dedicated his life to Christ is inevitably crucified and dead with his Lord. A devotee ascends to Golgotha carrying his own cross. Along the way to Golgotha, huge trees may obstruct you. Many tremble and fall in the middle of the road. They do not reach the summit of Golgotha. In other words, they do not reach the peak of their duty. They faint for fear of walking carrying their cross. The journey of ending one's life of one's own free will and dedicating one's life to Jesus Christ would have been a success. There are so many people who lay down their lives for meaningless theories and for people who are just as fleeting as themselves. But does not give due seriousness to matters relating to eternal life. We must dedicate our whole lives to the Lord. We must submit all our desires and aspirations to Christ. If any man will come after me, let him deny him, and take up his cross, and follow me (Matthew 16:24). We must come forward in the service of the Lord, surrendering not only what we have but also ourselves at the feet of Jesus Christ. This Lord fully deserves your time, money, and abilities.

He who gave his life for Jesus was not ashamed to speak of the gospel truth that Jesus Christ is the only Savior. Here is an example of how many of the things we do are not for our benefit. The one who not only abandons the world and its hopes but also abandons them with hatred and uproots future temptations deserves to be called a true disciple of Jesus. Such people should think that there is no one else to carry out this mission and that he should always be inwardly aware that he has been called for this purpose. Another aspect of this is that one must have a clear understanding of the calling. We are commanded and committed to continue the work of proclaiming the message of salvation of Jesus Christ. The symptom of those who have sacrificed their lives is to abandon our plans and submit to God's plans and give up our lives for the glory of God. A devotee doesn't care about wealth, status, position, privileges, expectations, comfort, convenience, man's aspirations, desires, and pursuits. Be willing to give up anything we desire to fit in with our breasts, such as dreams, education, family, and children. No mental anguish in rejection like a convict sentenced to cruel punishment. No fear of becoming the experience of those who sacrificed their lives. Have a lifestyle where you can see friends and loved ones who have sacrificed their lives and not be misled by their balance (John 1:11; Matthew 6:19, 10:37–38, 16:24, 19:29; Luke 9:23; 1 Corinthians 8:13).

As Paul says, willingness to sacrifice is the moment when the entire world and our comforts in the world are perishable, decaying and falling apart, remembering the weight of eternity. Be the one who takes his cross and serves his master without pay for the rest of his life, dying of our desires and aspirations at any cost, and therefore, first and foremost, forms a lifestyle that underscores that there is no deliverance from this master in life. No contract for a fixed period with an expiration period. One who serves his master until death? After the Ten Commandments, the first law that Israel gave to the children was the law of slavery (Leviticus 25:55; Deuteronomy 6:5). The word *slave* is used 112 times. An important criterion of discipleship is to hate life itself. That is, one cannot imitate Christ with what he thought was great to this day. I am the good shepherd; the good shepherd lays down his life for the sheep. Sacrifice your life for others.

The life of a devotee is more challenging than family life. This is a fact that is not clear in the language of the common man. Since the consecrated life is a gift of the Lord and inspired of the Holy Spirit, it becomes more powerful when challenges arise. Jesus was alone during the tribulation, though he had twelve beloved disciples with him. But Peter, saying unto them, we will go with him and die, and Peter shall not be offended. What's next after Jesus's death? The resurrection of Jesus was a turning point for the disciples. Despite their love for the Master, their fear of the Jews and the thought of being orphans led them to distance themselves from society. The resurrection of Jesus was the solution to all their worries. Faith is the best defense against the aggression of the devil.

CHAPTER 10

Conclusion

IT WAS EARLY in the morning, and it seemed like a dark evening with shadows, and the morning, which had been drenched in rain the night before, froze. Coming to the end of a long journey. A journey from the book of Genesis to Revelation. A magical world of sights and sounds, a journey through the senses. We have seen the success of those who are obedient, faithful to God, and the lives of those who fail because of disobedience. The plot of some was sad and depressing. One who is devoted to God is not hindered from deep sleep without any worries about the uncertainty of tomorrow. The hands of the devotee come to the rescue in times of danger, wondering what to do next. We have been on a journey since we were born. If you ask me where I am going, I will go to the heavenly Canaan. You have to proceed without heeding the pin calls.

There are still a lot of sights, and people left along the way. There are still days and nights left to walk. Not in a dream car, but through a handful of experiential lessons with a twist of direct knowledge. The fact is that some people miss the mark. In this journey, everyone travels in different ways. Some through the desert, some through the snowy mountains, some through the gorges, some through the plains. Still, others travel through rugged jungles, rocks, and thorns, some through royal streets, some through swamps, some through valleys, some through narrow and wide roads, but all have the same goal. Will those who travel through the scorching desert get tired of the extreme heat of sin, or those who travel through the icy mountains freeze in the extreme cold of sin? Will those who travel through rugged gorges stumble upon the rock of sin? Those who travel through lush jungles, lush swamps, and ocean of destructive waves are more likely to perish, but God will continue to give strength to those who want to lead a sinless life on high. Those who sacrifice their lives are destined to go through horrible experiences. The value of each is known when each is lost.

Sarojini Naidu, who was political activist, feminist, and poet, once was traveling by train when she met a French nun who ran a nearby orphanage. When asked how long she had been in India, she said it was thirty-two years. When asked if her parents were alive, she said she never went back to France. To the question of whether she should have gone and seen them, she was surprised to hear that the money spent on it would have been enough to meet the various needs of the orphans. Sacrifice, in a sense, is the act of giving up one's own pleasures and making sacrifices for the sake of others. It is possible to say without any doubt that God loved us unconditionally. The work that looks into the eyes of the beholder can never be sacrificed for the sake of their lives. Those who sacrifice their lives should not be enslaved by addictions. If we miss that goal, we may lose our election. Better a poor horse than no horse at all.

We have seen the history of those who dedicated their lives to God, walked with God, led their lives; faithfully traded the mission entrusted to them, and abandoned the mission halfway through. Some, like Uriah, are on the battlefield, giving up many of life's achievements and the comforts of this world. Uriah's heart was filled with thoughts of war, of the Lord's ark, and of his fellow soldiers on the battlefield. Would not the Uriah's today lain down their garments and weapons and make peace with their enemy Satan? It is a paradox that we see and cherish what the followers of Christ in the first century left behind as garbage. Those who bravely face excessive pressure by coping with situations at bad times. It means those who walk with God but live in fellowship and obligation to God alone, with no attachment to anyone else. Those who walk with God can mean those who fall. We have seen in the Bible the history of many who were apparently in decline and who acted as watchmen. Those who surrender to God are those who have killed themselves and lived valiantly despite all the hardships they have endured (Romans 13:13;

John 3:19). Martin Luther said I have held many things. I lost it all, but all that I have given into the hands of the Lord is now in my hand. Sunset is never the end of the sun. Just the beginning of a new dawn, the waves of darkness will be torn apart, and the golden glow of light will come.

Dedicated ones will be subjected to beatings, spitting, whipping, carnage, thorn bushes, insults, mockery, and crucifixion. The devotee should not run away from the world but should sanctify the world by being in the world, preaching to sanctify and liberate the social order around him. Dedicated are those who are self-sacrificing, those who swim against the current, and those who have left the world. One's beginning, end, and end are all from God. The Old Testament introduces the God who travels with man in his daily life. We see God walking with a pillar of cloud by day and a pillar of fire by night. That God was with us when we crossed the Red Sea and came to the land of Canaan. Whether he hid among the trees of Eden, or Hagar fled into the wilderness, God heard the voice of the lad. God would have done his work. A God who led the fugitive back and summoned the one who hid and said, "I am with you." In the Bible, we see God finding the little in us, regardless of the mistakes that come into our lives. God is the one who sees Cephas swaying like a reed, the powerlessness of the sons of thunder, the disbelief of Thomas, the heartbreak of a sinful woman, and the fullness of the mustard seed.

David had to go through many hardships because the sword did not leave his family because he was seduced by lust. Becoming a slave to sin, sin became David's master. Sin has a special attraction over righteousness, and Satan is the owner and captain of the ark of unrighteousness, and a believer must not enter into it without paying or paying, and if he steps into it, he will be bound by the chains of invisible sin (2 Timothy 1:9). We can light a candle to find the key to holiness. The streetlights ran out of oil, and the lights went out. May the Lord make it possible for many to end up burning as beacons of guidance that will not lead astray? It is not the sight of the outer eye, but the lack of light in the inner eyes that really blinds one. We are intrigued by the history of many saints who, despite having many, gave up everything for Christ.

Midday is more profound by weighing the day on the scales of the evening, but evening is feistier when you weigh the scales of noon. Wise man, can you say for sure which of these is livelier? You can see the tangible truths and pretend that you have not heard or seen for a long time, deaf or blind. The journey to find the truth by looking at the moralistic for that matter, do not forget that the train will not wait whether you board it or not. When you calculate your life by dividing, multiplying, adding, or subtracting the figures, you will get the same answer. Those who deny tradition must know that failure is inevitable if they try not to fall into the trap of tradition. Freedom from the bondage of obsolete rituals the dilapidated traditions of the social system dims the light of the individual. When you are within reach of the truth, do not try to avoid being distracted by a whirlwind of mischief. Instead of swallowing what we hear, we must make the quest to find the truth and to understand the facts properly. Break the shackles of duty, and try to leave yourselves in God. If you go down to the depths of these lines for a moment, you will surely understand the meaning and scope. New dawns will dawn again for you, and separations will give way to reunions. From the shadow of fear to the valley of relief.

Our life journey is often through dark paths. Life's sorrows can be like a torrential downpour. In the meanwhile, thunder and lightning from unexpected areas can make us feel discouraged. But there is one thing we must always remember: God has given us a lamp that can keep burning in any darkness or storm. We cannot light that lamp by ourselves or keep it burning during the storm; only God can do that. What is that lamp that God gives us to light? Faith. Yes, it is our faith in God. The bottom line is that our faith and trust in God often falters. Our faith is the lamp that God gives us. If we want the lamp that He gives to stay unquenchable, we need His blessing for that too. The fact is that He always gives us that blessing. We just need to accept it wholeheartedly with both hands. May we seek His blessing to keep the lamp of faith firm in God burning? Of course, if the lamp of faith is not extinguished in our lives, we can have the courage to move forward without being overwhelmed by any darkness or storm. God did not send us to this earth in vain. His presence is always with us wherever we are on this earth. He is always ready to help us in all our affairs. He will give us the strength to overcome adversity when we encounter it in our lives. But the fact is that we often forget all these things. As a man prepares a house for his bride, Christ has prepared a most magnificent new heaven and new earth for His bride. The beauty of our eternal home is so much greater than our senses can discover. Those who fought a good fight they can expect one or more of the following rewards:

1. To eat of the tree of life.
2. To receive a new name written in white stone.
3. To receive power over the nations.
4. Not to be hurt of the second death.
5. To eat of the hidden manna.
6. To be clothed in white garments.
7. To be a pillar in the temple.
8. The new name Jesus shall be written upon the forehead.
9. Granted to sit with God in His throne.

The faithful believers get the following crown. The crown of life, crown of incorruptible, crown of rejoicing, crown of righteousness, and victor's crown.

Every day we are confronted with the absurd emotional aversions of this world full of unrest and the cries of violent speed. Even before the golden glow of happiness fades, the shadow of sorrow spreads. Many people get tired when they face frequent fire tests and inspections. We do not understand the relevance and relevance of many things. The dry summer roads of life carry us forward with some hope, even when we are exhausted. Spring is waiting for some turn; some unexpected joys that were thought to have been abandoned in the past, some happiness. All the relationships seem to be like flowers burning in the sun, and some insinuate that even if they are filled with viruses, some of them are still alive. This world is a rented house. After living here for a while as tenants, we have to return to our own homeless paradise. Our citizenship is in heaven. The captain is unable to keep the car and call away. But according to their strength, they can only hold the stern and steer the ship. Let every reader remember that the philosopher Seneca said that no wind would be favorable if the sailor did not know which port he was going to. We must all appear before the judgment seat of Christ so that each one may receive what is due for what he has done in the body, whether good or evil. Those who once dedicated their lives to God can never be sold to another. How can you sell something you do not own? If your reading extends to the last page, let me humbly ask you one thing. Have you ever wondered for a moment where your eternity is? Knowing the shocking truth of the frightening mental thoughts of death, shouldn't this book be returned without a solution? May you complete the last chapter of your life and fill your life with the words, "Behold, I lay down my life for God, and may the Lord of hosts bless you abundantly." An invisible billboard is hung around the necks of those who have dedicated their lives to God. *Not for sale; sold out already.*

BIBLIOGRAPHY

Abrams, Judith Z. *Learn Talmud*. New Jersey: Jason Aronson Inc., 1995.

Goldin, Barbara Diamond. *The Family Book of Midrash*. Library of Congress cataloging, US, 1990.

Josephus, Flavius. *The Antiquities of the Jews*. 1668.

Kattikad, Fr. Bobby Jose. *Ramaneeyam ee jiivitham*, India: DC Books, 2018.

Kattikad, Fr. Booby Jose. *Ordinary*. Kottayam, India: DC Books, 2017.

Marsh, F. E. *1000 Bible Study Outlines*. Michigan: Kregel Publications, 1970.

Meier, Rabbi Levi. *Moses: The Prince, the Prophet*. Vermont: Jewish Lights Pub., 1999.

Nidhin, Joseph. *Assisi* magazine. Bharananganam, Kottayam, 2009.

Panthaplam, Fr. Jose T., *Jeevithavijayam*. Kerala: Allied Publications, 1997.

Pereira, Fr. Eugine H. *Jeevanum Velichavum*. Vellayambalam, India: Sterling Print House, 2009.

Schurer, Emil. *A History of the Jewish People in the Time of Jesus Christ*. Hendrickson Pub., 2008.

Shepherd, David R. *Manners and Customs of Biblical Times*. Tennessee: Boradman & Hollman Pub., 2000.

Swindoll, Charles R. *John the Baptizer*. Insight for living Ministries, 1991.

Swindoll, Charles. *Moses: A Man of Selfless Dedication*. Word Pub., 1999.

Willmington, Harold L. *Willimington's Bible at a Glance*. Carol Stream, Illinois: Tyndale House Pub., 1997.

ABOUT THE AUTHOR

PASTOR MANU PHILIP lives in South Florida for the last thirty-six years. He authored six books, and he is currently working on two other books. He was awarded twice for different books a Fokana Special Literary Award for 2020–2022 and was also awarded in Kerala Pentecostal North American Writers Forum. He wrote several inspirational faith and spirituality articles and travel reports in various Christian magazines. He is a retiree and presently volunteering as a clergy in Memorial Hospital Miramar.

Printed in the USA
CPSIA information can be obtained
at www.ICGtesting.com
LVHW090810020224
770695LV00001B/63

9 798891 307964